MOON

WANDERLUST
Road Trips

40 BEAUTIFUL DRIVES AROUND THE WORLD

CONTENTS

UNITED STATES

9 MONTEREY

END
MI 230

CARMEL
8 ★ POINT LOBOS
★ GARRAPATA STATE PARK

1

BIG SUR 7

★ JULIA PFEIFFER BURNS STATE PARK

6 PIEDRAS BLANCAS

5 CAMBRIA

1

4 SAN LUIS OBISPO

3 PISMO BEACH
MONARCH BUTTERFLY GROVE

UNITED STATES

San Francisco
Las Vegas
Chicago
Dallas
Houston

 LOCATION

California's west coast

 ROUTE

Santa Barbara – Monterey

LENGTH

230 mi (380 km)

TIME

One day is enough to reach Monterey from Santa Barbara, but why rush? Take a few days to enjoy the many dreamy sights along this route.

YOU'LL LOVE

The sweetness of California and the superb panoramas from the jagged coasts.

PACIFIC COAST
HIGHWAY
THE CALIFORNIA DREAM ROAD
FROM SANTA BARBARA ⟶ TO MONTEREY

Stretching a total of 650 mi (1,000 km) between San Diego and San Francisco, California State Route 1 (or Highway 1) is part of a select club of the most beautiful roads in the world. Experience the California way of life as the state's beautiful coastline unrolls in front of you. The stretch between Santa Barbara and Monterey offers spectacular scenery between two charming towns. Depart from Santa Barbara, among the palm trees, to take El Camino Real, the route of the old Spanish missions. Farther on, Highway 1 continues in solitude. Sprayed by the waves of the Pacific, the road rises, twisting up the side of the coast, hugging cliffs, and winding past hidden coves with golden sand and forests of sequoias. A true ode to wild California.

1
★ LA PURÍSIMA MISSION

2
SOLVANG

START
MI 0

1 SANTA BARBARA

START/END OF ROAD TRIP

STOP ●

LANDMARK OR POINT OF INTEREST ★

ROAD 1

ROAD TRIP ═══

SANTA BARBARA: THE AMERICAN RIVIERA

It all starts in **Santa Barbara (1).** The journey begins on the promenade along East Cabrillo Boulevard, in the shade of palm trees as tall as skyscrapers. Joggers and rollerbladers slide past each other along the concrete ribbon that meets the wide sand carpet of East Beach. Beach volleyball players give it their all against the backdrop of the Pacific. At the end of the beach, Stearns Wharf, the oldest (1872) and longest pier in California, reaches into the sea with its 2,300 ft (700 m) of planks resting on a forest of 2,307 wooden pillars. On the other side of the pier, West Beach, wide as an airfield, welcomes the outrigger canoes of the local clubs.

Marching away from the ocean, State Street forms the backbone of downtown Santa Barbara. From the very first steps, Spanish colo-

nial-revival style buildings, built after the devastating earthquake of 1925, assert the city's Hispanic heritage. The old Arlington Theater, with art deco touches, echoes the nearby County Courthouse and its Spanish influences. Down the street you'll find the Presidio, one of the four strongholds of Spanish California, built in 1782, with its authentic adobe walls.

A stone's throw away, the Santa Barbara Museum of Art houses works by Chagall and Matisse. Captured by the 1980s soap opera Santa Barbara, the city, which saw the birth of American cinema before Hollywood, is home to one of the highest concentrations of high-income earners in the United States. Over the years, Kevin Costner, Tom Cruise, Leonardo DiCaprio, and Kirk Douglas have been among them.

CALIFORNIA: LAND OF MISSIONS

A stopover at Mission Santa Barbara (1820) opens a window to the past. Travel back in time as you take in the neoclassical facade decked out in pink columns, and the interior of heavy beams, colorful stuccoes, and depictions of crucifixions. Water gurgling in a mossy fountain almost sounds like prayer.

As early as the 16th century, the mythical California invented by the conquistadores proved to be a disappointment. A Franciscan priest, Junípero Serra, continued their conquest

through the forced conversion of the indigenous people who lived here. Between 1769 and the 1820s, 21 missions were built along the Camino Real, the "royal road," each about a day's ride from each other. Today, many major cities bear their names: San Diego, Santa Barbara, Santa Cruz, San Francisco, and more.

Most of the missions have survived centuries and earthquakes. To the north of Santa Barbara, near the vast flower and strawberry fields of Lompoc Valley, **La Purísima Mission**

(1812) recreates the daily life of yesteryear, with its sheep and chickens.

The reddish tile roofs and light pink walls enclose the dormitories of the soldiers who watched over the monks, the apartments of their commander, and the craft workshops. The indigenous people, forcefully converted, worked there day after day for the "salvation" of their souls. Don't be surprised if this place feels haunted.

PISMO BEACH: KINGDOM OF BUTTERFLIES

Located inland, at the foot of the wooded sierras of Santa Ynez, **Solvang (2)** stands out in the Californian scene. A windmill, half-timbered houses, bakeries, clog-makers, and a replica of Denmark's Little Mermaid statue. . . . Is this a movie set? Almost. This town, founded a century ago by Danes, has become a must-see. Stop by for some a pea soup, and continue your drive north.

Route 101 returns to the Pacific Ocean at **Pismo Beach (3).** It's a typically Californian resort town, with wide, straight avenues, motels, fast food restaurants, and RV parks home to snowbirds (retirees fleeing cold winters of the northern states).

They're not the only ones who make the trip. At the **Monarch Butterfly Grove,** the eucalyptus trees, bathed in the smell of minty dry leaves, are home to hundreds of the orange-and-brown butterflies who return each November. The monarch is part of a special phenomenon: Each autumn, it travels between 600 and 3,000 mi (1,000 and 5,000 km) to reach the grounds where it will spend the winter. Traveling 20 mi (35 km) per day on average (with peaks of 80 mi/130 km!), the butterfly takes between one and four months to reach its final destination.

The population born east of the Rockies reaches as far as the Mexican Sierras. The ones born in the west fly down to the Californian coast. The butterflies stay there until February or March, before starting their long ascent back up north, which the next four or five generations will continue. Their genetic memory is astounding.

HEARST CASTLE: THE PALACE OF *CITIZEN KANE*

In **San Luis Obispo (4)**—also born around a Spanish mission—Highway 1 branches off to the north. Progressing between the ocean and grassy rolling hills, it reaches the pleasant village of **Cambria (5),** another great place to stop. The town features brick buildings, antique shops dating back at least to the Nixon era, a saloon, and an art deco liquor store.

The next day, reservation in hand, knock on the door of Hearst Castle. On the itinerary: a visit to the incredible second home of William Randolph Hearst, newspaper magnate of the last century. Perched on a ridge at the end of a winding road accessible only by bus from the visitor center, this sprawling estate holds 115 rooms (including 38 bedrooms and 41 bathrooms). Construction began in 1922, and it had yet to be completed when Hearst died in 1951.

The castle overflows with masterpieces gleaned from all over Europe. It's eclectic, over-the-top, and bombastic, with its Roman swimming pool with blue mosaics and its personal zoo where antelopes, kanga-roos, giraffes, and zebras frolicked. Hearst Castle was such a sight that playwright George Bernard Shaw described it as "what God would have built if he had had the money!"

Charlie Chaplin, Clark Gable, and Cary Grant all dragged their boots here . . . and of course, critics of the house still showed up, rain or shine. Hearst's life was also one of the main inspirations for Orson Welles's *Citizen Kane.*

PIEDRAS BLANCAS AND ITS ELEPHANT SEALS

It's 6am at **Piedras Blancas (6)** beach. The sun has barely risen above the Santa Lucia Mountains, a refuge for the last condors in California. Down below, a few elephant seals are already basking. Females and pups, long and plump, huddle together at the foot of the slope.

One after the other, the come onto the sand. Glistening with cold water, they observe the scenery for a moment, then make their way across the sand, wiggling their bodies, to crowd together in the rays of the rising sun. Farther on, at the edge of the surf, two juvenile males mimic the fights they've seen adults perform: Face to face, they throw themselves on each other, tossing their heads and bodies in large, sudden movements.

In a few years, once the animals have reached their full-grown size, this fight won't be so playful. Elephant seal males can weigh up to 4.5 tons and grow up to 20 ft (6 m) long! For the time being, most of the large males are offshore, waiting to come back to shore to molt.

Elephant seals were hunted for their fat—almost to the point of extermination—in the 19th century. They took refuge on Mexican islets, and they have gradually reconquered the North Pacific. In 1990, about 20 elephant seals took possession of this isolated beach at the foot of the coastal road. Now 17,000 of them frequent the place at one time or another during the year, particularly in late January, late April, and late October.

BIG SUR: VERTIGO ON THE ROAD

After Piedras Blancas, the most adventurous stretch of Highway 1 begins. Completed in 1937, the road here winds along the side of a cliff, crossing a succession of steep valleys, capes, and peaks. The view is plunging, the Pacific omnipresent, the vertigo constant.

When winter storms kick in, it's not uncommon for landslides to get in the way. Sometimes, a few days of work are enough to restore the track. Sometimes months of hard work are needed. A few years ago, Route 1 was cut off in two places for four months, effectively turning Big Sur into a makeshift island.

Shortly before reaching this point, a stopover is essential. At **Julia Pfeiffer Burns State Park,** the McWay Falls look like they're straight out of a movie scene. The falls, more plentiful in spring, flow from a wooded promontory onto a beige sand beach, lining the bottom of a peaceful cove. From the coastal path, perched high above under the leaves of eucalyptus trees, the view is breathtaking—and the smell intoxicating.

Finally, here is **Big Sur (7),** an artists' haunt since Henry Miller fled civilization for solitude here. Fir trees and sequoias cover everything. Roofs protrude from between the peaks, overlooking the ocean.

A narrow road descends slowly toward Pfeiffer Beach, another paradise: a wild immensity of gray sand, punctuated by black rocks and an islet pierced by a keyhole. In the morning, the cliffs are enveloped in fog, formed when the temperatures from the cold ocean makes contact with the warmer land.

CARMEL AND 17-MILE DRIVE

Head to **Garrapata State Park** for a chance to see frolicking otters. Otters were once hunted for their fur, and though the population was decimated, they are gradually reclaiming their old domain here and in **Point Lobos,** where they share the waters and coves with seals and sea lions. The float on kelp beds—large clumps of algae that can reach 300 ft (100 m) in length—moor themselves to the seaweed, and break shells with their expert paws.

Carmel (8), between pines and cypresses, is home to a wealthy population. The town's cute mission, among the oldest (1770), is surrounded by an abundant, serene garden of tall trees, wisteria, and a gurgling fountain. This is where Junípero Serra, the infamous missionary, chose to rest for eternity.

Take in a view through tree branches of the rocky, brittle coast, hemmed by the white foam of a not-so-peaceful ocean, along the famous **17-Mile Drive.** In sight: **Monterey (9),** the endpoint of this lovely drive.

Take your time to wander the beautiful Victorian homes of Pacific Grove and the old canneries of Cannery Row, passed down to posterity thanks to John Steinbeck. A can't-miss stop is the Monterey Bay Aquarium, a pioneer in the field of modern super-aquariums. And the mischievous sea lions of Fisherman's Wharf are endearing, too.

Big Sur

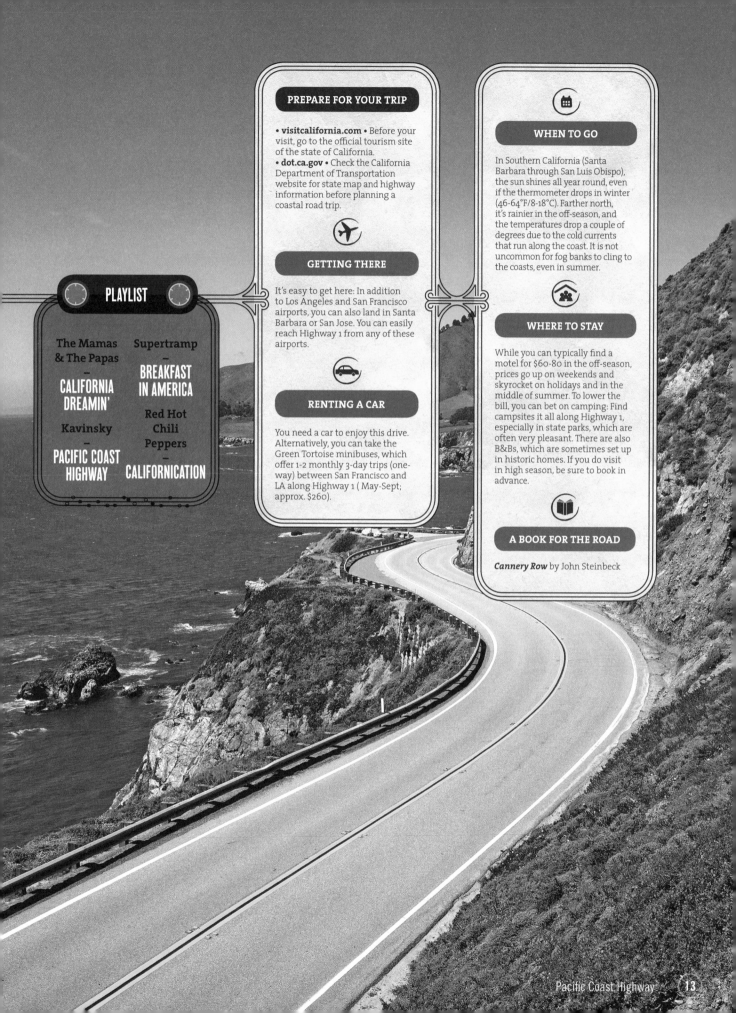

PLAYLIST

The Mamas & The Papas

CALIFORNIA DREAMIN'

Kavinsky

PACIFIC COAST HIGHWAY

Supertramp

BREAKFAST IN AMERICA

Red Hot Chili Peppers

CALIFORNICATION

PREPARE FOR YOUR TRIP

• **visitcalifornia.com** • Before your visit, go to the official tourism site of the state of California.
• **dot.ca.gov** • Check the California Department of Transportation website for state map and highway information before planning a coastal road trip.

GETTING THERE

It's easy to get here: In addition to Los Angeles and San Francisco airports, you can also land in Santa Barbara or San Jose. You can easily reach Highway 1 from any of these airports.

RENTING A CAR

You need a car to enjoy this drive. Alternatively, you can take the Green Tortoise minibuses, which offer 1-2 monthly 3-day trips (one-way) between San Francisco and LA along Highway 1 (May-Sept; approx. $260).

WHEN TO GO

In Southern California (Santa Barbara through San Luis Obispo), the sun shines all year round, even if the thermometer drops in winter (46-64°F/8-18°C). Farther north, it's rainier in the off-season, and the temperatures drop a couple of degrees due to the cold currents that run along the coast. It is not uncommon for fog banks to cling to the coasts, even in summer.

WHERE TO STAY

While you can typically find a motel for $60-80 in the off-season, prices go up on weekends and skyrocket on holidays and in the middle of summer. To lower the bill, you can bet on camping: Find campsites it all along Highway 1, especially in state parks, which are often very pleasant. There are also B&Bs, which are sometimes set up in historic homes. If you do visit in high season, be sure to book in advance.

A BOOK FOR THE ROAD

Cannery Row by John Steinbeck

WELCOME TO *Fabulous* LAS VEGAS NEVADA

ZION NATIOAL PARK

15 • KA

15

DEATH VALLEY

2

START/ END

1 LAS VEGAS

93

40

 LOCATION

Arizona, Utah, and Nevada

 ROUTE

Las Vegas – Las Vegas

 LENGTH

About 1,370 mi (2,200 km)

 TIME

Two weeks

 YOU'LL LOVE

The wide-open spaces, wild landscapes of red rock, Native American culture, and the image of a quintessential road trip.

START/END OF ROAD TRIP

STOP

★ LANDMARK OR POINT OF INTEREST

93 ROAD

ROAD TRIP

UNITED STATES

San Francisco

Las Vegas

Chicago

Dallas
Houston

12 · ARCHES

11 · CANYONLANDS

13 · CAPITOL REEF

24

14 · BRYCE CANYON

12

7 · MONUMENT VALLEY

10 · NAVAJO NATIONAL MONUMENT

LAKE POWELL

163

8 · MARBLE CANYON

98

89

160

ANTELOPE CANYON · 9

5 · CANYON DE CHELLY · 6

4 · GRAND CANYON

264

HOPI RESERVATION · 191

64

WILLIAMS · 3

THE ETERNAL WEST
LOOP FROM LAS VEGAS

Arizona, Utah, Nevada. This sacred trio is home to some of the most famous landscapes of the American West. Giant canyons or narrow crevasses polished by rain, stone arches and needles, rocks carved in red sandstone . . . a true polychromatic festival. The result: Southern Utah and northern Arizona are home to the largest concentration of national parks in the United States. Here is a unique corner, mythical and mystical, boundless, semi-desert and sparsely populated, alternating between sweltering summers and icy winters, all against the backdrop of Native American people and their culture.

LAS VEGAS: CAPITAL OF KITSCH

Before 1905, there was nothing here save for a dingy stopover for stagecoaches making their way to California. Then, the "iron horse" landed, and barracks rose from the ground at lightning speed. Anxious to marry off its cowboys as quickly as possible, Nevada liberalized its marriage laws. (Divorce followed.) To accommodate and occupy those who waited, hotels were built in **Las Vegas (1),** followed by casinos.

Since the end of the 1960s, Sin City has been constantly razing and rebuilding, including constructing amusement parks and concert halls to attract families. Today there are more than 150 casinos in and around Las Vegas.

The mecca of Vegas is the 4.2-mi (6.7-km) Strip, Las Vegas Boulevard—so nicknamed, they say, because you lose everything there, even your last shirt. When the neon lights turn on at nightfall, it's fun to cruise down the strip via car, from casino parking lot to casino parking lot. The Strip is home to well-known veterans of the 1970s: Caesars Palace, now in debt, and Circus Circus.

Between the two stand the posh Encore and Wynn, some of the tallest buildings on the strip, though they're missing their 4th and 13th floors—the number 13 is said to bring bad luck in the West, as does the number 4 in China. Next door, the Palazzo and the Venetian, all decked out in marble, house 7,050 suites—a world record! No need to go to Europe now; here you'll find St. Mark's Square and its pigeons, the Doge's Palace, and a section of the Grand Canal complete with gondolas. On the other side of the street: Treasure Island, the Mirage with its volcanic eruptions every 15 minutes, and then the Bellagio and its large musical fountain, reflecting the Eiffel Tower (a half-size replica) at Paris Las Vegas across the street. Next comes New York New York and its Big Apple skyline: a 42-story Empire State Building, a Statue of Liberty, and a Brooklyn Bridge, all crisscrossed by a roller coaster! On the other side of Tropicana Avenue, the Excalibur shows off with its neo-medieval turrets and fire-breathing dragon. At its neighbor, the Luxor, a glass pyramid stands behind a full-size sphinx.

DEATH VALLEY

As you drive through the desert, the superheated air distorts the pavement, creating the illusion of a wavy yellow line along the road. Mirages may cause improbable puddles of water to appear in front of your wheels. Every once in a while, you'll pass by towns, promising oases of air-conditioning and carrying memories of miners drawn by the promises of gold, silver, and borax (less profitable but more abundant). Finally, 130 mi (200 km) northwest of Las Vegas, on the border of California, **Death Valley (2)** unrolls its thirsty lands: an elongated basin wedged between two mountain ranges, dug so deeply into the earth that it sits at well below sea level (-282 ft/-86 m!). The highest recorded temperature here: 134°F (56.7°C). To the south stretches the Devils Golf Course, a lunar landscape where even the slightest blade of grass will never grow. Don't try to look for shade—there is none. Nowhere. A little farther, Dante's View offers a spectacular panorama over the valley. Try to go there at dawn: the last stretch of the road up to the viewpoint is very steep (a 14 percent grade), and during the hotter hours of the day, your engine is likely to overheat. At Zabriskie Point and Artist's Drive, eroded sections of the hills radiate rainbow colors—green, yellow, orange, pink, and purple—from the oxidation and decomposition of minerals. Keep driving north, past Furnace Creek, the main hub of the national park, and you'll come upon sand dunes, their gentle tides highlighted by the glow of the setting sun.

THE GRAND CANYON

Cross the Arizona border at the great Hoover Dam, built on the Colorado River. Follow 200 mi (300 km) of unremarkable road until you get out of the Mojave Desert and reach the pine trees and the relative freshness of **Williams (3),** an Old West village frozen in the era of the pioneers.

Enjoy the classic atmosphere before attacking the hour-long journey to the most famous natural wonder and national park in America: the **Grand Canyon (4).** When Spanish conquistador García López de Cárdenas stumbled upon it in the 16th century, he didn't see a wonder, but rather an obstacle that prevented him from continuing his quest for the seven cities of gold of Cibola—the fantasy of El Dorado. The gash, it's true, is a sizeable one: 277 mi (446 km) long. Over the years, the tumultuous Colorado River patiently dug out the arid plateau to a maximum depth of 6,000 ft (1,800 m), its excavation work revealing rocks that are 1.7 billion years old. From the Rim Trail, the view is spectacular. Down below, the cliffs multiply, forming waves, folds, and islets of rock as if suspended above a river you can only guess at, its wide bends hidden from view by an intermediate plateau. From Yavapai, Mather, Maricopa, Hopi, and Mojave Points, the views constantly alternate between emptiness and fullness, drawing invariably vertiginous landscapes. At The Abyss, the cliffs plunge down vertically 3,000 ft (1,000 m).

Several trails descend into the canyon. The popular Bright Angel Trail meets Indian Garden Campground halfway down, a haven of greenery where often, in the evening, friendly mule deer pass by. From Plateau Point, the whole Colorado River is revealed in all its majesty. Hikers with a permit can continue to the bottom. Because of the difference in altitude, the pines and firs of the upper areas give way to cacti. Prepare for a challenging ascent under the relentless sun the following day.

⑤ ⑥ ⑦

OPTION 1: HOPI AND NAVAJO COUNTRIES

Running 25 mi (40 km) along the South Rim of the Grand Canyon, Route 64 eventually veers off into a barren no-man's land. Half an hour later, the road joins Highway 89 in the same desert setting. It is on these lands of northeastern Arizona that the Navajo and Hopi peoples have always lived.

Tuba City is a town planted in the middle of the desert. The only river that passes through here, the Piute Creek, is dry most of the year; the rest of the time, it overflows and carries everything in its path with it. This is where Highway 264 begins, leading to the **Hopi Reservation (5).** Tired of invasions past and present, the tribe forbids photography, drawing, recording, and even taking notes on its territory. This might make your desire to discover the stone dwellings of the old villages of Walpi, Shungopavi, and Mishongnovi even stronger. Old Oraibi, in the Third Mesa, is said to be 2,000 years old.

The road leads into the heart of Navajo country, the largest of all the Native American lands in the United States (27,000 square mi/65,000 square km), spilling out into Utah and New Mexico. The Navajo Nation manages its own government, enacts its own laws, and has its own police and social services. Toward the north, at **Canyon de Chelly (6)** National Monument, the White House Ruin, backed by fantastic red sandstone walls, bears witness to the Ancestral Puebloans who once lived here. A hiking trail will take you there in about 2 hours.

Farther north, the Navajo people reign supreme over one of the most famous sites in the West, **Monument Valley (7)**, a legendary image from Western movies of the 1940s and 1950s—*Stagecoach* comes to mind. You'll encounter little traffic on U.S. 163, except for a few trucks and old pickups coming off dirt roads that seem to lead nowhere. On the edge of Utah, these towers of red sandstone rise up on an immense plateau strewn with scrub and rare trees with curved trunks. Some of the silhouettes are extraordinary, like a totem pole that seems to hang by a thread. At John Ford Point—named after the director of Westerns—the setting sun ignites the rock better than anywhere else. The only way to see the park without a Navajo guide is to drive the 17-mile unpaved loop road with pullouts for scenic views of the rock spires and lonely buttes.

OPTION 2: LAKE POWELL AND ANTELOPE CANYON

A more traditional choice, this northern route heads toward Colorado. The first stop (and a small detour) is **Marble Canyon (8),** where settlers crossed the river via ferry back in the day. Up next is the town of Page, founded for workers who built a dam nearby. Though the dam filled the immense red rocks of Glen Canyon with water, it also made it possible to travel by boat to the distant stone arch of Rainbow Bridge.

At the gates of Page, in Navajo territory, Route 98 passes between two natural wonders: the Upper and Lower sections of **Antelope Canyon (9).** No open gorge here, no giant cauldron, no feeling of vertigo, but instead two discreet narrow breaches, chiseled into the orange rock by sandy winds and rainwater. You can only enter the canyons on foot and in dry weather—and with a Navajo guide. As you squeeze through the thin slit in the rock, a narrow, winding formation takes shape around you, 1,300 ft (400 m) long and 120 ft (40 m) deep, with walls evoking frozen waves. Between shadow and light, you can see streaks of geometric lines in the sandstone that's been polished by the elements, with the hesitant sun coming to visit during the hottest hours. In Lower Antelope, you have to put in a bit more effort, crawling over the rocks, sliding down metal ladders, slipping through even narrower passages—bend down, stand up, and start again.

Farther along U.S. 160, **Navajo National Monument (10)** is home to ruins of two cities that date back to the 13th century, Betatakin and Keet Seel. Their mysterious builders, the Ancestral Pueblo people, settled here in the shelter of rocky overhangs and at the foot of vertiginous cliffs. Keet Seel was once home to at least 150 people! To reach either site, you must be accompanied by National Park Service staff, and be aware that the hikes down into the canyon and back up are strenuous.

Antelope Canyon

SOUTHEAST UTAH

In the far southeast corner of Utah, **Canyonlands (11)** National Park extends over an immense territory (527 square mi/1,365 square km) free of almost any human presence. On the menu: mesas, rock fortresses, even more canyons, and magnificent juniper trees with trunks twisted by the elements. To the north, easily accessible Dead Horse Point State Park features viewpoints that overlook Colorado, so high up that it feels like you're on an airplane. After that you'll come to Canyonlands' Island in the Sky, a rocky outcrop bounded by high cliffs. On one side flows the Colorado, on the other the Green River. Here, an easy trail leads to the dramatic Mesa Arch, which rises on the rim of a sheer 800-foot (243-meter) cliff. South of the park, it's best to rent a 4x4 to explore the endless landscapes dotted with cacti and rock carvings. Among dusty roads and thunderstorms, the whole West pulsates.

There are tamer parks here, too, like **Arches (12)** National Park. Paved roads and short hiking trails lead from one stone arch to another. You could spend days here—there are more than 1,500 arches, the highest concentration in the world. It's a symphony of astonishing shapes: the high walls of Park Avenue, gravity-defying Balanced Rock, Double Arch with its fine twin curves, Delicate Arch perched on the edge of a cliff. The landscapes seem frozen for eternity, but they're frozen in appearance only. In 1991, a piece of the gigantic Landscape Arch, one of longest in the world (290 ft/88 m), broke loose, further tapering this incredible line of suspended rock. In 2008, Wall Arch collapsed without warning on a balmy summer night.

ROUTE 12

The next stage of the drive is equally lonely. As soon as you rejoin I-70, you have to leave it again, in the midst of nothingness, to hop onto Highway 24. Whatever you do, don't forget to refuel before leaving: There are no living souls before Hanksville, 1 hour away. Just the heat and the land parched by the alternating frost and sun.

The town of Caineville is a little more cheerful. After that comes a real oasis: the poplars, apple trees, and peach trees of Fruita, in the small **Capitol Reef (13)** National Park, where herds of deer often roam at the end of the day. The heat here is intense, and sweat might run down your back as your gaze clings to the ramparts and castles of white and red rocks that evoke North African ksars. At Capitol Gorge, a trail weaves its way between the walls, reminiscent of the efforts of Mormon pioneers who once brought their wagons through en route to the promised land of the West.

In Torrey, ranches and pastures are making a comeback. It is in this valley where one of the most beautiful drives in the country begins: Highway 12, classified as a National Scenic Byway. The fabulous, ascending route crosses 9,200 ft (3,000 m), accumulating turns, canyons, and then forests of birch and pine trees. In this wild country where the mountain lion still roams, the only evidence of humankind is in hamlets and scattered farms. After Boulder, the section leading to Escalante (the gateway to a huge wilderness playground) becomes downright spectacular. For a while, the road plays a tightrope walker over a vertiginous ridge framed by two empty sections. The natural formations are inspiring: multicolored sand needles of Kodachrome Basin State Park, eroded cliffs of intensely red Red Canyon, and, the highlight, **Bryce Canyon (14)** National Park.

The Paiute people called this place "red rocks standing like men." Nature has surpassed itself here. Carving away into the plateau, runoff water gave birth to an army of hoodoos, which are exalted by the first and last lights of day. The maze is such that the outlaw Butch Cassidy, a native of the area, found refuge here on numerous occasions. Between the stone sentinels, pine trees soar. And in winter, the white snow sprinkled on the red rock offers a rare, beautiful contrast.

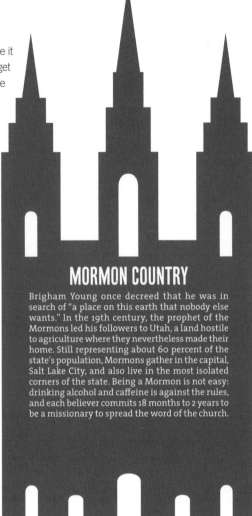

MORMON COUNTRY

Brigham Young once decreed that he was in search of "a place on this earth that nobody else wants." In the 19th century, the prophet of the Mormons led his followers to Utah, a land hostile to agriculture where they nevertheless made their home. Still representing about 60 percent of the state's population, Mormons gather in the capital, Salt Lake City, and also live in the most isolated corners of the state. Being a Mormon is not easy: drinking alcohol and caffeine is against the rules, and each believer commits 18 months to 2 years to be a missionary to spread the word of the church.

ZION AND BACK

Back on the plateau, Highway 89 invites a few detours to scattered sites: Cedar Breaks National Monument (less crowded than Bryce), the bright dunes of Coral Pink Sand Dunes State Park (best explored via ATV), and, beyond, one of the bastions of Hollywood's golden years: **Kanab.** All the West's cowboys and longhorns meet here the last week of August for the Western Legends Heritage and Music Festival.

Beyond, **Zion National Park (15)** announces itself in the shape of strange round rocks streaked with strata. The park encompasses the gorge of the Narrows, carved by the Virgin River—a trek that is only 20 ft (6 m) wide in places, and which you hike through with your feet in the water. Depending on the place and the season, the water can go up to your knees, up to your waist, or up to your chin!

Utah disappears from the rearview mirror a little farther along the four lanes of Highway 15. Two hours later, the first suburbs of Las Vegas emerge from a dreary and parched backdrop, facing the setting sun. Your circle is complete.

Bryce Canyon

PLAYLIST

Willie Nelson	Bruce Springsteen
–	–
ON THE ROAD AGAIN	**BORN IN THE USA**
Ray Charles	Steppenwolf
–	–
HIT THE ROAD JACK	**BORN TO BE WILD**

PREPARE FOR YOUR TRIP

- **travelnevada.com** •
- **visitlasvegas.com** •
- **visitarizona.com** •
- **visitutah.com** •
- **nps.gov** • The U.S. National Parks website.

GETTING THERE

Las Vegas has a sizable airport.

RENTING A CAR

You'll find the major car rental companies in Las Vegas, offering competitive rates, with unlimited mileage. Remember to refuel before embarking on longer stretches through the desert.

WHEN TO GO

April-June and September-October.

WHERE TO STAY

You have four options: camping (with some awesome scenery), classic motels, B&Bs (more expensive), and Las Vegas casino hotels.

WHERE TO EAT

Restaurants are everywhere you look in Vegas. Out in the desert, there are of course fast-food restaurants, a few cafés, and sometimes restaurants that look as if they sprung up out of nowhere. In Navajo country, you can taste local specialties (mutton stew, corn, and more).

A BOOK FOR THE ROAD

The Monkey Wrench Gang by Edward Abbey

NEWBERRY SPRINGS

SELIGMAN

KINGMAN

GALLUP

5
SANTA FE

END
MI 2,280

OATMAN

WILLIAMS
6

TWO GUNS

ALBUQUERQUE

66

SALOON

★ LOS ANGELES

7
SANTA MONICA

START/END OF ROAD TRIP

● STOP

★ LANDMARK OR POINT OF INTEREST

66 ROAD

═══ ROAD TRIP

UNITED STATES

San Francisco

Las Vegas

Chicago

Dallas
Houston

 LOCATION

The United States from east to west, from Illinois to California

 ROUTE →

Chicago – Santa Monica

 LENGTH ↔

2,280 mi (3,670 km)

 TIME 🕐

Minimum 3 weeks. One thing to note is that on Route 66, the speed is limited to 50-55 mph (80-90 km/h) outside urban areas. You can expect an average of 7 hours of driving per day, or 250 mi (400 km).

 YOU'LL LOVE ♥

The spirit of adventure on this mythical route, the motels and diners worthy of classic films, the variety of landscapes, the feeling of freedom.

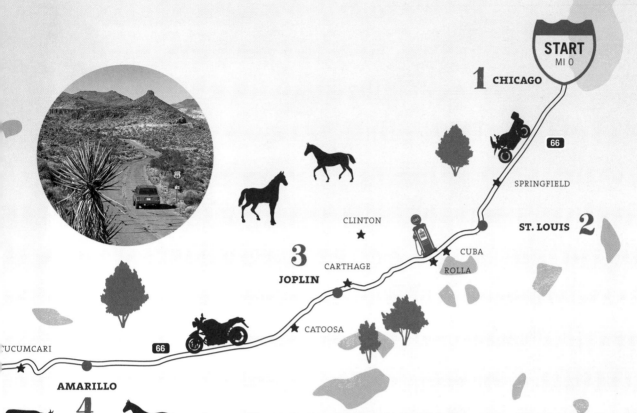

START
MI 0

1 CHICAGO

66

SPRINGFIELD

ST. LOUIS 2

CLINTON

3

CARTHAGE

CUBA

ROLLA

JOPLIN

CATOOSA

TUCUMCARI

66

AMARILLO

4

ROUTE 66
THE ULTIMATE ROAD TRIP
FROM CHICAGO ➤ TO SANTA MONICA

The gold rush, cowboys, beatniks, hippies, Harley-Davidsons . . . a retro bric-a-brac punctuated by motels, diners, out-of-service gas stations, ghost towns, and sprawling megalopolises. Route 66, a legendary road linking Chicago to Los Angeles, is a bit of all this at once. This enduring road is often straight for miles, setting out to conquer the West and the great outdoors, sometimes green, sometimes arid. Its breathtaking landscapes have seduced cinema (Easy Rider, Thelma and Louise) and literature (On the Road, The Grapes of Wrath). Called "Main Street of America" or "Mother Road" by John Steinbeck, Route 66 unrolls its ribbon of asphalt for more than 2,200 mi (3,600 km). It crosses eight states (Illinois, Missouri, Kansas, Oklahoma, Texas, New Mexico, Arizona, California) and three time zones.

CHICAGO – ST. LOUIS: FIRST MILES ON THE MOTHER ROAD

It's in the heart of **Chicago (1),** at the corner of Adams Street and Michigan Avenue, that Route 66 discreetly begins. You'll find only a modest sign to indicate the start of this legendary route.

The first compulsory stop, just a few blocks away, is Lou Mitchell's diner, a veritable institution of Route 66, where all women and children are rewarded with "milk duds" doughnut holes before being seated at a table. Then, head to the town of Cicero, the former stronghold of Al Capone, south of the city.

On the road, keep an eye out for vestiges of the golden era of Route 66. The first is a giant hot dog, followed a little farther by the Gemini Giant statue outside the Launching Pad drive-in restaurant, and then the statues of Marylin Monroe, the Blues Brothers, and more at the Polk-a-Dot Drive In. You'll see how restaurants had to compete with these imaginative sights to attract travelers in the 1950s. In Illinois, Route 66, which undulates between the fertile plains watered by the Mississippi and the Ohio Rivers, is very well signposted.

After a short stop to buy some delicious maple syrup at Funks Grove (known for its legendary matriarch, Glaida, who sadly died in 2020), you'll be on your way to **Springfield.** Get here by nightfall, the perfect time to test out the town's renovated drive-in movie theater. Turn off the headlights, turn the radio to 93.5 for audio, and dig into a plate of nachos while you watch.

The next day begins with a tour of the Old State Capitol and Abraham Lincoln's home, before winding through cornfields. A must-do is crossing the Chain of Rocks Bridge, now reserved for pedestrians. There, on the other side of the Mississippi River, rises the Gateway Arch, symbol of St. Louis.

ST. LOUIS – JOPLIN: CROSSING THE PLAINS OF MISSOURI

Notable stops in **St. Louis (2)** include the irresistible frozen custard at Ted Drewes and the majestic Gateway Arch, which offers a breathtaking panorama of the city. Head to **Cuba,** Missouri, and its astonishing murals, to spend the night there. As you set off the next day in the early morning, winding between farms and pastures, the two-lane road breaks away from the highway. On this bucolic section, you'll finally get a taste of the delicious thrill of the wild outdoors.

In **Rolla,** stop at the Totem Pole Trading Post. This service station, which has changed locations three times since its creation in 1933,

no longer delivers gasoline, but has turned into a souvenir shop/ flea market.

Up next is a little local oddity: Red Oak II. This reproduction of the original village of Red Oak, now a ghost town, was created by an eccentric man who now lives alone in the carbon copy of his native town. The place, deserted and surreal, might give you goosebumps. Before reaching **Joplin (3),** you'll pass through **Carthage,** whose drive-in always attracts crowds.

JOPLIN – AMARILLO: THE WILD WEST

Up next is Kansas. With barely 12 mi (20 km) of paved asphalt, Route 66 only grazes this state, a veritable gateway to the Great Plains. Farther on, bikers, with their bandanas flapping in the wind, stop to have a snack at Cars on the Route snack bar. Go visit the whale statue of **Catoosa,** Oklahoma, a former aquatic center, and treat yourself to some comfort food while sitting in the classic red leather booths at Tally's Café.

Leaving Tulsa, the road gets lost in the countryside, far from the highway. Here is Route 66 as you probably imagine it, setting out to conquer a horizon that never ends. The next day begins with a visit to **Clinton,** whose main point of interest is the Oklahoma Route 66 Museum. Then, set out to traverse the Panhandle, the narrow northern region of Texas crossed by Route 66. This land is home to ranches as far as the eye can see and herds lying on the edge of ocher ponds.

Along the way, you'll come across several ghost towns. One surprising sight is the strange cemetery of **Cadillac Ranch,** located west of Amarillo. The evening ends in **Amarillo (4),** at the inimitable hotel-restaurant The Big Texan Steak Ranch. Everything here is gargantuan, from the dining room, to the cowboy decor, to the portions, to the restaurant's famous offer: Anyone who finishes a 72-ounce (2-kilo) steak in less than an hour gets the meal for free.

FOCUS

Cadillac Ranch

Designed in 1974 by the artist collective Ant Farm and funded by a Texas billionaire, Cadillac Ranch traces the evolution of the automobile brand's line from 1949 to 1963. Ten Cadillac models, perfectly aligned, planted in the ground nose-first, are enthroned in the middle of an arid meadow.

AMARILLO – SANTA FE:
THE HIGHLANDS OF NEW MEXICO

In Amarillo, cowboy boots and Stetson hats are a must. Twice a week, the region's ranchers meet at West Stockyards, one of the largest cattle markets in the world. Cattle, horses, and even rabbits are auctioned off here.

In the auction room, the auctioneer, dressed in a plaid shirt and Stetson hat, speaks at such a speed that he seems to be humming. It's a well-established routine, punctuated by offers from buyers. Treat yourself to a small detour through the town's antique shops before heading to New Mexico. The scorched plains of Texas give way to large meadows planted with shrubs, from which mesas emerge.

The town of **Tucumcari** is home to some original and beautifully restored motels, such as the Blue Swallow Motel. In Santa Rosa, too, many vintage signs light up the sky. From here, you could cut across the state and go directly to Albuquerque. But the original Route 66 requires a detour through **Santa Fe (5)** and its adobe structures. The capital of New Mexico, Santa Fe is also the oldest city in the West, since its origins date back to 1610. It was a commercial crossroads for a long time, and now stays busy thanks to tourism. Its streets lined with houses in the style of Spanish pueblos and shops selling pottery, moccasins, and jewelry invite you to stroll.

SANTA FE – WILLIAMS: AT THE GATE OF THE GRAND CANYON

In New Mexico, Route 66 is bewitching, undulating between mesas and ghost towns on the vast plains. For 10 mi (30 km), it passes through **Albuquerque,** where it's named "Central Avenue."

In this city, Route 66 takes the name of Central Avenue. In the past, more than 100 motels with their neon lights were lined up along this stretch; you can still see some vintage signs. Some even indicate the presence of a long-gone building. There are also a few superb art deco buildings, such as the KiMo Theatre.

The day ends in **Gallup,** at the El Rancho Hotel. Inside, the monumental entrance with its Wild West décor sets the tone. The establishment opened in the 1930s to accommodate the Hollywood crowd, who came to shoot the outdoor scenes of Westerns in the surrounding area. The swarm of autographed photos covering the walls bears witness to this era.

The next day, the road plunges you straight into a film setting. The rust-colored valleys of the Painted Desert give way to the azure mounds of the Blue Mesa. It's a palette of colors that changes with the sun according to the time of day.

These lunar landscapes lead to Petrified Forest National Park, home to tree trunks dating from the Triassic period that have turned to fossils. Don't even think about discreetly taking a log for your fireplace— the rangers are watching. Farther on, leave behind the famous Meteor Crater, where a meteorite crashed more than 50,000 years ago, and head for **Williams (6).** En route, you'll pass the thrilling setting of **Two Guns,** a tiny deserted and barricaded town, near which stand the remains of an old zoo.

The International Balloon Fiesta takes place each year in Albuquerque. It's the largest gathering of hot air balloons in the world, where hundreds of hot air balloons rise above a Wild West landscape. The town of Gallup has a similar event, the Red Rock Balloon Rally. The experience is majestic and poetic.

WILLIAMS – SANTA MONICA: A BEACH AT THE END OF THE ROAD

The last city to be bypassed by the I-40 motorway, Williams is known for its proximity of the Grand Canyon and its train station, which leads directly there (on the condition that you reserve your ticket several months in advance). The city does everything it can to retain tourists. Diners, soda fountains, and souvenir shops make this small Arizona town feel like Disneyland.

The town of **Seligman** follows the same recipe, with the addition of painted eyes on old automobiles in homage to the cartoon movie Cars. The atmosphere is kitschy but entertaining.

In **Kingman,** stop for lunch at Mr D'z Route 66 Diner. All the classics are here: the leather booths, the jukebox, the '50s posters on the walls, and the cheerful waitresses. A burger and fries later, Route 66 gets lost in a Western setting. The ribbon of asphalt winds between arid hills.

In the middle of nowhere looms the city of **Oatman,** where roaming donkeys have long replaced gold prospectors. The town features classic Wild West décor: Everything is wood, from the saloon to the post office. The area is mostly deserted, but the inhabitants have a sense of showmanship. Twice a day, the main street is the scene of a duel (with blanks). It's a little cheesy, but effective. And after one last glance at the donkeys, here is California.

The first town to cross is Needles; be sure to fill up on gas, as there are no service stations for 92 mi (150 km) until Ludlow. After a final stop at the famous Bagdad Cafe in **Newberry Springs,** which served as the setting for a cult classic film of the same name, **Los Angeles** spreads its tentacles. Route 66 becomes I-15.

Contrary to popular belief, Route 66 does not end on **Santa Monica (7)** beach, but just before it, at the intersection of Olympic and Lincoln Boulevards. (There are no signs to indicate its end.) But don't let that prevent you from going to dip your toes in the Pacific, filled with the satisfaction of having come "to the end of the road."

*It's almost impossible to pass the town of Williams without giving in to the temptation to travel the 60 mi (100 km) or so that separate it from the South Rim of the **Grand Canyon.** This geological wonder of gigantic proportions, extending over 277 mi (450 km) in length, offers a striking spectacle.*

PLAYLIST

The Titans
—
STICK SHIFT

Canned Heat
—
ON THE ROAD AGAIN

The Rolling Stones
—
ROUTE 66

ZZ Top
—
LA GRANGE

PREPARE FOR YOUR TRIP

• **www.nps.gov/subjects/ travelroute66/index.htm** • The National Park Service's website for Route 66.

GETTING THERE

Direct flights to Chicago and Los Angeles are available from around the world.

RENTING A CAR

We all dream of traveling Route 66 in a convertible Ford Mustang, but it's a better idea to rent an SUV-type car, equipped with air-conditioning. Another option for motorcycle fans is the Harley Davidson. Note: Some rental companies might charge you an extra one-way fee.

WHEN TO GO

June and September are probably the best months. Skip July and August, when temperatures can reach more than 100°F (40°C) along parts of the road and prices are higher. Winter weather makes some part of the road impassible.

WHERE TO STAY

Here is a list of some typical motels that you will find on the road:

- **Wagon Wheel Motel:** *901 E Washington Blvd., Cuba, Missouri.*
- **Munger Moss Motel:** *1336 Route 66, I-40 exit 130, Lebanon, Missouri.*
- **Desert Hills Motel:** *5220 E 11th St., Tulsa, Oklahoma.*
- **Blue Swallow Motel:** *815 E Route 66 Blvd., I-40 exit 335, Tucumcari, New Mexico.*
- **Historic Route 66 Motel:** *500 W Route 66, Seligman, Arizona.*
- **Wigwam Motel:** *2728 Foothill Blvd., San Bernardino, California.*

WHERE TO EAT

Vintage-style diners:

- **Lou Mitchell's:** *565 W Jackson Blvd., Chicago, Illinois.*
- **The Ariston Cafe:** *413 N Old Route 66, Litchfield, Illinois.*
- **Tally's Café:** *1102 S Yale Ave., Tulsa, Oklahoma.*
- **Midpoint Cafe and Gift Shop:** *5100 Old Route 66, Adrian, Texas.*
- **Delgadillo's Snow Cap:** *301 AZ-66, Seligman, Arizona.*
- **Mr D'z Route 66 Diner:** *105 E Andy Devine Ave., Kingman, Arizona.*

A BOOK FOR THE ROAD

On the Road by Jack Kerouac

START
MI 0
1
CHICAGO

55

2
ST. LOUIS

MEMPHIS **3**

4 CLARKSDALE

55

END
MI 1,000
5
NEW ORLEANS

LOCATION

The middle of the U.S., north to south

ROUTE

Chicago – New Orleans

LENGTH

1,000 mi (1,600 km)

TIME

Between 15 days and 3 weeks—depending on your pace and your mood—with 2 days in Chicago and 3 days in New Orleans.

YOU'LL LOVE

The music, the Mississippi River, the big cities, the history, the food.

THE BLUES HIGHWAY
FROM CHICAGO ➤ TO NEW ORLEANS

This is the most famous of all musical pilgrimages, following 1,000 mi (1,600 km) from Chicago to New Orleans, in the footsteps of Muddy Waters, Chuck Berry, Buddy Guy, and Louis Armstrong: great musicians who, through blues and jazz, served as voices of African American people. Along the Mississippi River on Highway 61, this journey to the Deep South follows the legendary Blues Highway, passing through Memphis, to meet B. B. King and Elvis Presley. It's a journey through history and the larger-than-life landscapes of the United States. Travel over the hot asphalt, accompanied by the best blues standards. "Like a Rolling Stone. . ."

START/END OF ROAD TRIP	⛉
STOP	●
LANDMARK OR POINT OF INTEREST	★
ROAD	55
ROAD TRIP	═

UNITED STATES

San Francisco
Las Vegas
Chicago
Dallas
Houston
New Orleans

(1)

CHICAGO: THE HOME OF BUDDY GUY

It is not uncommon to hear saxophone notes flying through the air of the Windy City. **Chicago (1)**, the third largest city in the United States, is lively and pleasant. Here, the skyscrapers never feel suffocating.

This sweetness perhaps comes from the city's shady parks and its exceptional location on the shores of Lake Michigan, so vast it looks like a sea. Take in Chicago's full spread at the top of the Willis Tower: From the observatory, you get a stunning view of the city and the lake.

The symbol of Chicago is "The Bean," Anish Kapoor's bean-shaped stainless-steel sculpture, which attracts tourists who have fun taking pictures of their reflection, with the skyline as a backdrop. Take the opportunity to stroll through Millennium Park, dotted with sculptures. It is considered an open-air museum, but you can also visit a real one: The Art Institute of Chicago is a remarkable museum of modern art.

Take the time to walk through the West Loop, the former meatpacking district that has been converted into an arty haunt. After this long walk, you can rest in one of the city's 570 parks (!), such as the magnificent Lincoln Park.

By nightfall, the blues awakens; head to the aptly named Buddy Guy's Legends (700 S Wabash Ave.). Come early in the evening in hopes of grabbing a table in front of the stage. Photos of Buddy Guy are hung everywhere, as are the guitars of Keith Richards, Bonnie Raitt, Eric Clapton, and Carlos Santana. For a more intimate option, Blue Chicago (536 N Clark St.) has a program of local musicians. Like Buddy Guy's Legends, this is one of the last authentic addresses in town.

Chess Records at **2120 South Michigan Ave.:** *One of the major labels in the history of blues, rock 'n' roll, and soul offers guided tours. It was the studio of many of the greatest bluesmen, namely Chuck Berry, Muddy Waters, and Howlin' Wolf. The building is now home to Willie Dixon's Blues Heaven Foundation, a tribute to composer Willie Dixon who wrote many of his songs in Chicago.*

ST. LOUIS – MEMPHIS: THE START OF HIGHWAY 61

In **St. Louis (2),** known for its arch (the largest in the world), do not miss the National Blues Museum, before touring the (many) clubs in the city. Finally, it's time to join the legendary Highway 61. This is the road that inspired one of Bob Dylan's best albums (*Highway 61 Revisited*). Stretching 1,400 mi (2,300 km), it crosses the country from north to south, from Wyoming, Minnesota, to New Orleans, Louisiana. It is nicknamed the Blues Highway.

After 280 mi (450 km), the road reaches **Memphis (3),** cradle of the blues. The city, bordered by the Mississippi, can seem frozen in the 1960s. It's known for three "Kings": Elvis Presley, Martin Luther King Jr., and B. B. King. It is in Memphis that Elvis Presley walked through the doors of small Sun Studio (706 Union Ave.) to record the song "Blue Suede Shoes," among others.

Topped by a guitar, the brown-brick recording studio is hard to miss. Inside, everything recalls the universe of Elvis. Music plays in the background, and an old TV from the 1960s and a jukebox stand in the corner. The tour guides, full of interesting anecdotes, can tell you the history of the blues, from the cruel days of enslavement to the birth of certain mythical songs.

Stax (926 E McLemore Ave.), the other historic record label in town, has also been transformed into a museum. In the 1960s and 1970s, this is where recorded the greatest soul and rhythm and blues artists recorded their music: Otis Redding, Rufus Thomas, and Johnnie Taylor.

Less commercial, Stax is the emblem of the collaboration between white and Black artists. A re-creation of the original studio, stage costumes, guitars, and even Isaac Hayes's Cadillac are all on display in the museum.

Finally, the Memphis Rock 'n' Soul Museum (191 Beale St.) is worth a detour. The visit begins with a video comparing the birth of rock 'n' roll and soul in Memphis. The museum features a beautiful and rich collection of period objects: clothes, microphones, musical instruments, and more.

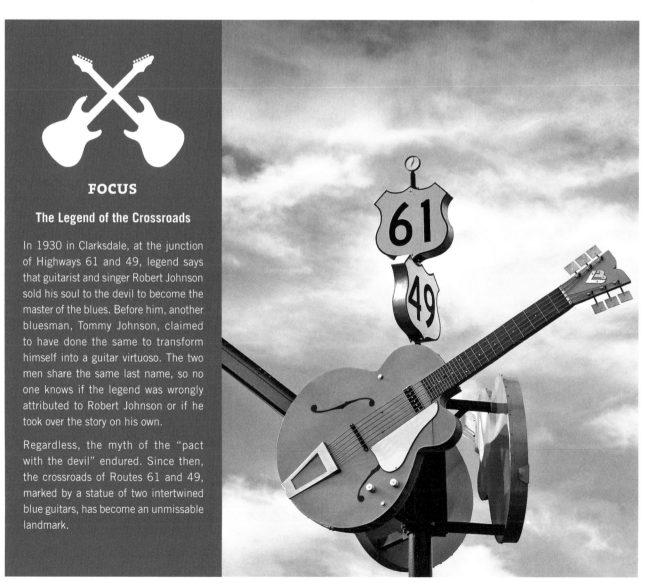

FOCUS

The Legend of the Crossroads

In 1930 in Clarksdale, at the junction of Highways 61 and 49, legend says that guitarist and singer Robert Johnson sold his soul to the devil to become the master of the blues. Before him, another bluesman, Tommy Johnson, claimed to have done the same to transform himself into a guitar virtuoso. The two men share the same last name, so no one knows if the legend was wrongly attributed to Robert Johnson or if he took over the story on his own.

Regardless, the myth of the "pact with the devil" endured. Since then, the crossroads of Routes 61 and 49, marked by a statue of two intertwined blue guitars, has become an unmissable landmark.

ELVIS PRESLEY'S LAIR

Memphis doesn't have Disneyland, but it does have an equally fun attraction: **Graceland.** It would take a good three hours to cover the entire property. You'll learn plenty of history from the audio guide provided as you board the minibus for Elvis Presley's house (3764 Elvis Presley Blvd.), one of the most visited places in the United States.

From the outside, the house is not particularly impressive. Large, white, and serious, it offers a pretty facade with colonnades. You'll immediately notice the huge garden and the ranch, which recall Elvis's passion for horseback riding.

In the kitchen, you can imagine the family meals that "the King" enjoyed so much. In his office, nothing has changed since his death. A video shows him sitting, surrounded by the same objects, giving an interview.

Then, there are the rooms that will leave you speechless with admiration: the famous "jungle," a reception room with wacky decorations, the magnificent TV room, all in yellow and black with mirrors on the ceiling, and the trophy room, whose walls are covered with plaques and records up to the ceiling.

The tour ends with the graves of Elvis Presley and his family, including his father, mother, and grandmother. The serenity of this flowered corner of the garden invites contemplation. Some visitors place a rose or a bouquet here in thoughtful silence.

LOVE AT FIRST SIGHT

Beale Street, Memphis's main thoroughfare, comes to life at night. Do not be fooled by its touristy and flashy side; you can still listen to good bands here, in bars that have remained in their original state. Some favorite spots? B. B. King's Blues Club (at 143), the Rum Boogie Cafe (at 182), and the Blues Hall next door.

MEMPHIS – CLARKSDALE: THE HEART OF THE BLUES

On the road between Memphis and Clarksdale, you leave Tennessee to enter the state of Mississippi. The landscapes are much greener. You'll notice the countless fields and swamps that already portend the bayous of New Orleans.

Clarksdale (4), in the heart of the rural U.S., feels lightyears away from the skyscrapers of Chicago. It's a quiet little town, at least during the day—in the evenings, memories of the blues linger at the juke joints, clubs that were essential in the development of Black music.

The city is worth a stopover for the interesting Delta Blues Museum (1 Blues Alley), where you can see Bobby Rush's shoes, Otis Redding's costumes, and vintage microphones and harmonicas. You'll remember this quote from McKinley Morganfield, aka Muddy Waters, proof of the immense influence of the blues: "You know the blues had a baby, and they named the baby rock and roll."

At the time when many establishments were reserved for white people, these kinds of clubs provided a safe haven for Black artists to meet, drink, and dance. Two of them have kept that spirit: Ground Zero Blues Club (387 Delta Ave.) and Red's Lounge (395 Sunflower Ave). The co-owner of the first is none other than actor Morgan Freeman. You'll fall in love with the establishment, which welcomes you in with sofas and a pool table at the entrance. The second joint has a whole different atmosphere. In this quirky bar, even more intimate, the soft lighting is 100 percent red. The stage is delimited by a simple carpet, to be as close as possible to the audience. During breaks, the singer takes the time to shake hands with each spectator. You can be sure: Nowhere else will you get closer to the soul of the blues than Clarksdale!

NEW ORLEANS: WHERE BLUES AND JAZZ MEET

How to end this musical journey in style? After a 330-mi (540-km) drive from Clarksdale, you arrive in the most French of American cities. Let's say it right away: **New Orleans (5)** has a gift for making people fall in love with it. The city's buildings with colonial architecture, decorated with pretty wrought iron balconies, give it quite the cachet! But it's not just that. Visitors fall head over heels for its gastronomy, where Spanish, French, and Creole influences blend together on the plate, its relaxed and festive atmosphere, its sunny climate, its steamboats, and its night markets.

Also noteworthy is its eccentric *je ne sais quoi:* The Historic Voodoo Museum is a must—even if the most popular spiritual ritual in New Orleans today is the throwing of plastic bead necklaces along the Bourbon Street.

There's perhaps no better introduction to New Orleans music than Preservation Hall, formed in 1961 expressly to keep the legacy of the city's distinctive style of jazz music alive for generations to come. Right off Bourbon Street, it's without question the most authentic music venue in the French Quarter. Otherwise, a lot of very talented street musicians bring the city to life. The tip will cost you less that a concert, and it's more fun!

In the evening, try going for a stroll along Frenchmen Street, less rowdy than Bourbon Street. Brass bands trumpet until the end of the night, mixing jazz and blues. Bamboula's (514 Frenchmen St.) offers live concerts. Many other bars dot the famous Frenchmen Street, but jazz has taken precedence over the blues. Regardless, you're guaranteed a great night out in New Orleans.

While in New Orleans, there are plenty of ways to get outdoors and explore. A quintessential experience is taking a tour of the bayous and swamps via an airboat or pontoon boat. Look out for the alligators!

NOT TO BE MISSED

PLAYLIST

Muddy Waters	Nina Simone
–	–
I'M READY	**BLUES FOR MAMA**
B. B. King	Elvis Presley
–	–
PLEASE LOVE ME	**BLUE SUEDE SHOES**
Buddy Guy	
–	
I'VE GOT THE BLUES	

PREPARE FOR YOUR TRIP

• **msbluestrail.org** • The website for the Mississippi Blues Trail.
• **visittheusa.com/trip/blues-highway** • More information on the Blues Highway.
• **louisianatravel.com** • Louisiana's official travel website.

GETTING THERE

Chicago has two large airports: Chicago O'Hare International Airport (ORD) and Chicago Midway International Airport (MDW).

RENTING A CAR

In Chicago, rent a car, motorcycle, or van to travel the Blues Highway with complete freedom. There are many rental companies in town and at the airport.

WHEN TO GO

Spring and fall are the best seasons. September and October are pleasant, when it's sunny and temperatures are mild. The Mississippi River is highlighted by the orange foliage of the surrounding trees. Avoid winter, which is harsh in Chicago.

WHERE TO STAY

- Be aware: Hotels in **Chicago** are expensive.

- In **Clarksdale,** stop at **Riverside Hotel** • *615 Sunflower Ave.*
• **riversideclarksdale.com** • This historic hotel hosted all the great Black blues singers who came to the city for their concerts during the early 20th century. If you want to sleep in the Muddy Waters room, ask for #5.

- In **New Orleans,** the city center is full of quality hotels. Count on at least $100 per double room with breakfast.

WHERE TO EAT

- **Pizzeria Uno** *(29 E Ohio St., Chicago)* and **Giordano's** *(three addresses in Chicago; the most central is at 730 N Rush St.):* This is where you'll find the best deep-dish pizza, the local specialty.

- **The Four Way Soul Food Restaurant** *(998 Mississippi Blvd., Memphis):* This restauarant is known as a former hangout for civil rights activists (including Martin Luther King Jr.), and the food here is great.

- **Larry's Hot Tamales** *(Sunflower St., Clarksdale):* Don't leave Clarksdale without tasting hot tamales, a local specialty.

- **Coop's Place** *(1109 Decatur St., New Orleans):* Come here for excellent inexpensive Creole and Cajun specialties. Try the delicious rabbit and sausage jambalaya or red bean rice.

A BOOK FOR THE ROAD

Blues Legacies and Black Feminism by Angela Davis

LOCATION

Florida

ROUTE

Miami – Key West

LENGTH

160 mi (260 km)

TIME

You can reach Key West from Miami in a few hours, but 2-3 days makes for a more enjoyable trip.

YOU'LL LOVE

Diving and big-game fishing, heavenly settings, and the Caribbean atmosphere.

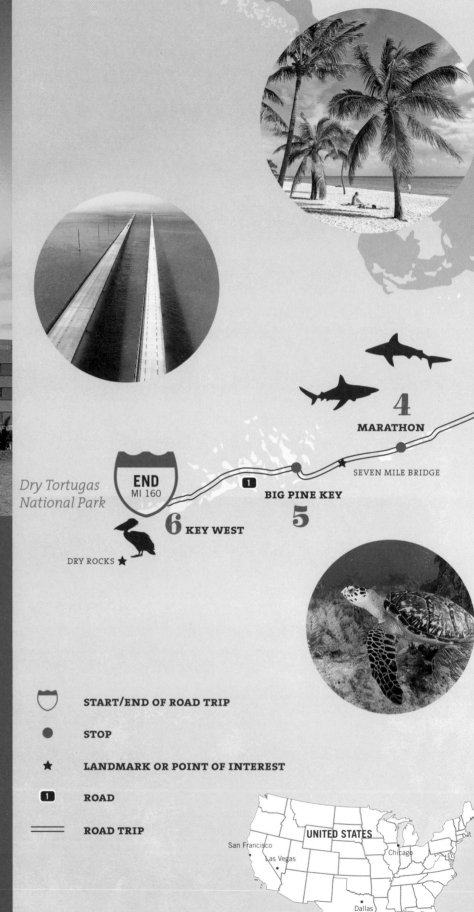

Dry Tortugas
National Park

END
MI 160

6 KEY WEST

DRY ROCKS ★

4 MARATHON

SEVEN MILE BRIDGE

1

BIG PINE KEY

5

START/END OF ROAD TRIP

STOP

★ LANDMARK OR POINT OF INTEREST

1 ROAD

ROAD TRIP

UNITED STATES

San Francisco
Las Vegas
Chicago
Dallas
Houston

START
MI 0

1
MIAMI

1

2
KEY LARGO

1

ISLAMORADA

3

THE KEYS
FLORIDA FROM ISLAND TO ISLAND
FROM MIAMI ➤➤➤ TO KEY WEST

Florida doesn't end in Miami! At the beginning of the 20th century, Henry Flagler, one of the richest men in the world, had the idea of building a railroad to link the necklace of coral islands and mangrove islets that stretch over some 100 mi (160 km) at the end of the peninsula: the Keys. Nowadays, you can get there and still keep your feet dry via the Overseas Highway, which replaced the defunct railway line, quickly destroyed by a hurricane. At the end of the road: Key West. Nestled under banyans and trees with huge red flowers, the city has retained the charm of its old wooden houses from an age gone by. The memory of shipwrecks, sponge fishermen, and Hemingway, who lived here for many years, lives on. It's a small tropical paradise under the Florida sun.

1

THE INVENTION OF FLORIDA

The road spans the 42 straits that separate the 43 islands of the Florida Keys chain. Some of the jumps are quite impressive: Between Knight's Key and Bahia Honda Key, the Seven Mile Bridge flies over the water for—you guessed it—7 mi (11 km)! On one side, the hues of the ocean vary from cobalt to sapphire; on the other, the gulf offers a palette of aquamarine. On the left is the Atlantic; on the right, the Gulf of Mexico. On both sides, there's coral as far as the eye can see and clumps of palm trees and mangroves. Above, the sun and the blue sky. It is the path of the Conch Republic, the edge of America lost in the Caribbean.

The causeway follows the path laid out in 1912 by the men of the Florida East Coast Railway Company under orders from Henry Flagler, the man who turned Florida into a tourist hot spot. To attract his first customers, he bought existing railway lines and developed them. A first hotel was built in St. Augustine, and then a second in Palm Beach. Soon **Miami (1)** began to grow, too.

The last link in the chain, the section toward Key West, was constructed at a huge cost in hopes of making this town an economic capital: The Panama Canal was set to be built soon, and Key West seemed like an ideal port for receiving goods. Unfortunately, in 1935, the railway line flew away under the battering of a particularly violent hurricane.

MYTHICAL KEY LARGO

Emerging from suburbs of Miami, your drive starts at the foot of the first bridge launched over Florida Bay. Here, a sign catches your eye: "Crocodile Crossing." Though alligators abound, there are only about 2,000 American crocodiles remaining, and many of them live here in the extreme south of Florida. Although they are protected by the federal government, these rare reptiles (which can reach up to 16 ft/5 m) are very sensitive to cold weather.

Farther on, you'll spot a "Pelican Crossing" sign. At the Florida Keys Wild Birds Center, said pelicans, white ibis, and injured egrets are rehabilitated on a protected bit of mangrove; it's fun to watch daily feedings. You might also find smart raccoons shopping here, too.

And here is **Key Largo (2),** an island that gave its name to a film well known by classic noir enthusiasts. Bogart and Bacall, led by John Huston, face off against lawless gangsters behind closed doors at a local hotel. Three years later, the director did it again with *The African Queen*. We find Bogey here again, alongside Katharine Hepburn this time, on a mission in East Africa. The little steamer featured in the film, an authentic vessel used in Africa in the mid-20th century, has finished its race in Key Largo. Restored, it now offers short sea trips for nostalgic fans.

A long snake of earth, Key Largo stretches nearly 30 mi (50 km) long but only 2 mi (3 km) wide at most. Like all of the Keys, the island is the remnant of an ancient reef that has been exposed by falling sea levels. Another reef grows offshore: Protected by the John Pennekamp Coral Reef State Park, it forms the largest barrier reef in North America. Hop on a boat tour to sail over the light swells to reach the **Dry Rocks,** located a good 5 nautical miles offshore. With your fins on and mask over your nose, slip into the water to discover a very strange resident: Christ of the Abyss, a bronze statue anchored here in 1965, at about 25 ft (7 m) deep, arms raised to the sky.

 NOT TO BE MISSED

At Jules' Undersea Lodge, you can stay in a former scientific research station, located at the bottom of a channel bordered by mangroves. Though the price is steep, at $800 per night for two people, this is your chance to stay in the world's first underwater hotel.

Jules' is only accessible to certified divers or to those who follow a short training to visit the place. Your luggage will be transported here for you in a waterproof suitcase.

Once you arrive, the activities are limited to the essentials: lazing around or watching the fish through the transparent window—except this time it's you who is in the fishbowl.

ISLAMORADA FROM BRIDGE TO BRIDGE, AND A STOPOVER TO SEE KEY DEER

Islamorada (3) is not just an island, but a series of islands. The island's name is said to come from Spanish explorers—"morada" means purple—who found purple sea snails washed up on shore, one legend has it.

After a hearty breakfast, only two activities remain on the agenda: taking a fishing charter out to catch tarpon, marlin, and swordfish, or visiting the unexpected History of Diving Museum, where you'll find a fantastic collection of scuba gear on display. At mile marker 50, you'll reach **Marathon (4),** the self-proclaimed capital of diving and the lobster Rueben (a sauerkraut-and-lobster sandwich). Ocean aficionados explore Sombrero Reef, guarded by a metallic red lighthouse, and the wreckage of the Thunderbolt, which has been sunk to create an artificial reef. On the program: brain coral, finger coral, lettuce coral, nurse sharks, and more.

Those without sea legs will be content to visit the Turtle Hospital, located on the roadside in a former motel from the 1960s. Between 50 and 100 turtles of 3 or 4 species are treated there each year. They repair shells damaged by boat propellers, try to remove hooks and plastics stuck in the turtles' intestines, and, a more difficult task, attempt to heal malignant tumors. Nine out of ten patients are treated for cancer caused by pollution of marine waters.

After the **Seven Mile Bridge,** buildings disappear and green predominates. Here are the Keys of yesteryear, bordered by mangroves, coral sand beaches (pretty Bahia Honda Key), and small bushy woods perched on tall roots—an adaptation to escape flooding from storms. These forests are known as hammocks.

Big Pine Key (5) is aptly named: This big, jagged island is covered in pine forests. The safari begins in the setting sun. Emerging from the cover, little Keys deer—endemic to this island and its neighbor, No Name Key—venture to the edges of the streets and onto the lawns to stock up on vitamin-rich grass, soaked in water by automatic sprinklers. Although it is forbidden to feed them, the animals have become accustomed to being around humans. They are regularly found in the gardens of the two B&Bs on the island and sometimes even in the supermarket parking lot (with tempting grassy flowerbeds)! At the end of Key Deer Boulevard, the street ends in dust. There, perched on a few dead trees, vultures, identifiable by their naked red heads, gather in flocks.

Islamorada

Ernest Hemingway Home & Museum

KEY WEST: HEMINGWAY'S CITY

One hundred and fifty miles (250 km) after leaving the continent, the journey ends in **Key West (6)** (population 25,000), the southernmost point of the United States, closer to Cuba than to Miami. Ernest Hemingway first set foot on the island in the 1930s after John Dos Passos described the "dreamlike crossing" of traveling through the Keys. Hemingway liked it so much that he decided to settle here.

The writer lived for 10 years in this port, where bootleggers smuggled Cuban alcohol during Prohibition. Between travel, frequent trips to sea, and numerous double whiskeys, Hemingway wrote some of his most famous novels here: *For Whom the Bell Tolls, A Farewell to Arms, The Snows of Kilimanjaro.*

Today, Key West is still paying homage to Hemingway, with its annual short story competition and lookalike contest, featuring the larger-than-life belly and white beard. Two bars compete for customers: Sloppy Joe's and Captain Tony's Saloon. At 907 Whitehead St., the novelist's home, now the Ernest Hemingway Home & Museum, was once one of the most beautiful homes on the island, with its fireplace, wine cellar, and swimming pool—the first in the Keys, which cost three times the price of the house. In the garden, about 60 six-toed cats stroll around, descendants of the master's original pet.

THE CONCH REPUBLIC

At the end of the street, a large marker in the shape of a buoy denotes the southernmost part of the island, as well as of the United States. It is decorated with the inscription: "90 Miles to Cuba."

This proximity excites and attracts many people, including immigrants from Cuba. As a result, in 1982, the United States Border Patrol set up a roadblock near the start of the Overseas Highway on the Florida peninsula, where all cars were stopped and searched for narcotics and people traveling illegally. Since this blocked the only road that accesses the Keys, the inspection point became a deterrent for tourists. The local government's complaints to federal authorities went unanswered, and in protest, Key West declared itself independent of the United States!

Thus was born The Conch Republic. The declaration established the pelican and the hibiscus as official bird and flower, as well as a separate currency and tourist visas for American vacationers. The media spread the news around the world. When the Conch government made a request for foreign aid from Washington, the roadblock was finally lifted, never to be seen again.

Smathers Beach, Key West

THE SPIRIT OF KEY WEST

Populated with Victorian and ginger-bread-style log homes, Key West is far from a classic American town. Drowned under tropical vegetation, the city is small, intimate, exotic, and colorful. Pink and mint-green buildings stand in harmony next to the turquoise water. During the day, see the island by bike, on a golf cart, or aboard the Conch Tour Train, which has crisscrossed old Key West since its inception after World War II. From the Audubon House & Tropical Gardens (built in 1849) to the Oldest House (built in 1829), you'll discover interiors of yesterday, the days of being a pioneer in the Keys.

Avatar of a past of hurricanes and sailors, the character in Key West has always been strong. These epitaphs on the graves at the old cemetery stand as proof: "I told you that I was sick." And, farther on: "At least I know where he sleeps tonight!" Home to artists and idealists, Key West has evolved over time into a haven of tolerance; today it remains one a favorite destination for LGBTQ+ travelers. The LGBTQ+ community comes together for the drag shows on Duval Street and for **Fantasy Fest,** the carnival organized for Halloween—glitter and feathers galore for the parade's costume contest! The locals are quite proud of this

tradition and compare it without hesitation to the Carnival in Rio. The party is rocked by the sounds of Conchtown rhythm, a cocktail of jazz, calypso, and blues, spiced up with Cuban salsa.

The other evenings of the year, everyone meets up in **Mallory Square** on the Sunset Deck, where, believe it or not, the most beautiful sunset in the world occurs. It is the pride of the islanders. Over a beer or a cocktail, watch the orange disc disappear beyond the horizon. And, when there are only a few purple traces left in the sky, the spectators cheer—but only if the performance was good enough.

A MUSEUM WORTH ITS WEIGHT IN GOLD

Among Key West's must-see museums is the Mel Fisher Maritime Museum, which exhibits a small part of the treasure recovered in 1985 from the wreck of the *Nuestra Señora de Atocha*, a Spanish galleon sunk in 1622 by a hurricane. On board: 1,041 silver ingots from the mines of Potosí, hundreds of Colombian emeralds, gold jewelry, and more. The whole thing, found after 16 years of research, has an estimated value of over $200 million! Some historical pieces are for sale on site (if you have a small fortune). You can even help finance new excavation campaigns and see conservation in action.

Fort Zachary Taylor Beach, Key West

DRY TORTUGAS: AT THE END OF THE KEYS

Where the road ends, the seaplane and the boat take over. Head for the seven islets of **Dry Tortugas National Park,** located 70 mi (110 km) from the hustle and bustle of the Sunset Deck, on the edge of the Gulf of Mexico. The archipelago is the most isolated national park in the United States.

Bathed by intense turquoise waters, Garden Island has been almost entirely occupied since 1850 by the immense, hexagonal Fort Jefferson, built to control navigation in the gulf and to ensure the protection of Key West.

A jail for rebels, drunkards, and horse and cattle thieves, the fortress also imprisoned Union deserters when the Civil War broke out. A Unionist stronghold in the open southern sea, it found itself isolated from everything, without regular supplies. Inhabitants began dying of malaria, tuberculosis, and dysentery. Its most famous guest, however, was a doctor. His name? Dr. Samuel Mudd, condemned for treating the broken leg of President Abraham Lincoln's assassin, John Wilkes Booth. At the entrance to his cell, an inscription once echoed Dante's Inferno: "Abandon Hope All Ye Who Enter Here."

Climb to the top of Fort Jefferson to see a few enormous artillery pieces and for a view of Bush Key, a few fathoms from Garden Island's golden beach and its coconut trees (camping is allowed on Garden Island). Between March and August, thousands of terns, pelicans, and brown and masked boobies swirl in the air.

PREPARE FOR YOUR TRIP

- **visitflorida.com** •
- **fla-keys.fr** •

GETTING THERE

Fly into Miami International Airport (MIA).

RENTING A CAR

A rental car is recommended for traveling the 165 mi (265 km) between Miami and Key West at your own pace. There are also daily connections via Greyhound buses.

WHEN TO GO

The driest period, which corresponds with high season, extends over most of the winter, with mild temperatures (average 68°F/20°C) and water temperatures around 72°F (22°C).
The rainy season is June-August; the downpours can be torrential. Hurricanes occur mainly September-November.

WHERE TO STAY

In recent years, lodging prices have increased significantly. While motels can still be found in the $60-80 range during the off-season (summer), prices soar in winter, especially on weekends—and even more so on holidays.
Several state parks in the Keys have campsites, but reservations must be made several months in advance. In Key West, the average rate for a double room is $250 a night. At this price, you could stay in an excellent hotel or in a B&B housed in an old colonial house; there are many choices. Again, it is imperative to book in advance for weekends and in high season (winter).

A BOOK FOR THE ROAD

The Old Man and the Sea by Ernest Hemingway

BLACK CANYON
OF THE GUNNISON
NATIONAL PARK

9

50

END
MI 305

10

GUNNISON

550

OURAY 8

BOX CANYON ★

7

IRONTON ★

RED MOUNTAIN PASS

SILVERTON 6

MOLAS PASS ★

COAL BANK PASS ★

PURGATORY 5

*Mesa Verde
National Park*

DURANGO 4

SALOON

550

AZTEC 3

*Chaco Culture
National
Historical Park*

550

550

CUBA 2

550

**START
MI 0**

1 BERNALILLO

LOCATION

The Southwestern United States

ROUTE

Bernalillo – Gunnison

LENGTH

305 mi (592 km). The most interesting section, stretching between Durango and Montrose, is 107 mi (172 km).

TIME

It takes a minimum of 2 days for the complete itinerary, including 1 day for the leg from Durango to Montrose, with the option of spending the night en route to Silverton or Ouray.

YOU'LL LOVE

Solitude, wide open spaces, high mountain passes, the thrill of ghost towns, and the shadow of the Gold Rush.

ROUTE 550
THE MILLION DOLLAR HIGHWAY
FROM BERNALILLO ⟶ TO GUNNISON

Born in the arid plains of New Mexico, Route 550 traverses vast, bleak expanses before reaching the Rocky Mountains. Then, it begins to rise, twisting and rearing up to cross the passes of the San Juan Mountains, reaching summits of 10,000 ft (3,000 m) and even 13,000 ft (4,000 m) in altitude. It was the promise of silver and gold at the end of the 19th century that drove men to begin building these incredible roadways, in defiance landslides and snowdrifts. A challenge so great, so costly, that the central portion of Route 550 has earned the nickname "Million Dollar Highway."

START/END OF ROAD TRIP	⬚
STOP	●
LANDMARK OR POINT OF INTEREST	★
ROAD	550
ROAD TRIP	═══

UNITED STATES

San Francisco
Las Vegas
Chicago
Dallas
Houston

THE START OF US 550 IN NEW MEXICO

It's a bit of a sad start for such a beautiful route: an exit on the Highway I-25 (number 242) in a dull plain setting, and then the town of **Bernalillo (1)** and its herd of motels and fast-food restaurants—though an air of the grandeur of the American West still exists here. In your line of sight: 160 mi (257 km) of four-lane roads unrolled in the abyss of the semi-desert plateaus of northern New Mexico, barely disturbed by a few old Native American pueblos and a handful of dusty trading posts. You'll pass the village of **Cuba (2)** with its Main Street USA planted with starry banners fluttering in the wind.

The memory of the Spanish past resurfaces in the large town of **Aztec (3).** In 1776, two Franciscans, looking for a route to the Californian missions, believed they had found the remains of a Mexican city here. There are no grandiose pyramids, but instead an excavation of buildings made up of more than 400 small rooms, classified a UNESCO World Heritage Site alongside other sites in the region. This is where Ancestral Puebloans lived in the 12th-13th centuries. On the ground, rounded foundations indicate the location of several kivas, their most sacred sanctuaries. The largest, supported on four columns, has been completely rebuilt.

DETOUR TO CHACO CULTURE NATIONAL HISTORICAL PARK

It would be difficult to find another spot farther away from everything. Follow a succession of tracks (County Roads 7900, then 7950) from Route 550 for 21 miles (34 km) to reach this bastion of Pueblo culture. Also classified by UNESCO, the site, lost in a dry canyon, was a great ceremonial and political center between 850 and 1250. The area of Pueblo Bonito—the best preserved—brings together some 600 rooms that were once stacked 4 to 5 floors high, and many *kivas*. The skillful construction, with meticulously adjusted dry stones, and the shape of the doors, slightly trapezoidal, might remind you of Inca buildings.

Little Molas Lake

DURANGO – PURGATORY: STORMING THE ROCKIES

You'll cross over the Colorado border driving 70 mph (110 kp/h) along yet another straight-line road, shiny trucks buzzing alongside you. In the southwest corner of the state, **Durango (4)** is nestled on the banks of the Animas River at an altitude of 6,522 ft (1,988 m), where the high plateaus give way to the unstoppable rise of the Rockies. The red-brick heart of this large town enthusiastically cultivates a Western mythos. The Victorian wallpapers of the Strater Hotel (1887) echo the red velvets of the Diamond Belle Saloon and the dynamic cowboy crowd of the Wild Horse Saloon. After taking a look at the old locomotives in the museum, jump onto the venerable Durango & Silverton Narrow Gauge Railroad, which steams along an improbable line carved in the middle of the mountain, originally built to quench the thirst for gold.

Route 550 also winds its way up the Animas River Valley, past Electra Lake, and then reaches the modest family ski resort of **Purgatory (5)** at 8,000 ft (2,400 m). Colorado abounds in places with names like this: Eureka, Gold Park, and Last Chance say a lot about the state of mind of the people who founded them. But times have changed, and a century later, Purgatory has turned into a winter paradise, with an average of 21.7 ft (6.6 m) of snowfall annually.

*Southwest Colorado is part of the Four Corners region, where it joins the states of New Mexico, Arizona, and Utah in a beautiful symmetrical pattern. It is in this arid area, now deserted, that Ancestral Puebloan culture flourished until the 13th century. One of the most beautiful sets of ruins left by these Indigenous people is scattered about 55 mi (90 km) west of Durango, around the high perched plateau of **Mesa Verde National Park** (classified as a UNESCO World Heritage Site). There, in the crevices of the mountain, nestle nearly 600 housing complexes, including the famous—and superb—**Cliff Palace,** hidden under a large rocky canopy, on the side of a deep canyon. In the modern era, it was rediscovered in 1888 by two cowboys looking for their lost cows.*

SILVERTON – IRONTON: THE MYTH OF GHOST TOWNS

Two passes follow one another. **Coal Bank Pass** (10,640 ft/3,243 m), reached amid a backdrop of pine trees and steep curves, is followed by **Molas Pass** (10,910 ft/3,325 m). The road then descends to **Silverton (6)** (9,318 ft/2,840 m), surrounded by mountains that are bleached until the dawn of summer. Silverton skillfully cultivates the essence of its bygone era, with a small grid of streets around a main artery highlighted by classic Old West buildings. The population has been cut fourfold since the heyday of the 1880s, when miners of all stripes gathered in the 29 saloons and brothels of the red-light district on the east side of Greene Street. Still, every day from early May to late October, the arrival of the old Durango steam train rekindles the memory of faded glories for a moment.

From Silverton, gravelly County Road 2 leads to the abandoned Old Hundred Gold Mine, from which an unsteady track climbs up the high slopes of the Rio Animas. Even in June, temperatures are still close to freezing and snowdrifts still pile up 6 ft (2 m) high. Continue along the county road until you reach Animas Forks (altitude: 11,200 ft/3,414 m), where a few old wooden huts reinforced with corrugated iron are falling into ruin. Some have been restored, including the large Walsh House, three stories high, once owned by lucky miner Thomas Walsh who discovered one of the largest gold mines in America. Walsh's daughter Evalyn Walsh McLean is known for once owning the famous Hope Diamond. In the city's height during the 1880s, it city was publishing its own newspaper and was served by the highest railway line in the United States.

Between 1878 and 1893, the U.S. government added the silver standard to the gold standard to secure the country's currency reserves. Demand for the metal—and prices—exploded overnight. In Colorado, mines multiplied to the point of flooding the market, which soon caused a crash. The ruin was immediate. In the mountains, the lodes were abandoned. In Animas Forks, and also in **Ironton** (on Route 550) and Tomboy, the miners packed up. A few independent ones clung on, without much hope of a bright future. One after another, mining towns fell into disrepair before dying for good. It is estimated that they are nearly 1,500 of these ghost towns across Colorado.

BIKE VERSUS TRAIN

For a break from the road, hop on the railroad. The Durango & Silverton Narrow Gauge Railroad, inaugurated in 1882 after only nine months of construction work in the mountains, resumed service with the rise of tourism. The ascent, over 44 mi (72 km), lasts nearly 3.5 hours, which leaves plenty of time to admire the landscapes, especially from the open cars. Even more nostalgic (and more expensive): a ride in the very Victorian Cinco Animas car, in "Presidential" class. The bravest travelers stick to the road, though. The Iron Horse Bicycle Classic Race has been celebrating the return of the railroad every spring since 1972. The challenge? Reaching Silverton by bike before the train, leaving Durango at the same time.

• durangotrain.com •

• ironhorsebicycleclassic.com •

OURAY – BLACK CANYON OF THE GUNNISON: VERTIGINOUS ROAD AND GRANDIOSE CANYON

At the beginning of 2014, Route 550 north of Silverton was closed for three weeks. Even in normal times, the **Red Mountain Pass (7)** (11,017 ft/3,358 m) closes as soon as a good foot of powder accumulates. Your only option is to make a (slight) detour back via Durango (217 mi/350 km!) to reach the town from the north. On the way down toward Ouray, Rote 550, carved into the cliffside by blows of dynamite, twists wildly above the void, in a sector exposed to about 20 avalanche corridors. It is this passage, torn from the mountain at the cost of colossal efforts and investments at the end of the 19th century, that legend says earned the route its nickname: the Million Dollar Highway.

The air wams up (a little) when the road reaches **Ouray (8).** The town, enclosed in a rocky amphitheater, also owes a lot to the mining boom of the late 19th century, which left hundreds of paths and trails clinging to the mountain. The shingled roofs, wooden facades of old hotels, gilded mirrors, stuffed pumas, and Victorian furniture paint a portrait of a once opulent place. In addition to the memories, there are hot springs, ice waterfalls, and the strange fall of **Box Canyon,** which can be reached via a suspended footbridge.

In Colorado, the human footprint feels very small, while nature looms large. **Black Canyon of the Gunnison National Park (9),** shaped by the Gunnison River, demonstrates this well. Descending steeply down the western flank of the Rockies toward the great Colorado River, the stream has carved a narrow canyon into the dark rock, reaching up to 2,600 ft (800 m) in depth. Crossed for the first time in 1901 on a rubber raft, its rapids were calmed by two dams built upstream. But reaching the bottom of the canyon on foot remains a real challenge. The Gunnison Route, the less arduous option, requires an hour and a half of sweat to descend an 1,800-ft (550-m) vertical drop, with pretty steep sections—including one where you have to use a chain attached to the wall to avoid the risk of slipping. At the bottom, the reward is a riverside oasis, isolated from the world by cliffs rising from the water. And the last stop of the road trip is the town of **Gunnison (10).**

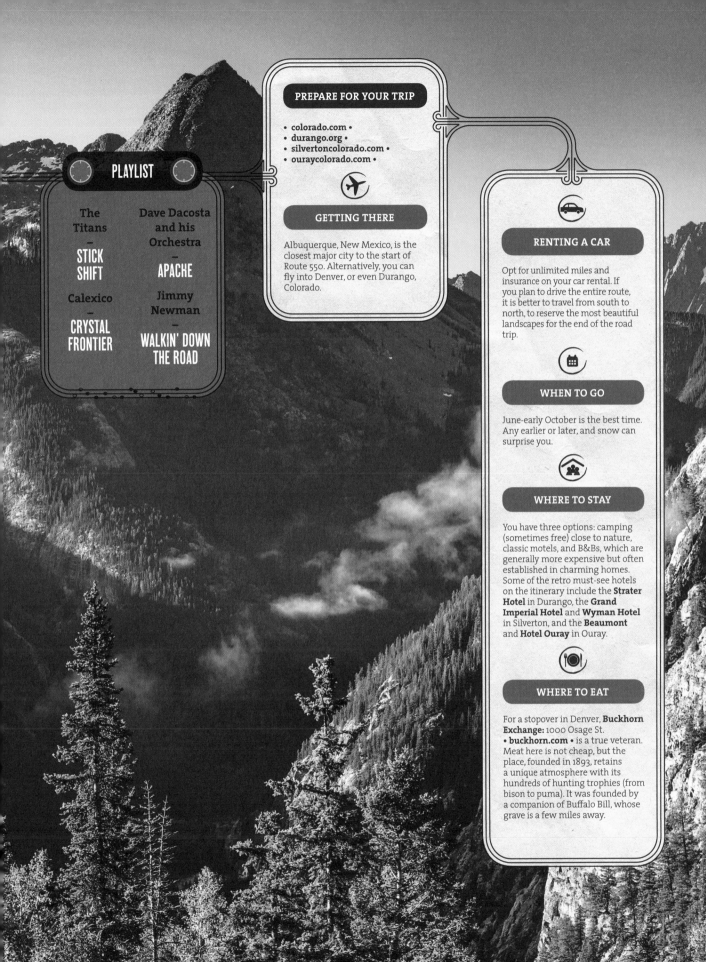

PLAYLIST

The Titans	Dave Dacosta and his Orchestra
STICK SHIFT	**APACHE**
Calexico	Jimmy Newman
CRYSTAL FRONTIER	**WALKIN' DOWN THE ROAD**

PREPARE FOR YOUR TRIP

- colorado.com •
- durango.org •
- silvertoncolorado.com •
- ouraycolorado.com •

GETTING THERE

Albuquerque, New Mexico, is the closest major city to the start of Route 550. Alternatively, you can fly into Denver, or even Durango, Colorado.

RENTING A CAR

Opt for unlimited miles and insurance on your car rental. If you plan to drive the entire route, it is better to travel from south to north, to reserve the most beautiful landscapes for the end of the road trip.

WHEN TO GO

June-early October is the best time. Any earlier or later, and snow can surprise you.

WHERE TO STAY

You have three options: camping (sometimes free) close to nature, classic motels, and B&Bs, which are generally more expensive but often established in charming homes. Some of the retro must-see hotels on the itinerary include the **Strater Hotel** in Durango, the **Grand Imperial Hotel** and **Wyman Hotel** in Silverton, and the **Beaumont** and **Hotel Ouray** in Ouray.

WHERE TO EAT

For a stopover in Denver, **Buckhorn Exchange**: 1000 Osage St. • **buckhorn.com** • is a true veteran. Meat here is not cheap, but the place, founded in 1893, retains a unique atmosphere with its hundreds of hunting trophies (from bison to puma). It was founded by a companion of Buffalo Bill, whose grave is a few miles away.

2
HOʻOKIPA
BEACH PARK

3
HAʻIKU

1 PAIA

36

START
MI O

TWIN FALLS

360

5
WAIKAMOI
NATURE TRAIL

4

6 GARDEN OF EDEN

11 PUAʻA KAʻA STATE
WAYSIDE PARK

12 HANAWI FALLS —

13
HALEAKALĀ NATIONAL PARK

 START/END OF ROAD TRIP

 STOP

 LANDMARK OR POINT OF INTEREST

36 ROAD

 ROAD TRIP

LOCATION

On the island of Maui

ROUTE

Paia – Hana

LENGTH

64 mi (103 km)

TIME

The drive takes 2.5 hours, but you need
1 day to fully enjoy the trip.

YOU'LL LOVE

The tropical setting, the abundant
waterfalls, and the wild coast.

HAWAII

THE ROAD TO HANA
FROM PAIA ➤➤➤ TO HANA

AUMAHINA
ATE WAYSIDE PARK

HONOMANU BAY *7*

KEʻANAE *8*

WAILUA *9*

UPPER WAIKANI FALLS *10*

14 **KAHANU GARDEN**

360

15 **WAIʻĀNAPANAPA**

END
MI 64

16 **HANA**

RED SAND BEACH ★

HAMOA BAY ★

WAIMOKU FALLS ★

MAKAHIKU FALLS ★ ★

ʻOHEʻO GULCH

★ KAUPO

In the center of the Hawaiian archipelago, Maui is a two-headed island. Made up of two volcanoes, it's dry and sunny in the west, and humid and tropical in the east. Here, skirting the colossal cone of Haleakalā, a narrow road winds its way between plantations, deep valleys, black lava cliffs battered by furious waves, and a dense forest dotted with multiple waterfalls (and their pools). It's Hawaii straight out of a postcard, discovered over the course of 620 curves and twists and a succession of 59 bridges.

PAIA – HAʻIKŪ: GOLDEN SAND AND XXL WAVES

Between sugarcane fields and the Pacific Ocean, there is something of a tropical western feel in the old wooden storefronts of the small town of **Paia (1).** The gentle sense of tropic serenity is reinforced by an old Japanese Buddhist temple. But this calm town has a wild side, as it's known as the world capital of windsurfing. The most beautiful spots on the island are just around the corner from town, and there's no better place to start than **Hoʻokipa Beach Park (2),** just a few miles down the road.

Here, a ribbon of golden sand (popular with turtles) is bordered by a cliff and huge waves. From the lookout, you can admire windsurfers, surfers, and kitesurfers moving fast, flying or struggling through the eddies of the ocean, with lifeguards keeping watch. A little farther east, in **Haʻiku (3),** one of the biggest waves in the world is formed: Jaws, aka Peʻahi, entered under both names in the Big Wave World Tour. In winter, the wave can reach more than 60 ft (20 m) high!

TWIN FALLS: FANTASTIC NATURE

The Hana Highway, aka Route 360, really begins in the middle of nowhere. Slipping between two walls of greenery, it immediately sets the tone for the trip: a long, slow, winding cruise. You will understand the slogans on T-shirts sold throughout the island: *I survived the Road to Hana.*

Make your first stop at the Twin Falls Farm Stand, a food truck with its name painted on a surfboard, where you can sip on a fresh coconut before leaving with a pineapple or a bunch of bananas. Hike up to the overlooks and make a big splash in the pool of the two waterfalls that make up the **Twin Falls (4).**

Back when sugarcane ruled day-to-day life on Maui, the powerful Alexander & Baldwin Company built 75 mi (120 km) of channels and tunnels in the middle of the mountains to water its plantations. The Hana Highway was built around an ancient Hawaiian trail and gradually took shape, starting in 1877 and completed in 1926. The road was finished when the eastern tip of the island could finally be reached. As for the irrigation network, you can still discover some sections along the way, notably at Miles 8.1 and 8.4.

WAIKAMOI NATURE TRAIL – HONOMANU BAY: A GARDEN OF EDEN

Silhouettes of Norfolk pines and fragrant eucalyptus trees frame the road, towering over bumpy green pastures. The ocean shines to the left, and the ribbon of tar twists and turns, crossing ravines drowned in vegetation. At Mile 9.5, the **Waikamoi Nature Trail (5)** rises between pandanus, bamboo, fruit-heavy mango trees, heliconia, elephant ear philodendron, and ti plants, offering some lovely views. The soil, intertwined with roots, is muddy, slippery, almost spongy. No doubt about it: The trade winds pour their rains here in abundance. At Mile 10.5, this profusion of nature finds a semblance of organization at the well-named **Garden of Eden (6).** On the menu: 25 acres (10 hectares) of (almost) domesticated jungle—for the price of admission.

As you continue your drive, you'll be facing **Honomanu Bay (7).** You can make out its crescent shape from scenic rest areas at **Kaumahina State Wayside Park,** where the blue-green depths of this large pristine bay are framed by shaggy mountains. The scenery features single-track passages and bridges, secret streams, cliffs draped in vegetation and lianas, trees with large red flowers. It's stunning. A little farther on, you'll find a black sand and pebble beach.

KEʻANAE PENINSULA – WAILUA: THE HAWAIIAN WAY OF LIFE

A bunch of palm trees and some houses clustered around a lava stone church dating from 1860: This is **Keʻanae (8),** a small town built on a strip of lava and dominated by the Haleakalā volcano. The volcano stands in the background, with all its protective power. This area, now silent, was once one of the most populous on Maui. The splendid patchwork of taro fields spread out over the peninsula's flats still bears witness to this history. If you've never tried taro, it's a tuber that's central to the Polynesian diet that some say tastes similar to a sweet potato. It's also grown at the Keʻanae Arboretum in the valley above.

After a slice of banana bread at Halfway to Hana and a smoothie from Uncle Harry's, you'll reach a fork in the road that will take you to **Wailua (9).** This charming village is established on a sort of coastal platform bordered by geometrically arranged taro fields, which can be admired from a little farther on, at Mile 19.2. Soak up the peace emanating from the white Saint Gabriel's Church, also known as Coral Miracles Church, the nearby Our Lady of Fatima Shrine, and a small garden.

UPPER WAIKANI FALLS – HANA LAVA TUBES: WATER AND FIRE

No less than 18 waterfalls have been identified along the road to Hana. Some are small (like the Twin Falls), while others are more impressive but often unreachable, as it is difficult to penetrate the backcountry. All the more reason to enjoy the beautiful **Upper Waikani Falls (10),** superb in their setting of black rock, ferns, and red torch ginger flowers. Other waterfalls follow at **Pua'a Ka'a State Wayside Park (11)** and then at **Hanawi Falls (12)** at Mile 24. View the magnificent Hanawi Falls from a bridge over the stream, or hike up to the pool and jump in for an icy swim.

If you've had enough of soaking in the waterfalls and are curious to see the insides of a volcano, head to **Haleakalā National Park (13).** When an eruption enters its secondary phase, the lava flows, less and less fluid, continue to circulate under the hardened crust, through tunnels that eventually empty when the magma dries up. Here, the lava tube, which formed 960 years ago, is the longest on Maui (2 mi/3.2 km) and one of the 20 largest in the world. You can explore a small part of the tube, equipped with a flashlight.

Are you craving ripe mango or freshly picked papaya? Fruit stands, scattered on the edge of the Road to Hana, are multiplying. There's no salesperson, just a box to slip the money in before leaving with your harvest. It's all on the honor system.

KAHANU GARDEN – WAI'ĀNAPANAPA STATE PARK: GARDEN AND UNTAMED NATURE

The large **Kahanu Garden (14)** evokes Hawaiian paradise before colonization. There are no plants from other continents here, only endemic species or those brought by the first Polynesian inhabitants of the archipelago. One plant to note is the breadfruit tree, with its fruits nearly the size of a volleyball.

You'll also find Pi'ilanihale here, the largest heiau (Hawaiian temple) on Maui, which dates back to the 13th century. It features a colossal, stepped platform measuring 413 ft (126 m) by 338 ft (103 m).

Leave this Eden behind and imagine a wild bay oscillating between turquoise and lapis lazuli, whimsically shaped rocks covered with the intense green of the naupaka plant, and a jet-colored beach . . . and here it is at **Wai'ānapanapa (15),** protected by one of the most beautiful natural parks on Maui. During heavy swells, waves infiltrate holes dug into the lava bed, emerging in geysers. These are called blowholes.

HANA AND BEYOND

Here, at the eastern end of the island, is the end of the Road to **Hana (16):** a timeless village of 1,235 inhabitants, slumbering between a small bay fringed with brown sand and the impressive mass of Ka'uiki Head. The vegetation is lush, even overpowering. With the exception of the Cultural Center & Museum (with a reconstructed Hawaiian village), there aren't many sights to see—it's more about the atmosphere. Follow an unkempt path clinging to the coastline to **Red Sand Beach**—remarkable with its rust-colored sand—or climb up to scenic overlooks to savor vast panoramas of the Pacific.

Even though the road has reached Hana, it isn't over yet. Continue to the pretty gray sand of **Hamoa Bay,** the beautiful **Wailua Falls** (80 ft/24 m tall), and then **'Ohe'o Gulch,** where a dozen interconnected waterfalls and pools descend. The gulch is also called Seven Sacred Pools—although they are neither seven, nor sacred. As a bonus, the muddy hike leads 0.5 mi (800 m) to **Makahiku Falls** (184 ft/56 m) and, even higher (2 mi/3 km) to **Waimoku Falls** (400 ft/122 m). You'll work up a nice sweat, between bamboo, mango trees, and ti plants, with the constant company of mosquitoes. Finally, all that remains is to turn back or return via the south coast track, via **Kaupo.**

NOT TO BE MISSED

The cemetery of the Palapala Ho'omau Church in the hamlet of **Kipahulu,** *past Hana, is home to a strange parishioner: Charles Lindbergh. The man known for crossing the Atlantic by plane died here in 1974, 47 years after his famous feat.*

PREPARE FOR YOUR TRIP

• **roadtohana.com** • Everything you need for your road trip in Hawaii.
• **gohawaii.com/islands/maui** • A wealth of information on the islands of Hawaii.
• **mauiguidebook.com** • Thematic info, recommendations for accommodations, and everything else to prepare for your visit.
• **nps.gov/hale** • Real-time information to help you plan your Haleakalā hikes.

GETTING THERE

To reach Hawaii, most people fly out of Los Angeles or San Francisco. While there are direct flights to Maui's **Kahului Airport** (OGG) from the West Coast, a layover in Honolulu may be necessary.

PLAYLIST

Israel "IZ" Kamakawiwo'ole
—
OVER THE RAINBOW

Elvis Presley
—
BLUE HAWAII

Kolohe Kai
—
EHU GIRL

Jack Johnson
—
BETTER TOGETHER

RENTING A CAR

Renting a car is easy in Hawaii. All the big companies are present at Kahului Airport, and the daily rates are pretty low. In high season (winter and June-August, to a lesser extent), it's advisable to book ahead. In general, the return by the south coast of the Road to Hana (via Kaupo) is authorized only for 4WD vehicles.

WHEN TO GO

May-early October.

WHERE TO STAY

The options for accommodations between Kahului Airport and Hana are limited. The **Wai'ānapanapa State Park campsite** is heavenly, and you can also rent a bungalow (reserve ahead!); there is another campsite in Kipahulu. Otherwise, in Hana and its surroundings, you have the choice between several very good B&Bs (**The Guest Houses at Malanai, Hamoa Bay Bungalows, Ekena,** etc.), studios and apartments at the **Hana Kai Maui** resort, and the luxury rooms of **Travaasa Hana.** The cheapest accommodations (hostels and motels) are clustered around **Kahului,** the administrative capital of the island.

WHERE TO EAT

Every now and then along the route, you'll find stalls and food trucks offering banana bread, hot dogs, burgers, sandwiches, ice cream, and smoothies to cool off. These include **Halfway to Hana** stand (Mile 17) and **Coconut Glen's** (Mile 27.5). Near Hamoa, **Huli Huli Chicken** is perfect for some good chicken or barbecue pork ribs, Hawaiian style, in a friendly atmosphere.

A BOOK FOR THE ROAD

The Descendants by Kaui Hart Hemmings

16

DETOUR TO THE HALEAKALĀ VOLCANO

Occupying two-thirds of the island, **Haleakalā** ("house of the sun") is an authentic giant. It culminates at 10,023 ft (3,055 m), but measured from its oceanic base in the deep Pacific, it stands at 29,704 ft (9,053 m)—one of the tallest mountains in the world. It's a young mountain, formed from eruption after eruption, emerging from the water only 900,000 years ago. At the top, reached after 1 hour of hairpin bends, a Dantean landscape spreads before you: lava needles, secondary cones, lunar soil tinged with red or gray, covering one of the largest calderas in the world, reaching about 20 mi (30 km) in circumference. The most recent eruption dates back to 1790. Many visitors come here to admire the sunrise (you must depart from the coast at 4am!) before riding a mountain bike along the slope or plunging into the belly of the monster on dusty trails.

OTHER ROAD TRIPS IN THE UNITED STATES

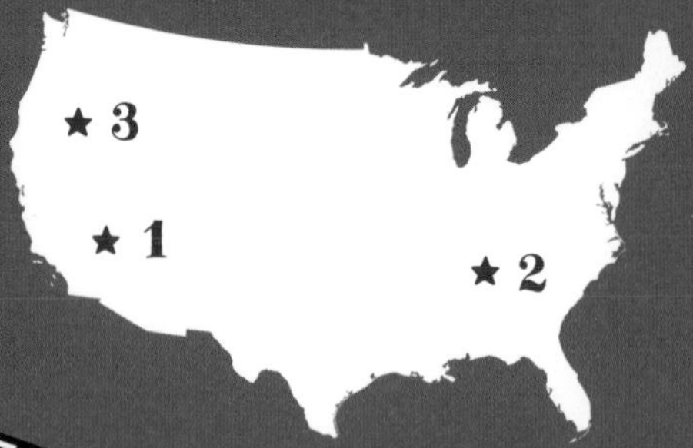

★ 3

★ 1

★ 2

ROUTE 6

Route 6 is the second longest highway in the United States. Allow at least 6 weeks to travel this route in order to visit all the points of interest. At 3,199 mi (5,100 km) long, it crosses the country from east to west, passing through 14 states. At its two ends are the towns of Bishop, California, and Provincetown, Massachusetts.

This road plunges deep into the U.S., where small towns and rural areas follow one another. Several notable sites punctuate the trip, such as Humboldt-Toiyabe National Forest near Sparks, Nevada. In Provincetown—a favorite of LGBTQ+ travelers—you can climb the Pilgrim Monument, a 253-ft-high (77-m-high) bell tower. The granite building commemorates the arrival of Pilgrims in 1620.

But one of the most interesting states to drive through is Pennsylvania. You'll pass Pine Creek Gorge, so deep it's nicknamed The Grand Canyon of Pennsylvania. There is also the Kinzua Bridge, 2,052 ft (625 m) long—before it was partially destroyed by a tornado in 2003, that is. It was built in the early 20th century and has been transformed into a pedestrian walkway.

①

HIGHWAY 101

U.S. Highway 101 follows the Pacific coast for nearly 363 mi (584 km) in Oregon, along the northwest coast of the Unites States. The great outdoors is on the agenda, with two parks that offer an off-road getaway. Oswald West State Park is popular with surfers, who make their way through coniferous forest to reach the beach. Ecola State Park, near Cannon Beach, is known for stunning Haystack Rock, a huge rock that pierces the waves.

In Reedsport, the Oregon Dunes National Recreation Area is home to about 40 mi (60 km) of sand dunes. Sea lions have chosen to settle in the rocks near the town of Florence. During winter, they take shelter in a cave that you can visit for an up-close look.

It is not only nature that performs wonders here. Highway 101 is marked by numerous bridges, unique in that they were all designed by the same engineer, Conde McCullough (1887-1946). In 1936 alone, he had five built for Highway 101. His masterpiece is the Yaquina Bay Bridge in Newport, with its blend of art deco and Gothic influences.

NORTH

US 101

③

②

GREAT RIVER ROAD

Created in 1938, this route is almost as long as the river it accompanies. The Great River Road, which runs along the Mississippi, is 2,069 mi (3,330 km) long. In the 19th century, trade in the vicinity of the river led to the rise of steamboat. Today more than 70 museums and sites, scattered in the 10 states crossed by the road, recall this rich history.

The Great River Road crosses two nature reserves, the Chickasaw National Wildlife Refuge and the Reelfoot Lake State Park, and the site of Fort Pillow Historic State Park. At the end of the Civil War, Union troops, mostly African Americans, were massacred here by the Confederates.

But the Great River Road also celebrates more peaceful moments—for example, over a glass of wine, in the vineyards of Minnesota or Wisconsin. This route has also inspired many artists. American composer Ferde Grofé was inspired by places around the river, from Lake Itasca to the Gulf of Mexico, in his work *Mississippi Suite* (1926).

CANADA

Jasper National Park

JASPER 9
END MI 200

16

8 ATHABASCA FALLS
MOUNT EDITH CAVELL
7

MEDICINE LAKE

MALIGNE LAKE

93

6 ATHABASCA GLACIER

⬡ **START/END OF ROAD TRIP**

● **STOP**

★ **LANDMARK OR POINT OF INTEREST**

1 **ROAD**

═══ **ROAD TRIP**

▪▪▪▪▪ **DETOUR**

1

CANADA

Edmonton
Vancouver
Winnipeg
Montreal
Ottawa
Toronto

LOCATION

Western Canada, in the heart of the Rockies

ROUTE

Banff – Jasper

LENGTH

About 200 mi (300 km), including 140 mi (230 km) on the famous Icefields Parkway (Highway 93).

TIME

A day if you're in a hurry, but that would be a shame! One week will let you take advantage of the many stops for hiking, rafting, and more.

YOU'LL LOVE

The grandiose landscapes, the flora and fauna, the great outdoors.

THE HEART OF THE CANADIAN ROCKIES

FROM BANFF ⟶ TO JASPER

Banff to Jasper is a traveler's dream! The crossing of the Rockies follows one of the most beautiful roads in the world. Covering nearly 200 mi (300 km), unforgettable panoramas of chiseled and grandiose landscapes follow one another: sparkling blue lakes, rivers, forests as far as the eye can see, peaks with sharp ridges, waterfalls, and glaciers. The land is also home to varied and abundant wildlife—bears, caribou, elk, and more. The stage is set for an unforgettable road trip in a land of pioneers, where the magic of the great outdoors is still alive.

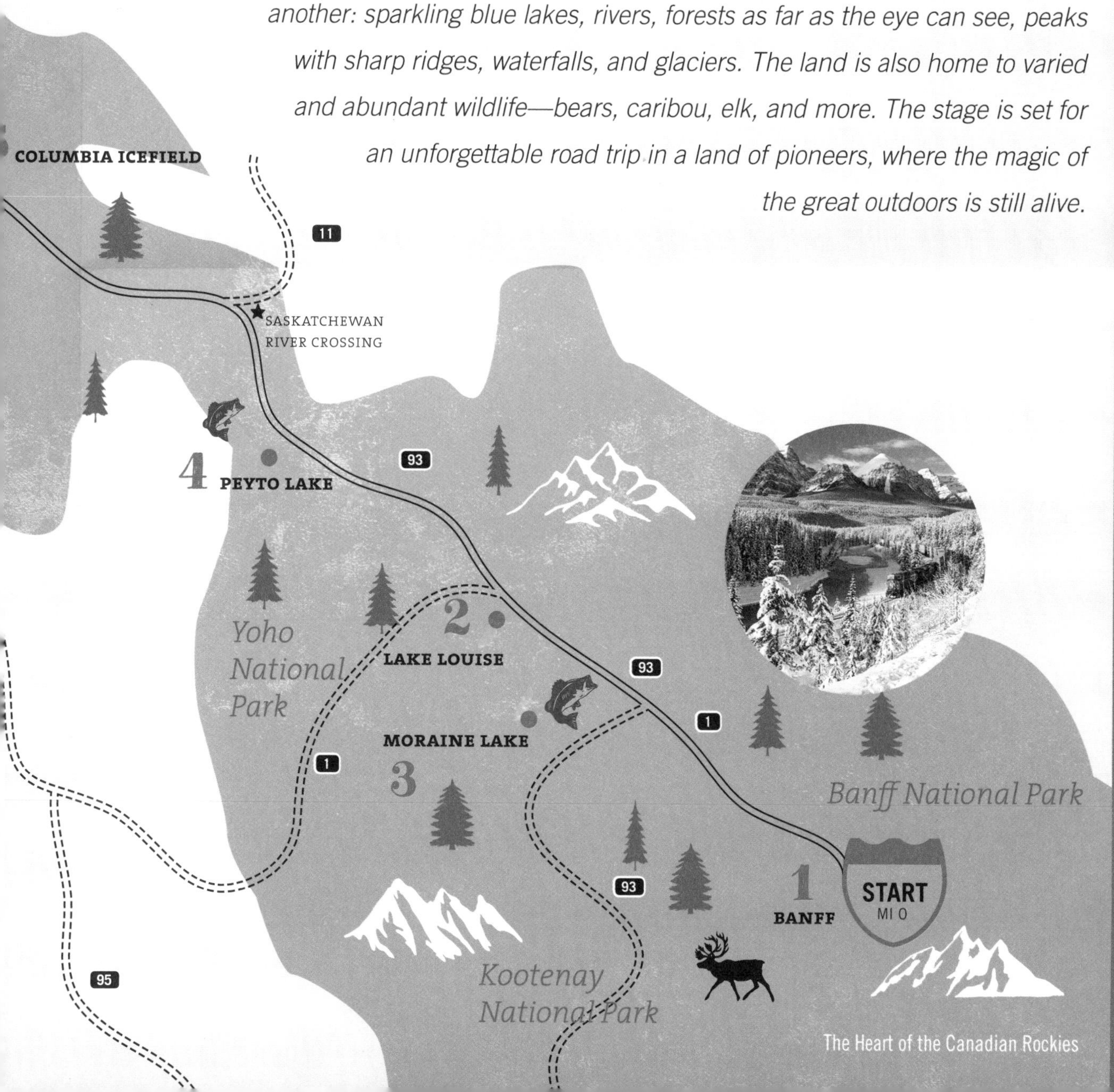

COLUMBIA ICEFIELD

11

★ SASKATCHEWAN
RIVER CROSSING

93

4 PEYTO LAKE

Yoho National Park

2

LAKE LOUISE

93

MORAINE LAKE

3

1

1

Banff National Park

START
MI 0

1
BANFF

93

95

Kootenay National Park

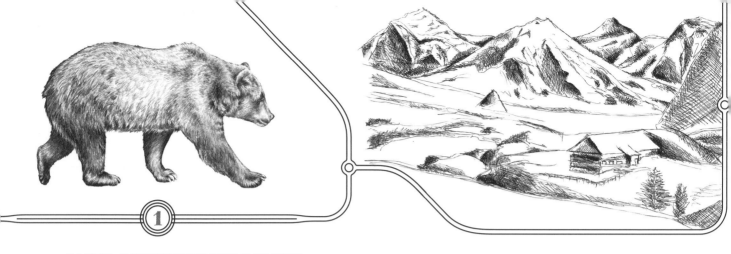

BANFF: GATEWAY TO THE ROCKIES

Gateway to the Rockies, 75 mi (120 km) from Calgary, Banff was born from an unexpected discovery: In 1883, workers on the transcontinental railway stumbled upon a cave with natural hot springs. To take advantage of the popularity of hot spring treatments, Canada decided to create the country's first national park. This was the beginning of a success story that continues today: With more than 3 million visitors a year, the charming mountain resort of **Banff (1)** is one of Canada's major tourist destinations, but not so much for hot springs anymore. The original thermal baths have been transformed into a museum (Cave and Basin National Historic Site) and only one swimming pool remains open to the public: the Banff Upper Hot Springs, where you can splash around (water at 104°F/40°C) in the open air on the slopes of the aptly named Sulfur Mountain.

Today, people come to Banff for the exceptional natural setting of the UNESCO-listed national park, its relaxed village lifestyle, its summer festival, and the countless trails in the surrounding area, which you can cross on foot, by bike, or by canoe. No less than 800 mi (1,300 km) of marked trails of all levels are available to hikers in Banff National Park—enough to recharge your batteries before embarking on this magnificent road trip.

*To take it all in, hop on the **Banff Gondola**, a cable car that rises 2,300 ft (700 m) in 8 minutes. From the top, you'll see a breathtaking 360-degree view of six mountain ranges, the **Vermilion Lakes**, and **Lake Minnewanka**, as well as the tumultuous Bow River, where you can go rafting once back down below.*

Banff Upper Hot Springs

LAKE LOUISE: JEWEL OF THE ROCKIES

On the road 36 mi (58 km) north of Banff, **Lake Louise (2)** appears. It's a popular tourist destination, but above all, it's a Canadian icon. Instantly recognizable, this mountain lake perched at an altitude of 5,680 ft (1,731 m) looks like it was pulled directly out of a landscape painting, so harmonious are its shapes and its setting. Its turquoise waters, in tones that vary according to the seasons and the light, rest at the base of a circle of mountains covered with fir trees, against a backdrop of glaciers and eternal snow. This beautiful, almost unreal landscape has drawn crowds during summer since the construction of the imposing Fairmont Château Lake Louise in the early 20th century. It's advisable to arrive early in the morning—spend the night there if possible—and hike up to a viewpoint first thing: Take the path up to the Big Beehive (a superb panorama), or even hike to the spectacular Victoria Glacier, which overlooks the lake. Less famous than Lake Louise, **Moraine Lake (3),** 7 mi (12 km) to the south, holds its own against its illustrious neighbor. More isolated—completely inaccessible in winter—it is bordered by severe rocky cliffs that plunge into bright blue waters, contrasting with the deep green of the surrounding conifers. An unforgettable, eminently romantic spectacle.

Moraine Lake

Peyto Lake

⑷   ⑸ ⑹

ON THE ICEFIELDS PARKWAY

From Lake Louise, the famous Icefields Parkway heads north toward Jasper, a route through splendid scenery that lives up to its reputation for 144 mi (232 km). Every bend in the Icefields Parkway looks even more beautiful than the last: a feast of pristine lakes including the sublime **Peyto Lake (4),** glaciers, and mighty mountains, all framed by wide valleys. Only a few rudimentary hostels, campsites, a handful of hotels, and a gas station dot the road. At times you'll drive without passing another car for miles, and you'll feel like you're completely alone in the world. After 75 mi (120 km), the forests give way to lunar landscapes, which serve as a prelude to the spectacular **Columbia Icefield (5),** which extends over more than 100 square mi (300 square km) and is more than 984 ft (300 m) thick—the equivalent of the Eiffel Tower—in some places. It includes eight large glaciers, the most famous of which is the **Athabasca Glacier (6).**

FOCUS

The Columbia Icefield's
Spectacular Athabasca Glacier

Located on the watershed, this imposing glacier is unique, as it feeds rivers whose waters flow into three oceans: the Pacific, Atlantic, and Arctic. The **Ice Explorer,** a bus with huge wheels, allows you to travel along the ice and reach the glacier. It can be crowded with tourists, but it's still a special experience! If you don't want to ride the bus, you can admire the glacier on your own, approaching it from the Icefield Center. Warning: It is **forbidden and dangerous** to walk alone on the glacier!

IN JASPER NATIONAL PARK

Continue along the Icefields Parkway. The must-sees along the way include **Mount Edith Cavell (7)** (with many invigorating hikes) and the impressive **Athabasca Falls (8),** 100-ft-high (30-m-high) waterfalls that tumble down a narrow canyon. The road ends in **Jasper (9).** Surrounded by impressive mountains, this small town is a paradise for hiking, cycling, mountain biking, kayaking, and rafting. At the gateway to the city, the Jasper Skytram cable car takes you up to nearly 8,000 ft (2,500 m) to The Whistlers and its superb panorama of the region. A little farther north, the open-air Miette Hot Springs are worth visiting. But above all, you will be able to explore the splendid national park itself. Heading southeast about 30 mi (50 km) from Jasper is another must-see wonder of the Canadian Rockies: **Maligne Lake,** arguably the most intimate of the region's lakes, set against a backdrop of snow-capped peaks. It's a landscape with the serenity of a Japanese woodblock print, sure to inspire contemplation.

Along the way, you will pass **Medicine Lake,** which is oddly dry in winter. It is fed by the underground water network of Maligne Lake, which overflows in summer. When the water levels withdraw, the lake becomes a plain streaked with streams of water. It's like a gigantic natural bathtub that has been magically emptied.

PREPARE FOR YOUR TRIP

- **icefieldsparkway.ca** •
Info on the road.
- **banfflakelouise.com** •
Banff Lake Louise Tourism Board.
Info and downloadable brochures.
- **tourismealberta.ca** •
Alberta Tourism Board.

GETTING THERE

Calgary International Airport is the closest large airport to Banff.

RENTING A CAR

Rent your car in Calgary, and either do a loop or return it in Vancouver. Car rentals are also available in Banff and Jasper.

WHERE TO STAY

- **Banff Centre:** 107 Tunnel Mountain Drive, Banff.
- **banffcentre.ca** • An astonishing amalgam of a cultural center, a campus for resident artists, several performance venues, and also a hotel and three restaurants for all budgets (Three Ravens Dining Room is very good).
- **Hotel Athabasca:** 510 Patricia St., Jasper. • **athabascahotel.com** •
A good hotel in the heart of Jasper, open since 1929. Vintage vibe.

WHERE TO EAT

- **The Maple Leaf Grill:**
137, Banff Ave., Banff. An elegant bistro with fine cuisine based on local products (Alberta beef, bison, salmon, etc.).
- **Bruno's Cafe & Grill:**
304, Caribou St., Banff. Burgers, pizza, wraps, sandwiches—a whole range of options at low prices.
- **Evil Dave's:** 622, Patricia St., Jasper. Generous and hearty options, good craft beers, modern decor, and great service.

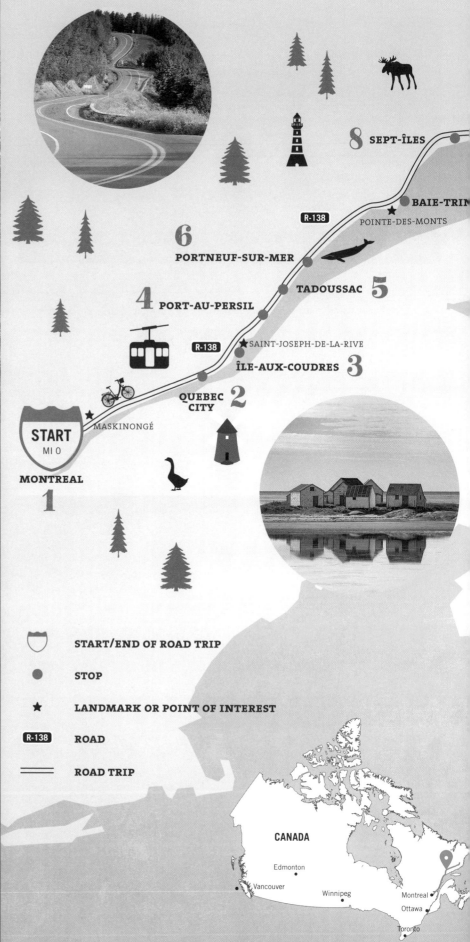

LOCATION

Quebec, in eastern Canada

ROUTE

Montreal – Kegashka

LENGTH

863 mi (1,389 km)

TIME

7 days minimum

YOU'LL LOVE

The bustle of Montreal, the timelessness of Quebec, the warmth of Quebecers, the great outdoors of the North Shore, the whales, and the adventure of reaching the end of the road.

8 SEPT-ÎLES

BAIE-TRIN

★ POINTE-DES-MONTS

R-138

6
PORTNEUF-SUR-MER

4 PORT-AU-PERSIL

TADOUSSAC 5

R-138

★ SAINT-JOSEPH-DE-LA-RIVE

ÎLE-AUX-COUDRES 3

QUEBEC CITY

2

START MI 0

MASKINONGÉ

MONTREAL

1

⬡ START/END OF ROAD TRIP

● STOP

★ LANDMARK OR POINT OF INTEREST

R-138 ROAD

═══ ROAD TRIP

CANADA

Edmonton

Vancouver

Winnipeg

Montreal

Ottawa

Toronto

★ BLANC-SABLON

R-138

10
NATASHQUAN

END
MI 863

11
KEGASHKA

AUX
ROQUETS ★
MINGAN
ARCHIPELAGO **9**

Anticosti Island

NEWFOUNDLAND ★

ROUTE 138
FROM MONTREAL ➤——→ TO KEGASHKA

It's not just a road; it's also a challenge, a test of patience. Over the course of several days, you'll see the banks of the monumental St. Lawrence River unfold, followed by its immense, salty estuary. On one side, water and whales. On the other, fields, blueberries, the boreal forest, and then the beginnings of the tundra in the distance at the gates of Labrador. More than for any other road trip, the main focus here is not the destination—a dead end—but the journey through all the charms of Quebec, from the city to the wild expanses.

Granny by A'Shop for the Mural Festival 2013

MONTREAL: CANADA WITH A FRENCH ACCENT

Though it officially begins at the New York State border, Route 138 really comes to life in **Montreal (1).** The route is named Sherbrooke Street within Montreal, and it serves as the backbone here, sliding through the city from west to east. It cuts between the French-speaking city's tidy skyscrapers, between the green belvedere of Mount Royal and the Place Ville Marie, which bustles with suit-and-tie workers and bicycle couriers zigzagging through traffic. It's lined with large museums and numerous department stores, and you'll cross it on a walk from Chinatown to Little Italy, through the remains of the red-light district, which has been reclaimed by theaters.

In spite of the city's fast pace, Montrealers know how to live and catch their breath: with a good *broue* (beer) at the terraces of Saint-Denis, or via BIXI (bicycle rentals) on the banks of the St. Lawrence River and the Lachine Canal. Montreal is an island surrounded by islands. On the island of Notre-Dame, you can bathe in clear water on a sandy beach in the shade of potted palm trees. And surfing is just a stone's throw away at the foot of the Pont de la Concorde (Concorde Bridge), with a view of the buildings of the old city. Montreal is a global city, timeless, constantly changing, and diverse.

MONTREAL – QUEBEC CITY: VIA THE CHEMIN DU ROY

Unfolding over 170 mi (280 km) between Montreal and Quebec City, this route lovingly follows the curves of the great St. Lawrence River, along which the settlers of New France established their long plots of land (called *rangs*) so that everyone could have access at the river. It is on this "grand rue" of bygone days that present-day Quebec took shape. Throughout the land, the stone mansions of lords, a few mills, monasteries, churches, and parish houses serve as relics of rural life under the yoke of religion. Snow geese, on the other hand, don't mind the history: Descending from the far north, they stop in droves near **Maskinongé** each fall, then again in spring during their great migration (2,000 mi/4,000 km one-way!). At last count, there

were 850,000 of them, along with geese and ducks, colonizing the riverbanks and the 103 islands of the great Lac Saint-Pierre, formed by an outflow of the St. Lawrence River. The area, 90 percent untouched, has been classified as a biosphere reserve.

After this breath of fresh air, Route 138 enters **Quebec City (2),** the capital of the province, which initially feels like a typical North American suburb. You have to leave the main artery to find the nucleus of Old Quebec, curled up behind its old walls and grassy slopes. Straight lines give way to charming curves and nostalgic names. In the lower town, around the Place Royale, cobbled streets, alleys, and stone buildings dating to the 17th and 18th centuries feel

lost in time; at times, you might think you're in northern France. In this very French-feeling maze, Notre-Dame-des-Victoires (1688) declares its seniority: It is the oldest stone church in North America. Then, you'll spot the funicular climbing the cliff, pouring its passengers onto the planks of the large Terrasse Dufferin, which faces the statue of explorer Samuel de Champlain. It's a theatrical setting at the foot of the famous Château Frontenac—an extravagant Victorian hotel with copper roofs, posted on a lookout point above the Chemin du Roy. "Nothing seemed to me so beautiful and so magnificent as the position of Quebec City," wrote Louis de Buade de Frontenac long ago.

LOVE AT FIRST SIGHT

Just downstream from Quebec City, a long strip of land stretches along the St. Lawrence: Île d'Orléans. French-Canadian singer Félix Leclerc sings about the peaceful island in his song "Le tour de l'Île"—Leclerc is buried on the island. The activities change with the seasons: You can visit in the spring for a taste of syrup in the maple groves, or at the beginning of autumn for the intense colors. Take a quiet walk along the path that traces the periphery of the island, through villages of noble stone, watched over by bell towers and by old mansions.

CHARLEVOIX – TADOUSSAC: TIMELESS QUEBEC

Charlevoix is a fascinating region—its geography was shaken up 350 million years ago by the impact of a huge meteorite. Route 138 continues its romantic stroll along the river here, with an atmosphere of deeply rooted Quebec tradition. The warm welcome and the sweetness of life have attracted many artists and craftsmen to this region, especially to Baie-Saint-Paul. From here, take a detour along Route 362, which hugs the escarpments along the St. Lawrence River where Route 138 turns inland. Route 362 passes **Saint-Joseph-de-la-Rive,** where you can take a boat to **Isle-aux-Coudres (3)** and its mills of yesteryear. You'll pass between farms and white wooden houses in **Saint-Irénée,** and

rejoin Route 138 in **Cap-à-l'Aigle,** known for its lilacs. Then, the charming hidden hamlet of **Port-au-Persil (4)**—ranked among the most beautiful villages in Quebec—is up next, home to spruce trees, little rapids, a small white church, and a small beach strewn with rocks. On the other side of the road: 12 mi (20 km) of river and tidal flats that can be explored at low tide.

Past Baie-Sainte-Catherine, Route 138 comes up against a major obstacle: the mighty Saguenay River, emerging from a fjord-like canyon. There's no bridge here, but a ferry will take you across the river to the large village of **Tadoussac (5)** (from *Totoustak,*

meaning "where the water comes out" in the Indigenous language of Montagnais), moored in a landscape of rocky, forested hills. One of the earliest trading posts of New France was founded here in the 16th century. Located along rue du Bord de l'Eau, the trading post been faithfully reconstructed, with fences and wooden shanties where French and Indigenous people exchanged beaver pelts for necklaces of glass beads. The town is also home to pretty wooden chapel (1750) that recalls the efforts—often in vain—of the missionaries to settle here and convert the Indigenous population.

THE CALL OF THE FOREST

Baie-Comeau, the industrious paper capital of Manicouagan, marks the beginning of an extraordinary adventure. From here, Route 389 runs due north, through 350 mi (570 km) of unbroken forest, toward the mining towns of Fermont and Labrador City, passing the ghost town of Gagnon and the large Manic dams. Much of the route is unpaved, and some sections are narrow, twisty, and bumpy. The journey enters English-speaking land at the paved Trans Labrador Highway (Route 500), continuing on until the military town of Goose Bay (310 mi/500 km). A dead end? Not since 2009 and the inauguration of Route 510, which connects to the Labrador Sea: 370 mi (600 km) more, including 250 mi (400 km) without a living soul.... And after that? You can continue via ferry to Newfoundland—a simple hop, skip, and a jump—or return to Quebec on the ferry, which travels from port to port along the Lower North Shore every week. After 32 hours of navigation, you'll reach Kegashka, the terminus of Route 138. The loop is complete. As a bonus? Spot a few icebergs drifting along the coast with the Greenland Current.

• relaisnordik.com •

TADOUSSAC – MANICOUAGAN: WHALE ENCOUNTERS

In Tadoussac, the story is sometimes told of a ship whose passengers, in a hurry to get ashore after a long transatlantic voyage, disembarked on a group of islets facing the port. When the rocks they were standing on began to sink, they realized they were standing . . . on the backs of whales! Though the number of whales in the area has unfortunately plummeted due to once-intensive hunting, every summer, many cetaceans still make their way up the river for an uninterrupted feast of plankton and krill, abundant in these waters. From the shore, in a boat, in a Zodiac (rigid inflatable boat), in a kayak, or even in a seaplane, it's possible to see a dozen species, including small white belugas, of which about a thousand remain. In Les Bergeronnes and **Portneuf-sur-Mer (6),** two less-touristy towns farther north on Route 138, your chance of meeting a colossal blue whale (115 ft/35 m!) increases.

Most visitors turn back once they reach Tadoussac. A pity. Still following the St. Lawrence River, Route 138 enters the heart of the Manicouagan and the North Shore, a region half the size of France and home to fewer than 100,000 people! Here it is, the Quebec you've dreamed of, with infinite landscapes of water and forest unrolling all around you. Along the way, the towns, named after the great outdoors—Chute-aux-Outardes, Les Islets-Caribou, etc.—become more and more scattered, smaller and smaller. After passing the pretty **Pointe-des-Monts** lighthouse, where the people used to fire cannons to guide ships in the fog, you'll reach **Baie-Trinité (7),** where the National Shipwreck Center confirms how dangerous it is to navigate this area. From here, you can no longer see the Gaspé Peninsula on the other side of the river: Suddenly, the estuary has widened to more than 60 mi (100 km)!

SEPT-ÎLES – LA MINGANIE: ON INDIGENOUS LAND

The large city of **Sept-Îles (8),** 556 mi (895 km) from Montreal, has only been served by road since the 1960s. Sept-Îles is on the territory of the Indigenous inhabitants of Montagnais, who are called Innu. The Shaputuan Museum bears witness to their thousand-year-old culture, centered on caribou hunting, while the Old Fur Trading Post of the Hudson Bay Company, founded around 1673, magnificently takes us back to the era of fur trading. Hidden behind a high fence, the few reconstructed wooden buildings, including a church, come to life in the summer thanks to costumed guides. To better understand the Indigenous residents and their traditions, you should come in early August for the Innu Nikamu dance festival; Crees and Inuit are also usually invited.

Shortly after Sept-Îles, the most spectacular region of the North Shore begins: Minganie. Route 138 winds its way through ever-increasing solitude, with charming villages bordering on the microscopic and gas stations becoming more and more precious. You'll cross the rapids and the fall of the Manitou River in an implacable setting of black spruce trees, rocks, and icy spray. Farther on, from Longue-Pointe-de-Mingan or Havre-Saint-Pierre, you can embark on a trip to the **Mingan Archipelago (9),** classified as a national park, known for its mushroom-shaped rock monoliths carved by glacial erosion. Some of these islets, where eider ducks (yes, as in eiderdown) nest, shelter wild campsites, paths, and footbridges running over the moor and in the bogs. A delight! In August, the **Île aux Perroquets** offers a bonus: a puffin colony.

Manitou River

ACADIA AND THE END OF THE ROAD

Rather than Quebec's fleur-de-lis flag, it is a French flag with a gold star that proudly flies over Havre-Saint-Pierre. In 1713, Acadia, the first French colony in North America (which was located in what is today Nova Scotia and New Brunswick, on the southern side of the Gulf of St. Lawrence) fell into the hands of the English. Two generations later, the king's troops forcefully expelled the remaining French farmers. This event is known as the Great Upheaval. Some ended up in Louisiana, others in Belle-Île off the western coast of Brittany. A few ended up here on the North Shore, which was mostly deserted at the time. Once landowners, they became fishermen, catching lobster and snow crab. Here, Route 138 seems at times to float on fluffy white waves of cottongrass, flying over dwarf spruce trees and peat bogs that look like tundra. It was only in 1996 that the road was extended to **Natashquan (10),** meaning "where the bear is hunted," 790 mi (1,270 km) from Montreal. The isolated beauty of the village is captured beautifully by the singer-songwriter Gilles Vigneault. Under the influence of the famed singer, the Montagnais (the Indigenous residents of Natashquan) cultivate their traditions with a restored old school and emblematic boathouses. But Route 138 continues on: In 2013, it connected the 138 inhabitants of **Kegashka (11)** to the rest of the country. This is now the terminus of Route 138. The end of the world? Not quite. Every week, the ferry takes over, going from port to port along the Lower North Shore coastline, all the way Labrador.

PLAYLIST

Nelly Furtado	Felix Leclerc
–	–
I'M LIKE A BIRD	**LE PETIT BONHEUR**
Arcade Fire	Gilles Vigneault
–	–
WAKE UP	**NATASHQUAN**

PREPARE FOR YOUR TRIP

- quebecoriginal.com •
- lecheminduroy.com •
- tourisme-charlevoix.com •
- tourismecote-nord.com •
- quebecmaritime.ca •

GETTING THERE

Flying into Montréal–Trudeau International Airport (YUL) is easy.

RENTING A CAR

Car rentals in Canada have unlimited mileage. That's good news, especially since you will have to make the return trip, at least partially: There are no car rental companies east of Sept-Îles.

WHEN TO GO

From June to early October.

WHERE TO STAY

Accommodation prices in Quebec are reasonable. In the city, the options are endless: youth hostels, motels, small and large hotels, not to mention bed and breakfasts and daily apartment rentals and Airbnbs. Along the river, you can choose camping, motels, or lodges according to your means.

WHAT TO EAT

Quebec cuisine is based on fresh seasonal products from both land and sea, and has been evolving for the last 20 years. Classic hearty dishes include *tourtière* (pie), beans with bacon, soups, game, and salmon. Urban areas have many international restaurants.

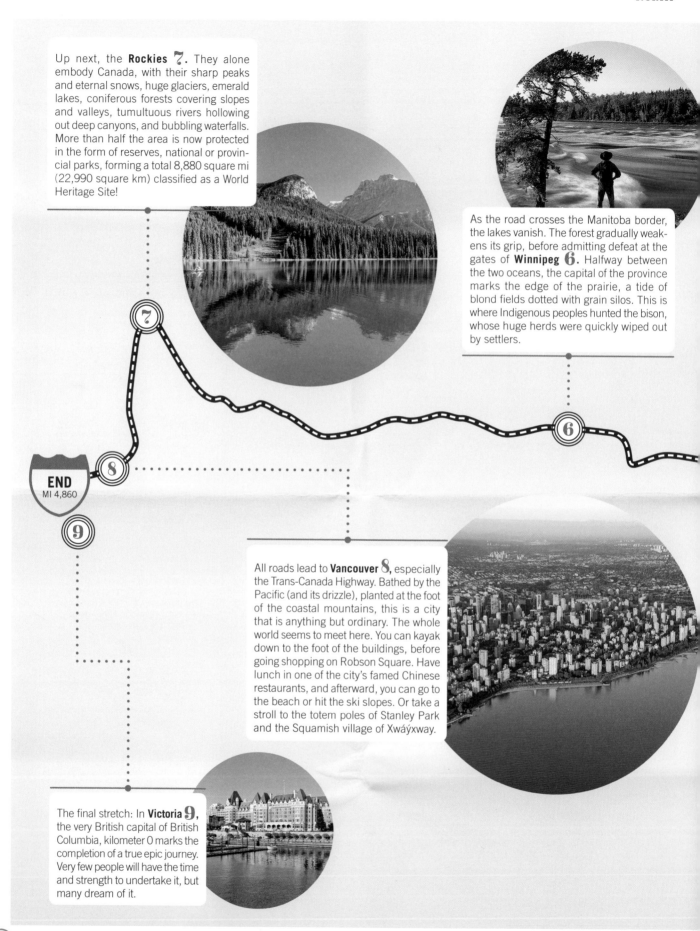

Up next, the **Rockies 7.** They alone embody Canada, with their sharp peaks and eternal snows, huge glaciers, emerald lakes, coniferous forests covering slopes and valleys, tumultuous rivers hollowing out deep canyons, and bubbling waterfalls. More than half the area is now protected in the form of reserves, national or provincial parks, forming a total 8,880 square mi (22,990 square km) classified as a World Heritage Site!

As the road crosses the Manitoba border, the lakes vanish. The forest gradually weakens its grip, before admitting defeat at the gates of **Winnipeg 6.** Halfway between the two oceans, the capital of the province marks the edge of the prairie, a tide of blond fields dotted with grain silos. This is where Indigenous peoples hunted the bison, whose huge herds were quickly wiped out by settlers.

END
MI 4,860

All roads lead to **Vancouver 8,** especially the Trans-Canada Highway. Bathed by the Pacific (and its drizzle), planted at the foot of the coastal mountains, this is a city that is anything but ordinary. The whole world seems to meet here. You can kayak down to the foot of the buildings, before going shopping on Robson Square. Have lunch in one of the city's famed Chinese restaurants, and afterward, you can go to the beach or hit the ski slopes. Or take a stroll to the totem poles of Stanley Park and the Squamish village of Xwáýxway.

The final stretch: In **Victoria 9,** the very British capital of British Columbia, kilometer 0 marks the completion of a true epic journey. Very few people will have the time and strength to undertake it, but many dream of it.

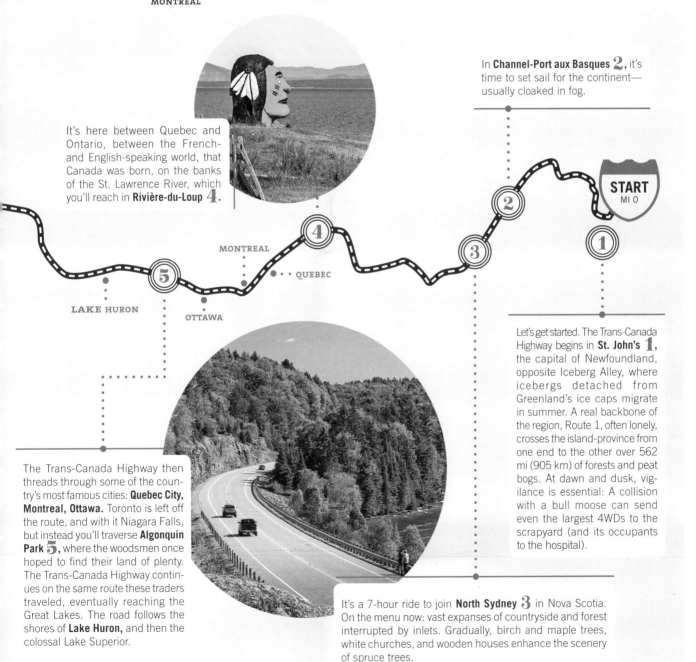

TRANS-CANADA HIGHWAY
FROM COAST TO COAST
FROM THE ATLANTIC ➤➤➤ TO THE PACIFIC

More than a road, this is an idea: uniting an entire country with one strip of pavement, from the Atlantic to the Pacific, through six time zones. Created in 1962 by connecting provincial highways, this axis maintained by the Canadian federal government has a major claim to fame: It's the longest "national" road in the world. It's an astonishing transcontinental route that links two islands, Newfoundland to the east and Vancouver Island, British Columbia, to the west.

VANCOUVER QUEBEC CITY MONTREAL

N
O E
S

In **Channel-Port aux Basques 2**, it's time to set sail for the continent—usually cloaked in fog.

It's here between Quebec and Ontario, between the French- and English-speaking world, that Canada was born, on the banks of the St. Lawrence River, which you'll reach in **Rivière-du-Loup 4**.

START
MI 0

MONTREAL
QUEBEC
LAKE HURON
OTTAWA

Let's get started. The Trans-Canada Highway begins in **St. John's 1**, the capital of Newfoundland, opposite Iceberg Alley, where icebergs detached from Greenland's ice caps migrate in summer. A real backbone of the region, Route 1, often lonely, crosses the island-province from one end to the other over 562 mi (905 km) of forests and peat bogs. At dawn and dusk, vigilance is essential: A collision with a bull moose can send even the largest 4WDs to the scrapyard (and its occupants to the hospital).

The Trans-Canada Highway then threads through some of the country's most famous cities: **Quebec City, Montreal, Ottawa.** Toronto is left off the route, and with it Niagara Falls, but instead you'll traverse **Algonquin Park 5**, where the woodsmen once hoped to find their land of plenty. The Trans-Canada Highway continues on the same route these traders traveled, eventually reaching the Great Lakes. The road follows the shores of **Lake Huron,** and then the colossal Lake Superior.

It's a 7-hour ride to join **North Sydney 3** in Nova Scotia. On the menu now: vast expanses of countryside and forest interrupted by inlets. Gradually, birch and maple trees, white churches, and wooden houses enhance the scenery of spruce trees.

OTHER ROAD TRIPS IN CANADA

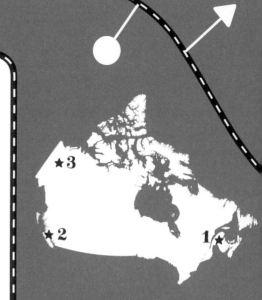

Infinite.
Unlimited. Without Borders.

There are many adjectives, but it's still impossible to define the legendary grandeur of Canada: nearly 4 million square mi (10 million square km), three-quarters of which is uninhabited. The size of the rivers, the harshness of the interminable winter, the theatricality of the landscapes subjected to the annual mischief of the late-summer heat—nothing is rational. Nothing is on a human scale. . . .

At the heart of these vast spaces, the myths of the Far North, captured by Jack London, and of the conquest of the West collide. The forest and the lakes (there are more than a million!) dominate the imagination. But the vastness of the boreal forest hides the jagged coasts of the Atlantic, the endless Prairie, the white peaks of the Rockies and their emerald lakes, the century-old trees and the wild beaches of the Pacific. And, in the far north: 15 degrees of latitude covered by tundra, all the way to the pole. A wild road, inaugurated in 2017, goes up to the Arctic Ocean. Canada is a country of countless odysseys.

THE GASPÉSIE TOUR

This is a sensible pick: an 550-mi (885-km) loop that winds along the coast of the great Gaspé Peninsula, sandwiched between the St. Lawrence River and its immense gulf. Where does the sea begin, and where does the river end? It's hard to say for sure, but one thing is certain: the waves here taste like salt—until winter freezes them. The small population lives in little fishing ports—you can see the cod they've spread out to dry—located at the mouth of secluded valleys with names that conjure images of adventure: Manche-d'Épée (Sword Handle), Cap-d'Espoir (Cape of Hope), L'Anse-au-Griffon (Griffin Cove), Ruisseau-Castor (Beaver Creek). . . . Here, one of the last herds of woodland caribou lives in the heart of the Chic-Choc Mountains. At the tip of the peninsula, where the last of the Appalachian Mountains drop off in high cliffs, Bonaventure Island (a national park) is home to the largest colony of northern gannets in the world: More than 50,000 mated pairs live there, calling out in concert. The iconic Percé Rock, an impressive block of granite with an arch through it, is nearby. The best time to go is late September–early October, when the second summer sets the forest colors ablaze.

ON THE ALASKA HIGHWAY

Less than 2 hours from the mainland, Vancouver Island is home to many getaways. And even though it's the end of the Trans-Canada Highway, it's where an even more beautiful, more intimate journey begins. Route 19, the only axis through this territory, winds north for 300 mi (500 km). A few rare roads branch off toward the west coast—the main one to the Pacific Rim National Park Reserve, its wild beaches strewn with logs and a thick coat of rain forest. Farther north, the island begins to open up to the Inside Passage and its armada of rocky and wooded islands. At Telegraph Cove, where houses on stilts hug the edge of the cove, you can embark on a trip to see orcas, as well as sea lions, seals, and bald eagles. Black bears and grizzly bears prowl around, too. And the tallest totem pole in the world (174 ft/53 m) stands against the wind a short distance away on Cormorant Island, among the 'Namgis First Nation population.

From Port Hardy, the Northern Adventure ferry slips through a labyrinth of fjords, straits, and islands until it reaches Prince Rupert, at the gateway to Alaska. Here, some succumb to the call of the North. Others take the long road to the Rockies, crossing through the territory of the Gitxsan people, where the land is as beautiful as it is underrated.

THE NORTHERNMOST ROAD IN THE WORLD

The motto of Canadian bridges and roads seems to be "Keep going north." In 1979, one of Canada's most challenging roads was born: the Dempster Highway. The road starts on the outskirts of Dawson City, a famous gold-mining town in the Yukon, and ends in the town of Inuvik in the Northwest Territories, located on the delta of the immense Mackenzie River. Total distance: 400 mi (700 km). This "autoroute" as our Quebec neighbors say, is not very comfortable: Cars are scarce, and trucks run on a raised bed of gravel to protect the permafrost and prevent the road from sinking during thaws. Paving with tar would be impossible here: The fluctuation between warmer temperatures and cold winters (-18°F/-28°C on average in Inuvik in January) means the pavement would constantly need to be redone.

To withstand the Dempster, you need to have nerves of steel, especially if it rains (think ice rink). And remember that the whole point of the trip is the journey, not the destination. Along the way, there's the motel-restaurant-rest-stop-laundromat-billiard oasis of Eagle Plains (230 mi/370 km from Dawson City), the Arctic Circle sign, a ferry to cross the Peel River, and the wooden church and cemetery of the old Hudson Bay Company trading post at Fort McPherson. And then, there's still a ferry to cross the Mackenzie River, plains bordered by huge mountains, sometimes moose, often mud, mosquitoes, and always dust. And as a bonus: a new stretch of road, 75 mi (120 km) more, up to Tuktoyaktuk, an Inuit village on the shores of the Beaufort Sea, overlooking the Arctic Ocean. Latitude: 69° 25' 24''. Before 2017, you could only get there in winter via an ice road.

LATIN AMERICA

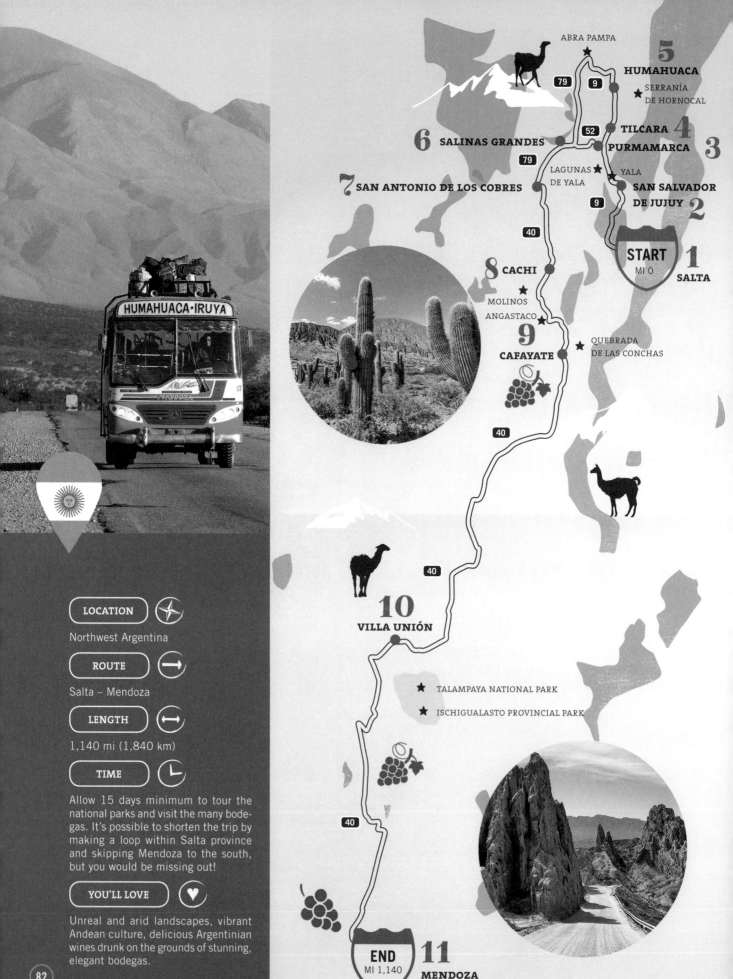

ABRA PAMPA

5
HUMAHUACA
★ SERRANÍA
DE HORNOCAL

79 9

52 **TILCARA** **4**
PURMAMARCA **3**

6 **SALINAS GRANDES**

79

7 **SAN ANTONIO DE LOS COBRES**

LAGUNAS ★
DE YALA

★ YALA
**SAN SALVADOR
DE JUJUY** **2**

9

40

START
MI 0

1
SALTA

8 **CACHI**

★ MOLINOS
ANGASTACO

9
CAFAYATE

★ QUEBRADA
DE LAS CONCHAS

40

40

10
VILLA UNIÓN

★ TALAMPAYA NATIONAL PARK

★ ISCHIGUALASTO PROVINCIAL PARK

40

END
MI 1,140

11
MENDOZA

LOCATION ✦

Northwest Argentina

ROUTE →

Salta – Mendoza

LENGTH ↔

1,140 mi (1,840 km)

TIME 🕐

Allow 15 days minimum to tour the national parks and visit the many bodegas. It's possible to shorten the trip by making a loop within Salta province and skipping Mendoza to the south, but you would be missing out!

YOU'LL LOVE ♥

Unreal and arid landscapes, vibrant Andean culture, delicious Argentinian wines drunk on the grounds of stunning, elegant bodegas.

NOROESTE
ARGENTINO
FROM SALTA ➤➤➤ TO MENDOZA

With its canyons covered in scrubby desert vegetation, the Noroeste Argentino offers an extraordinary, quintessentially Western atmosphere: earthy red color palettes, hoodoos, and high plateaus. An alien universe, almost bare, where water and wind have shaped spectacular landscapes. Bordered by Chile, Bolivia, and Paraguay, some residents of this region still speak Quechua, the language of their ancestors. Farther south, around Cafayate and Mendoza, wine is in the spotlight. Visiting some of the wineries, here called bodegas, you'll be able to taste some beautiful Argentinian grapes. This itinerary through a mythical region departs from Salta.

Córdoba

Buenos Aires

ARGENTINA

Comodoro Rivadavia

El Calafate

START/END OF ROAD TRIP	
STOP	●
LANDMARK OR POINT OF INTEREST	★
ROAD	9
ROAD TRIP	═══

FROM SALTA TO SAN SALVADOR DE JUJUY

Located in the heart of the Noroeste region at an altitude of 1,200 m (4,000 ft), at the foot of Cerro San Bernardo, **Salta (1)** is the largest city in Northwest Argentina. One of the prettiest colonial cities in Argentina, it's nicknamed *la linda,* or "the beautiful."

Founded in 1582 by the Spanish, a major stop on a traditional trade route to Bolivia and Peru, Salta flourished in the 18th and 19th centuries, as evidenced by its stately homes and churches and impressive old convent. Buildings are adorned by elaborate wooden balconies, porches, and carved gates; decorative interior patios surround *aljibes,* or traditional cisterns; and the exquisite scent of orange trees permeates the air. Still an active commercial city, Salta has maintained a pleasant, authentic atmosphere, lively day and night, young and traditional at the same time.

After enjoying the city for 2 or 3 days, it's time to hit the road and head north. A great route to take is the beautiful Ruta de la Cornisa (Ruta 9), a twisting, narrow road around Cerro San Bernardo. It's not easy to find from Salta, so don't hesitate to ask for directions and about conditions: The route is often impassable during the rainy period. Winding through thick tropical forests, it takes 2-2.5 hours to cover the 90 km (60 mi) separating Salta from **San Salvador de Jujuy (2).** Along the way, stop at picnic areas in the middle of superb, verdant landscapes.

The quicker route is to take Autopista 9 to General Guemes, and then Ruta 66 to Jujuy.

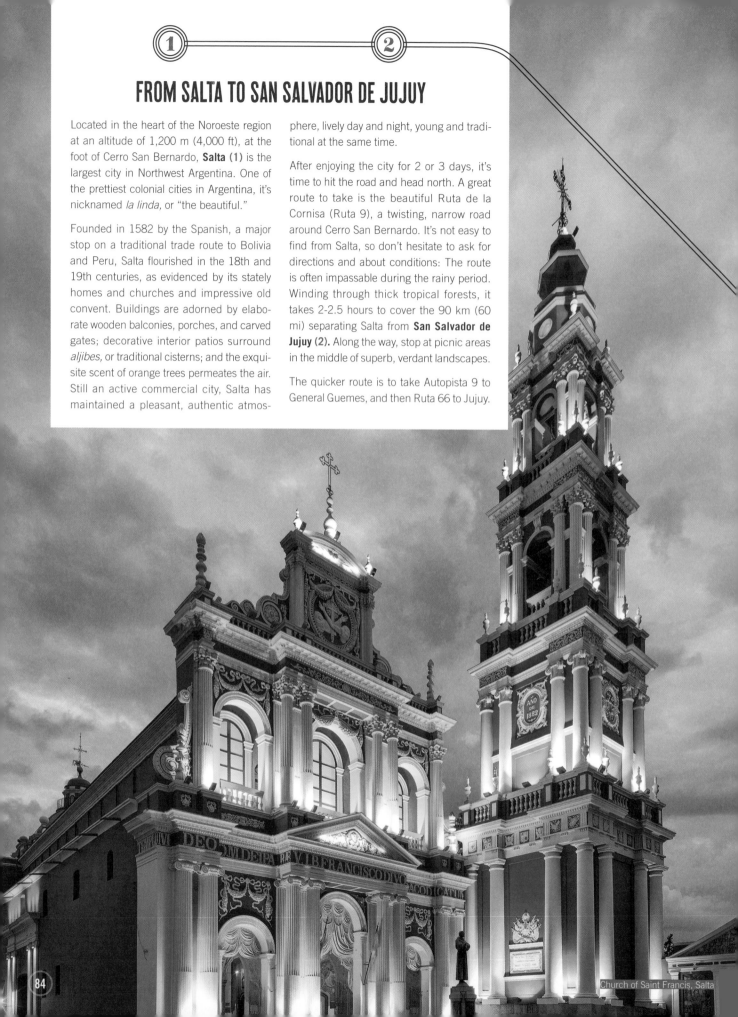

Church of Saint Francis, Salta

IN THE HEART OF THE QUEBRADA DE HUMAHUACA

About 10 mi (20 km) outside San Salvador de Jujuy, you'll pass the small village of **Yala,** a few beautiful houses surrounded by subtropical forest. Local fisherfolk meet here on weekends to fish for trout. You might want to stop by the **Lagunas de Yala,** surrounded by lush, green mountains.

Farther on, the verdant landscape becomes bare, thinning to the candelabra-like silhouettes of cacti. You'll pass the adobe hut villages of Volcan and Tumbaya.

Finally, you'll enter the fantastic Quebrada de Humahuaca, a wild, bewitching valley seemingly frozen in time. Listed as a UNESCO World Heritage Site in 2003 for its biodiversity and cultural history, the *quebrada* has seen no less than 10,000 years of human history, with hundreds of archaeological sites still unexplored.

On the intersection of magnificent Ruta 52 is **Purmamarca (3),** a large village surrounded by a rocky gorge known as Cerro de los Siete Colores (the Hill of Seven Colors). Small houses of adobe and cactus wood harmonize with the landscape; this "virgin land" (*purmamarca* in Quechua) is today the subject of growing tourist interest, with hotels and posadas popping up like mushrooms. Luckily, a constant concern for preservation and the environment means this tourism boom has not affected Purmamarca's serenity.

A few miles farther north, just before the Paleta del Pintor (Painter's Palette) region at an altitude of 8,085 ft (2,465 m), a small road leads to the village of **Tilcara (4).** Tilcara, which means "shooting star" in Quechua, is another booming town that deserves a stop, especially to walk up to its *pucará,* a fortress from the Inca period built at the top of a hill. The city is certainly the busiest in the *quebrada,* with an

DETOUR TO ABRA PAMPA

Head toward Salinas Grandes by driving north from Humahuaca, in the direction of Bolivia. You'll reach 12,400 ft (2,780 m) in elevation before getting to Abra Pampa, a large village battered by the wind, before continuing higher still, where the highlands (puna) take over. From Abra Pampa, you can either head back via Ruta 40, which begins in La Quiaca on the Bolivian border, or Ruta 11, less than half a mile north of Abra Pampa.

These two tracks cover 90 mi (140 km) of high plateau landscapes before meeting up with Ruta 52 near Salinas Grandes. It's a good alternative to Ruta 9 if you are not afraid of going a little off-grid. You'll pass remote villages, dashing vicuñas (relatives of the llama), and fuzzy Suri alpacas.

influx of young South American backpackers and foreign tourists, especially during Enero Tilcareño, or pre-Carnival, in January, but also during Carnival itself, Holy Week, and the festival celebrating Andean fertility goddess Pachamama in August.

On the banks of the Río Grande, **Humahuaca (5),** at an altitude of almost 10,000 ft (3,000 m), is the most populated village of the *quebrada* of the same name. The village has retained its authentic character with cobbled streets, adobe houses, churros, and llama wool sweaters. If you are lucky enough to come in February, during Carnival, you'll see age-old traditions that are very much alive, even though Buenos Aires seems lightyears away. You won't be able to miss **Serranía de Hornocal,** the famous 14-colored mountain, 15 mi (25 km) farther east.

SALINAS GRANDES: THE SALT DESERT

Once you've had your fill of the stark, alien north, go back to Purmamarca via Ruta 9 and get on Ruta 52, which climbs toward Chile. Between Purmamarca and Salinas, the drive offers magnificent panoramas of hoodoos, multicolored rocks, and precipices. After crossing the Potrerillos pass at 13,680 ft (4,170 m), you descend to a high plateau at 11,650 ft (3,550 m). You'll cross Ruta 79 before reaching what looks like a mirage: a white expanse as far as the eye can see known as the **Salinas Grandes (6).**

As you approach, you'll see rows of pools filled with turquoise water in which the sky and mountains are mirrored. All around, salt harvesters are covered head to toe to protect themselves from the sun that bakes Argentina's biggest salt flat. To make the most of the sunset over the Andes, leave in the afternoon, when the chances of a clear sky over the *salinas* are highest. Though fog often covers the pass that leads to the salt flat, when the clouds dissipate the spectacle is magnificent.

Next, head for **San Antonio de los Cobres (7)** and the legendary Ruta 40, located at an altitude of 12,385 ft (3,775 m). Soon you'll be descending farther south.

THE CALCHAQUÍES VALLEYS

The Río Calchaquí burrows into several very different valleys. A fabulous track through this region leads to Cafayate via the villages of **Cachi (8), Molinos,** and **Angastaco.** To fully appreciate this route, check the weather forecast and the condition of Ruta 40 between Cachi and Cafayate before setting off (some sections may be closed if it has rained too much recently). In the event of unfavorable weather conditions, rent a vehicle with four-wheel drive that can easily cross difficult passages; don't forget the spare tire and a full tank of gas. You'll find gas stations in Cachi, Molinos, and Angastaco.

CAFAYATE AND THE QUEBRADA DE LA CONCHAS

Leaving the stunning, moon-like Calchaquíes Valleys, you'll arrive in **Cafayate (9),** a small town surrounded by vineyards and bodegas. Leaning against the foothills of the cordillera at an altitude of 5,450 ft (1,660 m), Cafayate is a happy marriage of nature and culture. Formerly used mostly for grazing, winemakers have succeeded in growing vines and producing good wines on these scenic highlands. This is a quiet, homey stopover after hours of stony and dusty tracks.

To leave Cafayate without tasting some of its wines would almost be sacrilege. The region is known for Torrontés grapes, whose vines can grow at elevations of up to 10,000 ft (3,000 m) and produce complex and floral wines. Look out for the Torrontés or char-

donnay made by Michel Torino and the Torrontés Viejo and Cafayate Reserva Blanco from Etchart Wine. If you prefer a bolder red, try Don David's cabernet.

Cafayate is an excellent starting point for visiting the magnificent **Quebrada de las Conchas,** 10 mi (15 km) northeast of the city. Allow at least a half day to enjoy these beautiful landscapes, timing your visit to enjoy the beautiful early morning light or the cool sweetness of the late evening. A landscape worthy of classic Western movies, roamed by wild cats and snakes, the scenery is among the most spectacular in Northwest Argentina. Water and wind have shaped it bit by bit into often surreal formations, varying in shades from ocher to pink to red.

ROUTE 40 TO MENDOZA

Some 400 mi (600 km) south along Ruta 40 (a relatively short distance in a large country like Argentina, but still a long stretch!), stop at **Villa Unión (10),** a quiet village at the foot of the Andes mountain range. In the last few years, it has become the privileged base for the nearby **Talampaya National Park** and **Ischigualasto Provincial Park.** Grandiose geological landscapes dating to the Triassic Period, these two parks are so beautiful and astonishing that they are both classified as UNESCO World Heritage Sites. On the program: lunar landscapes and red and white rock formations; many animals, including guanacos (another relative of the llama), rheas (large flightless birds related to the ostrich and emu), and maras (a kind of giant hare); and traces of fossils in what's known as the Valley of the Moon.

Avoid the area in the summer, when the thermometer climbs to more than 110°F (45°C), even in the shade. The best period to visit is July-August.

After a long journey, you'll finally arrive in **Mendoza (11),** the country's fourth largest city, at the crossroads of the incredible Ruta 40 and the no less legendary Ruta 7, which connects Buenos Aires to Santiago de Chile. The earthquake of 1861, which killed more than 10,000 people here, left only rare vestiges of the city that existed before. But the quake also resulted in modern and airy town planning in the city, designed in 1863 by Jules Balloffet, a French surveyor.

The province of Mendoza is the main wine-producing region in Argentina, with more than 1,000 vineyards beginning literally on the city's doorstep. The first grapes were planted in the 19th century by European immigrants, many of them Italian, but the wine scene in Mendoza really hit its stride in the last 30 or so years. The result is an area of astonishing contrasts between historic family-run bodegas and ultramodern factories producing Malbec shipped around the world.

IF YOU WANT TO GO FARTHER
THE ANDEAN ROAD →

Don't miss this unique opportunity to traverse the heart of the Andes! Tracing its way from Mendoza to Santiago de Chile, Ruta 7 is one of those mythical routes that invites you to wander, by bus, car, motorbike, or bicycle. On the route: Aconcagua, the highest mountain in the Americas; the incredible natural rock arch of Puente del Inca; the winding path climbing to Christ the Redeemer, perched at an altitude of 12,657 ft (3,858 m). Grandiose panoramas and guanacos will keep you company along the way.

Another possibility: Continue on Ruta 40 to its terminus (see the next road trip).

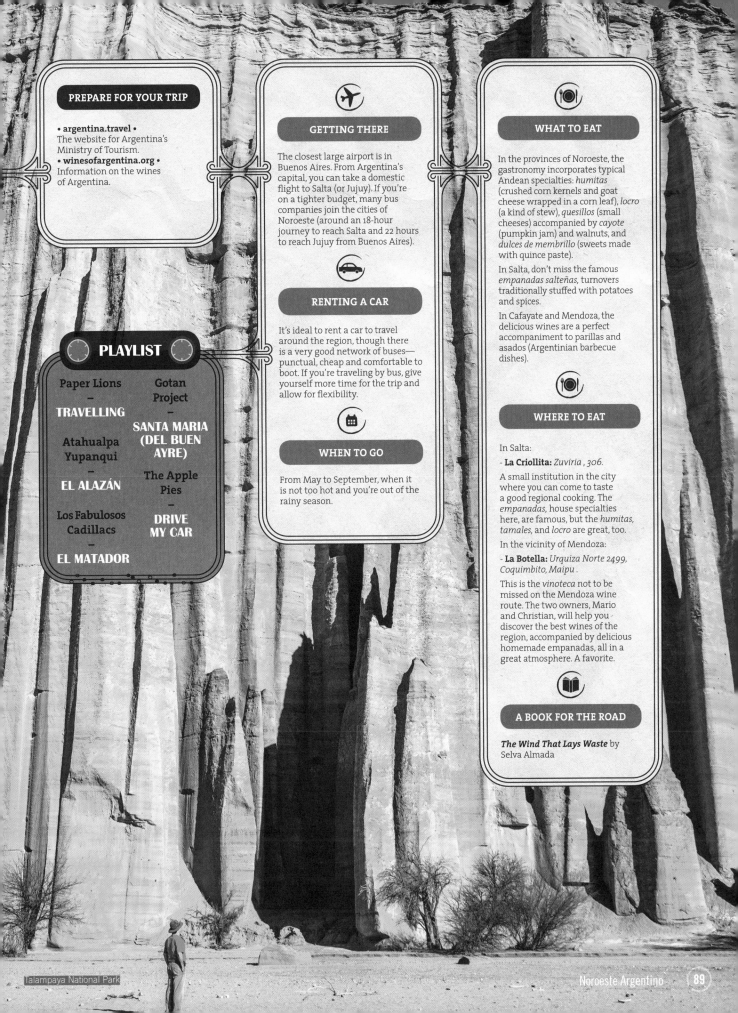

PREPARE FOR YOUR TRIP

• **argentina.travel** •
The website for Argentina's Ministry of Tourism.
• **winesofargentina.org** •
Information on the wines of Argentina.

PLAYLIST

Paper Lions – **TRAVELLING**	Gotan Project – **SANTA MARIA (DEL BUEN AYRE)**
Atahualpa Yupanqui – **EL ALAZÁN**	The Apple Pies – **DRIVE MY CAR**
Los Fabulosos Cadillacs – **EL MATADOR**	

GETTING THERE

The closest large airport is in Buenos Aires. From Argentina's capital, you can take a domestic flight to Salta (or Jujuy). If you're on a tighter budget, many bus companies join the cities of Noroeste (around an 18-hour journey to reach Salta and 22 hours to reach Jujuy from Buenos Aires).

RENTING A CAR

It's ideal to rent a car to travel around the region, though there is a very good network of buses—punctual, cheap and comfortable to boot. If you're traveling by bus, give yourself more time for the trip and allow for flexibility.

WHEN TO GO

From May to September, when it is not too hot and you're out of the rainy season.

WHAT TO EAT

In the provinces of Noroeste, the gastronomy incorporates typical Andean specialties: *humitas* (crushed corn kernels and goat cheese wrapped in a corn leaf), *locro* (a kind of stew), *quesillos* (small cheeses) accompanied by *cayote* (pumpkin jam) and walnuts, and *dulces de membrillo* (sweets made with quince paste).

In Salta, don't miss the famous *empanadas salteñas*, turnovers traditionally stuffed with potatoes and spices.

In Cafayate and Mendoza, the delicious wines are a perfect accompaniment to parillas and asados (Argentinian barbecue dishes).

WHERE TO EAT

In Salta:

- **La Criollita:** *Zuviria* , *306*.

A small institution in the city where you can come to taste a good regional cooking. The *empanadas*, house specialties here, are famous, but the *humitas*, *tamales*, and *locro* are great, too.

In the vicinity of Mendoza:

- **La Botella:** *Urquiza Norte 2499, Coquimbito, Maipu* .

This is the *vinoteca* not to be missed on the Mendoza wine route. The two owners, Mario and Christian, will help you discover the best wines of the region, accompanied by delicious homemade empanadas, all in a great atmosphere. A favorite.

A BOOK FOR THE ROAD

The Wind That Lays Waste by Selva Almada

Talampaya National Park

START
MI 0

1
SAN MARTÍN DE LOS ANDES

40

2
BARILOCHE

EL BOLSÓN **3**

4 ESQUEL

40

40

EL CHALTÉN ★

5
EL CALAFATE
PERITO MORENO GLACIER ★
END
MI 1,000

LOCATION

Southern Argentina, through the regions of Rio Negro, Chubut, and Santa Cruz

ROUTE

San Martín de Los Andes – El Calafate

LENGTH

1,000 mi (1,600 km)

TIME

Allow at least 1 week, or even 10 days, to enjoy the many national parks and hikes that Patagonia has to offer.

YOU'LL LOVE

The vast lakes, breathtaking land-scapes, delicious craft beer and choco-late, and numerous hiking possibilities.

RUTA 40
TOWARD PATAGONIA

FROM SAN MARTÍN DE LOS ANDES ⇒→ TO EL CALAFATE

Patagonia is a dream destination for adventurers of all stripes. Synonymous with endless spaces, wild lands, and the end of the world, Patagonia is above all a desert territory, with less than one inhabitant per square mile. This land fascinates, with its wide-open spaces and the diversity, beauty, and richness of the ecosystem it supports. As you gaze over the horizon from the desert plains to the Andes mountain range, it's hard to remain unmoved by the serene beauty of these skies, mountains and high lakes, and jagged coasts. From San Martín de Los Andes to the famous glacier Perito Moreno, Argentina's Ruta 40 is filled with wonders.

Córdoba

Buenos Aires

ARGENTINA

Comodoro Rivadavia

El Calafate

START/END OF ROAD TRIP	
STOP	●
LANDMARK OR POINT OF INTEREST	★
ROAD	
ROAD TRIP	

SAN MARTÍN DE LOS ANDES – BARILOCHE: ON THE ROAD TO THE SEVEN LAKES

In a superb natural setting between Lanín National Park and Lago Lácar, **San Martín de los Andes (1)** is one of the most exclusive ski resorts in the Andes. The city is also known for having welcomed Ernesto "Che" Guevara and Alberto Granado, who, during their legendary motorcycle journey across part of the South American continent, found refuge here in January 1952. Today, the wooden hut they stayed in has been transformed into a small museum that evokes the life of the budding revolutionary.

Lanín National Park, one of the largest in the country, is traversed by many marked trails, a hiker's dream in the summer. In the northern part of the park, Huechulafquen and Paimún Lakes create a picture-perfect environment, surrounded by black volcanic-sand beaches and snow-capped peaks. But the highlight is undoubtedly Lanín, considered a "young" volcano by those who study them, which culminates in 12,388 ft (3,776 m).

Those up for a strenuous hike can attempt to ascend the volcano. If you're more in the mood for rest and relaxation, head to the spa at Lahuen Co for a thermal soak.

Then, onto Villa La Angostura, located on the north shore of Nahuel Huapi Lake. The mythical Ruta 40 is at its most wonderful in this corner of the Andes Mountains, nearly 60 mi (100 km) of lakes surrounded by a wild environment, where the mountains are beautifully reflected on the surface of the water, which is sometimes turquoise blue, sometimes deep black.

After 120 mi (200 km) of lakes, mountains, and pine forests, wooden chalets, fondue, craft beers and chocolate await you. No, you are not in Switzerland, but in **Bariloche (2),** Argentina, though you'd be forgiven for getting confused. Superb Nahuel Huapi Lake has almost the same proportions as Lake Geneva, and its horizon is also framed by jagged, high mountains.

This charming little town in the Río Negro makes its living mainly from tourism: In winter, it is a chic ski resort for Argentines; in summer, visitors escape to the shores of the lake when temperatures elsewhere get unreasonable. It's also a popular spot with recent graduates, which is why Bariloche is home to some of the best nightclubs in the country. Europeans often shun this corner of Argentina, thinking it too similar to the Alps. But it's a beautiful, spectacular, and wild region, perhaps best seen from Cerro Campanario—which ends with a breathtaking panorama, with lakes as far as the eye can see.

NOT TO BE MISSED

Isla Victoria

A 40-minute drive from Bariloche takes you to Isla Victoria, in the heart of Nahuel Huapi Lake. The island is covered in a magnificent forest, the Bosque de Arrayanes. Its rare trees are covered in a cinnamon-colored bark dotted with surprising white spots. If you're lucky, you might even come across a pudu, the smallest deer in the world, adorably reminiscent of Disney's Bambi.

In winter (July-August), the Road of the Seven Lakes is often closed due to snow. It's also possible to travel this route by bus.

Nahuel Huapi Lake

EL BOLSÓN – ESQUEL: PARADISE ON EARTH

Eighty miles (130 km) south of Bariloche, on the border between the provinces of Río Negro and Chubut, is **El Bolsón (3).** The road here is beautiful, skirting Gutiérrez and Mascardi Lakes before descending into a deep valley bordered by forests. El Bolsón is situated in a long fertile valley crossed by the Quemquemtreu ("rolling stone" in the Mapuche language) River and bordered by two large mountains, Nevado and Piltriquitrón.

Attracted by the gentle landscape and a microclimate favoring the growth of fruit trees, hippies from all over the world settled in El Bolsón in the early 1970s to live in communities dedicated to crafts and organic farming. Today, El Bolsón is a small, quiet village that hasn't forgotten its roots, a peaceful, ecologically-minded community. The pretty little huts scattered around the surrounding hills are often built by the inhabitants themselves using local materials.

To top it all off, the city brews delicious craft beers, and it truly comes alive in the first days of March for the Fiesta del Lúpulo, or the Festival of Hops.

Twenty-five miles (40 km) south of El Bolsón, the Epuyén Valley is like an oasis, with its proudly standing poplars and beautiful lake. **Esquel (4)** is a small city in a beautiful valley at the foot of the Precordillera mountains, founded in the late 19th century by the descendants of the first Welsh immigrants to the area. Today, there are still a few red-brick houses, good pubs, and a traditional Welsh festival celebrated on July 28. Otherwise, the village is a good base for hikes in the surrounding peaks or in nearby Los Alerces National Park.

HIKING

Of all the hikes in the area, the most spectacular might be the ascent of Cerro Piltriquitrón (7,415 ft/2,260 m). This is not an easy Sunday stroll—the second part of the climb in particular is for experienced hikers. On the way, you'll pass El Bosque Tallado, where logs that survived a fire in the 1970s have been carved into sculptures by local artists.

EL CALAFATE: GATEWAY TO THE GLACIERS

More than 600 mi (1,000 km) south of Esquel, at the foot of the Andes mountain range and on the edge of Lago Argentino, **El Calafate (5)** is the first stop for visiting Los Glaciares National Park. It's in the heart of the windy Pampas, fertile lowland plains that take their name from a shrub with yellow flowers and black berries, very widespread in the region. (The berries also make an excellent jam.)

This modest pioneer village, founded in 1927 and surrounded by flat fields, has experienced tremendous development over the decades thanks to tourists eager to see the glaciers. Like many new towns in Patagonia, its small grid of streets is lined by low buildings made of wood or sheet metal, which can withstand the region's changeable climate and frequent, buffeting gusts of wind.

> **NOT TO BE MISSED**
>
> **Punta Walichu**
>
> *These caves are famous for their cave paintings of people and animals—more than 10,000 of them— left by the indigenous Tehuelche people. These frescoes in open-air caves are right on the edge of Lago Argentino. At sunset, the light shines directly on the paintings and magnifies their beauty.*

The glaciers are well signposted, 30 mi (50 km) from El Calafate. All of them (Perito Moreno, Upsala, Viedma, etc.) are really the extremities of the gigantic Campo de Hielo, an immense, 220-mi-long (350-km-long) glacier that straddles Argentina and Chile.

You'll never tire of admiring the waters of Lago Argentino, an unforgettable shade of milky blue and turquoise. Walking along its shores, lined by dead trees that could not withstand successive glacial floods, you'll feel like you're traveling in another world.

The highlight of the show is undoubtedly **Perito Moreno,** the most spectacular of the Andean glaciers and the easiest to access. If you have little time and can't see all the glaciers, this is the one to see. A real monster, 9 mi (14 km) long and 2.5 mi (4 km) wide, it rises 160-200 ft (50-60 m) above the water level of the lake. It's difficult to remain insensitive to this majestic beauty, imposing from afar and face-to-face. A UNESCO World Heritage Site, Perito Moreno is one of the liveliest glaciers in the world, a real force of nature! It creaks, cracks, and rumbles, and even the smallest block that comes loose from it falls with a crash. The collapse of a large enough ice sheet into the water can cause a mini-tsunami that floods the shores.

Falling ice is more common in the late afternoon, when the glacier has been warmed by the sun. It's easy to spend hours observing it without getting bored. Another point in Perito Moreno's favor is that the chance to see a glacier at so close up and at such a low altitude is very rare. In the northern hemisphere, in Alaska, Iceland, or Norway, you have to climb to an altitude of over 10,000 ft (3,000 m) to see anything similar.

Another (more expensive) way to see the glacier up close is to take a boat tour. Viewed from below, Perito Moreno's impressive facade towers over you like a massive blue wall, and you'll find yourself in the heart of the action when a piece of ice falls apart.

The other glacier not to be missed in the area is Upsala. Bigger than the city of Buenos Aires, it is one of the largest glaciers in the southern hemisphere. Upsala comes from the name of the boat belonging to a Swedish expedition from Uppsala University, which sailed these waters in the early 20th century. The front of Upsala rises about 230 ft (70 m) over the surface of the lake, with another 1,600 ft (490 m) under the water, which is over 1,000 m deep at this point; the visible part of the glacier only represents one-eighth of its total height. The glacier recedes more gradually than Perito Moreno, and it's usually not accessible by boat due to the icebergs floating on the lake.

MUSEO DEL HIELO

Visit the Museo del Hielo Patagónico before heading to Los Glaciares National Park to learn more about the formation of the Andean glaciers. The architecture of the museum, clearly visible from Ruta 11, recalls a glacial moraine. Its 200,000 sq ft (60,000 sq m) is housed in three pavilions, an auditorium, and a café, with a splendid view of Lago Argentino.

DETOUR TO EL CHALTÉN: IF YOU CAN'T GET ENOUGH

The paved, 140-mi (220-km) access road to **El Chaltén** is superb; panoramas of snowcapped mountains mingle with turquoise glacial waters and the always-blowing wind. It's without a doubt one of the most beautiful corners of Patagonia. At the slightest ray of sunlight, the landscape becomes magical. You'll cross the desert steppe, with the occasional appearance of some guanacos and rheas, to get to this small village at the end of everything, in the heart of the Andes and at the foot of Monte Fitz Roy. Far from the tourists of El Calafate, El Chaltén is especially loved by hikers and mountaineers. It is notably the starting point for all excursions around Fitz Roy (11,289 ft/3,441 m) and Cerro Torre (10,295 ft/3,138 m). The Tehuelche called Fitz Roy Chaltén ("Volcano"), as its peaks are often hidden in thick clouds. With their granite walls, the two mountains are the ultimate challenge for climbers.

People also come here to enjoy the quiet pace of life and the beautiful surroundings. Less experienced hikers can enjoy long walks in a dreamy setting, while the more seasoned might try a two-week expedition on the largest glaciers in the world.

DECEMBER – FEBRUARY

December to February is the high season in this region. Note that many establishments here close their doors from May (sometimes April) to September.

Monte Fitz Roy

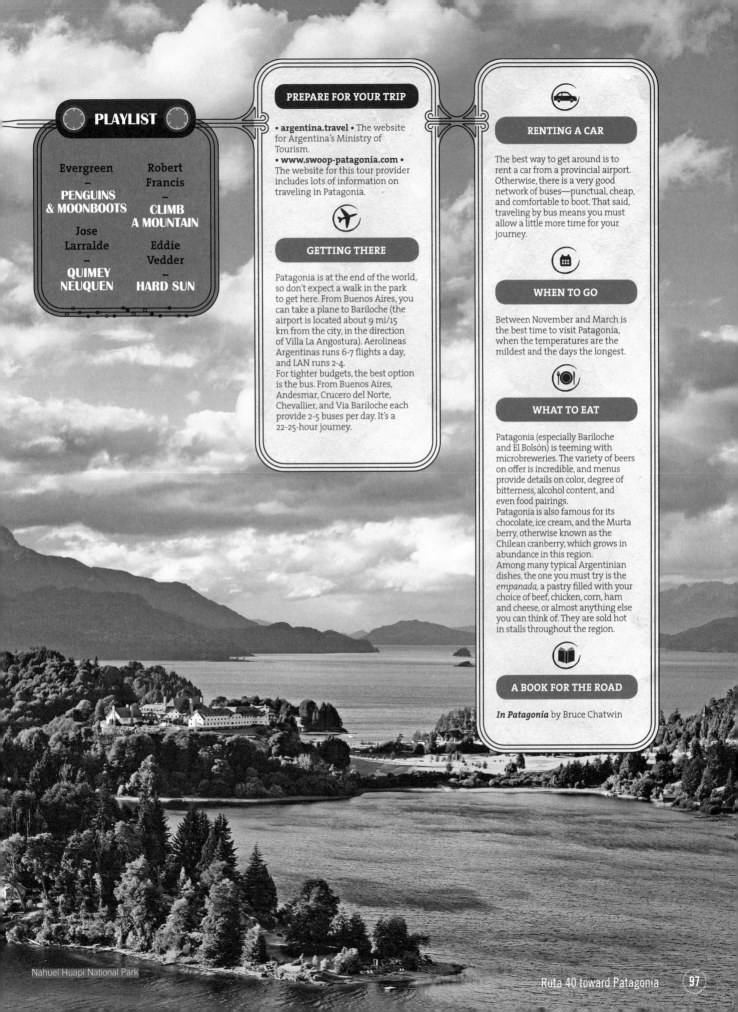

PLAYLIST

Evergreen
–
**PENGUINS
& MOONBOOTS**

Robert
Francis
–
**CLIMB
A MOUNTAIN**

Jose
Larralde
–
**QUIMEY
NEUQUEN**

Eddie
Vedder
–
HARD SUN

PREPARE FOR YOUR TRIP

• **argentina.travel** • The website for Argentina's Ministry of Tourism.
• **www.swoop-patagonia.com** • The website for this tour provider includes lots of information on traveling in Patagonia.

GETTING THERE

Patagonia is at the end of the world, so don't expect a walk in the park to get here. From Buenos Aires, you can take a plane to Bariloche (the airport is located about 9 mi/15 km from the city, in the direction of Villa La Angostura). Aerolineas Argentinas runs 6-7 flights a day, and LAN runs 2-4.
For tighter budgets, the best option is the bus. From Buenos Aires, Andesmar, Crucero del Norte, Chevallier, and Via Bariloche each provide 2-5 buses per day. It's a 22-25-hour journey.

RENTING A CAR

The best way to get around is to rent a car from a provincial airport. Otherwise, there is a very good network of buses—punctual, cheap, and comfortable to boot. That said, traveling by bus means you must allow a little more time for your journey.

WHEN TO GO

Between November and March is the best time to visit Patagonia, when the temperatures are the mildest and the days the longest.

WHAT TO EAT

Patagonia (especially Bariloche and El Bolsón) is teeming with microbreweries. The variety of beers on offer is incredible, and menus provide details on color, degree of bitterness, alcohol content, and even food pairings.
Patagonia is also famous for its chocolate, ice cream, and the Murta berry, otherwise known as the Chilean cranberry, which grows in abundance in this region.
Among many typical Argentinian dishes, the one you must try is the *empanada*, a pastry filled with your choice of beef, chicken, corn, ham and cheese, or almost anything else you can think of. They are sold hot in stalls throughout the region.

A BOOK FOR THE ROAD

In Patagonia by Bruce Chatwin

Nahuel Huapi National Park

5 TOCAÑA

4 COROICO

END
MI 50

3 YOLOSA

Camino de la Muerte

54

3

LA CUMBRE 2

3

3

START
MI 0

1

LA PAZ

LOCATION

Western Bolivia

ROUTE

La Paz – The Yungas

LENGTH

About 50 mi (85 km)

TIME

At least 3 hours

YOU'LL LOVE

The feeling of being a true adventurer, the Andean peaks, and the landscapes covered by the semi-tropical forest.

CAMINO
DE LA MUERTE
FROM LA PAZ ⟶ TO THE YUNGAS

How can you resist a name like that? The "Death Road" is not all that long, but it is definitely spectacular: Descending the altiplano in tight curves, it is constantly close to the void, with the semi-tropical massif of the Yungas and the Amazon Rainforest on the horizon. This route attracts a lot of mountain bikers, but it can also be traveled by car. It's better to skip the convertible for this drive: Along the way, you'll pass under several waterfalls.

BOLIVIA

La Paz

Cochabamba

Santa Cruz
de la Sierra

START/END OF ROAD TRIP

STOP ●

ROAD 3

ROAD TRIP

LA PAZ: A CAPITAL ON HIGH

The adventure begins in the highest capital in the world, with cob-blestone streets, colonial architecture, and unfinished brick buildings clinging to the sides of a windy, pebbled, and unwieldy basin. More than 2 million people are crowded into the anthill of **La Paz (1):** the poorer residents live in El Alto, at more than 13,000 ft (4,000 m) above sea level (it's colder here), while the richest live "down" (still at 10,500 ft/3,200 m and still cold at night). It's a strange city, at once both spread out and curled up at the foot of the mountains, where oxygen is lacking and diesel fumes perfume the ambient air. Newcomers may find themselves struggling to catch their breath the first few days.

La Paz is above all a nerve center, a meeting point, where Bolivian farmers and their products arrive and try to survive. On Calle Tumusla, the crowded sidewalks form a vast marketplace for sec-ondhand clothes, imported shoes, and inexpensive sunglasses. In the alleys, sometimes steep enough to require stairs, you'll find the shops and stalls of the Mercado Negro (Black Market). Farther on, at the crossroads of Linares and Santa Cruz, you'll find the beginning of the famous Mercado de las Brujas, or "Witches' Market." A few old women, dressed in heavy pleated skirts and bowler hats, sell medic-inal herbs, amulets, dried frogs (a token of good luck), coca leaves, and herbal teas. Roving sellers pass by chanting their sales pitches.

In the evening, the city seems to want to catch its breath on the plaza of the venerable Basílica de San Francisco, its colonial facade engraved with pre-Columbian symbols. The great Avenida Mariscal Santa Cruz runs up against the church, offering a contrary message between the honking horns and the traffic jams. The road rules are chaotic here, and driving is about cutting a path between the cabs, buses and their clouds of smoke, the *micros,* and the *trufis* (minibuses).

② LA CUMBRE: THE BEGINNING OF THE CLIMB

Minibuses struggle their way up the mountains out of La Paz, overtaking covered trucks and buses traveling at a snail's pace. Along the way, you'll pass the Incachaca dam, fed by the waters of melting winter snow. Finally, you'll reach the pass of **La Cumbre (2)** (15,300 ft/4,670 m). A small lake, shrouded in clouds, reflects a few Andean peaks with white summits. Scattered snowfields dot the bare and windswept landscape. A few alpacas graze, haughty guardians of their desolate home. The cold is startling, but the air is pure.

Heading due east, the road twists and turns over a sea of clouds, waterfalls, houses, and bushes appearing around the bends.

DEATH ROAD

Little by little, the dry valleys and the austere altiplano give way to more abundant and temperate vegetation. At Kilometer 54, you get to the heart of the matter: the Camino de la Muerte itself. Leaving the pavement of the new *carretera,* or highway, inaugurated in 2007, the original track, sometimes muddy, sometimes stony, but always tortuous, rushes downstream. Progressing down the side of the mountain, it narrows until it barely allows the passage of a vehicle. It passes under a icy waterfall, and sometimes even falling stones after a heavy rain. Vertigo is almost guaranteed, with your hands clammy on the wheel.

The road was built in the 1930s during the Chaco War (which saw Bolivia lose a quarter of its territory) by Paraguayan prisoners. For a long time, it was one of the few roads linking the altiplano to the Amazon. In its macabre heyday, it was responsible for an average of 100 deaths per year, and twice as many accidents. In 1983, an overloaded bus toppled over the side, killing 100 people. The empty shells of trucks lying in the ravines bear witness to attempts of impatient drivers who tried to pass on too-narrow sections (especially near the Curva del Diablo). Only the careful, calm, and experienced drivers survive.

A 1995 report by the Inter-American Development Bank describes the Camino a los Yungas—the road's "official" name—as the most dangerous road in the world. This was enough to convince decision-makers to finance an alternative route, now used by all long-distance traffic. On the Camino de la Muerte, only a few local buses, 4WDs driven by regulars, and worn-out trucks remain, and every day they are accompanied by numerous mountain bikers who come to enjoy the *carretera*. It is for them that protective barriers were recently installed.

THE CAMINO DE LA MUERTE BY BIKE

Several specialized tour operators based in La Paz offer day trips. You reach the La Cumbre pass by minibus, before getting on your bike in the intense cold. Half an hour later, adios to the pavement, hello to the camino: a steep, slippery, dizzy track. Don't let yourself get stressed out; take your time. And even as the Camino de la Muerte has become a tourist attraction, accidents still happen here. So be careful!

Look for • Evolution Ride Spirit • and • Xtreme Downhill • on Facebook.

THE YUNGAS: LAND OF COCA

Descending from the Camino de la Muerte, the vegetation grows denser. Here, you're in the middle of a cloud forest, nourished by the mists, fogs, and rains that coat the eastern side of the Andes for much of the year—especially during the southern summer. Between 4 ft (1.2 m) and 7 ft (2 m) of rain falls here each year.

The road ends after 105 mi (32 km) in the village of **Yolosa (3),** 11,500 ft (3,500 m) (vertical drop) below the La Cumbre pass, where cyclists end their adventures in a swimming pool at one of the posadas that have sprung up in recent years. Some extend their stay on site at the refuge of La Senda Verde, a private sanctuary for animals injured or pulled from the clutches of poachers, where volunteers work year-round to feed spider monkeys and capuchins and brush the shells of turtles.

In **Coroico (4),** the main small town in the area, located a little higher up on a natural balcony, the air is sticky during the day. To beat the humidity, dive into the invigorating waters of the Tres Cascadas and the Pozas del Vagante, or treat yourself to a rafting or canyoning trip. Another activity is a visit to the town of **Tocaña (5),** a village of 150 inhabitants, descendants of enslaved Africans who survived the silver mines of Potosí. They're known for the *saya,* a song and dance punctuated by drums. Along the way, you'll pass some coca plantations. The Yungas region is responsible for or two-thirds of Bolivia's coca production. Former Bolivian President Evo Morales, a former leader of a *cocalero* union, promoted the use of the plant during his 2006-2019 term. Under his presidency, the UN granted Bolivia the right to market coca at home for chewing leaves, herbal teas, and local sodas (Coka Quina and Coca Colla). The United States has pushed back against this, especially as part of its War on Drugs.

SENTIDO CONTRARIO

To try to limit damage on the Amazon road, a strange code of the road prevailed until 2017 on certain narrow stretches beyond Coroico: Vehicles did not pull over on the right when they passed another vehicle, as everywhere else in the country, but instead on the left, UK style.

WHERE TO STAY

As long as you are not too picky, you can find plenty of inexpensive accommodation in Bolivia—like a bed for less than $4, a double room from $8-10 in *alojamientos* and *hospedajes. Hostales* generally offer better comfort, with private bathrooms, but only the nicer hotels have heating. After driving the Camino de la Muerte, you can stay in Yolosa, at the Hotel Villa Verde or in the huts of the animal refuge La Senda Verde (you'll be awakened by the monkeys at dawn!). Otherwise, Coroico, a 15-minute drive away, offers a more choices.

WHAT TO EAT

Dishes here are hearty. Potatoes and corn are a part of every meal, perhaps accompanied by French fries, rice, quinoa, eggs, fried chicken, and/or meat (especially beef, llama, or alpaca). Soups are featured in almost all inexpensive lunch menus (about $1.50-2). An even cheaper option is a *salteña* (turnovers stuffed with meat or vegetables) or *anticuchos* (beef heart skewers).

A BOOK FOR THE ROAD

Affections by Rodrigo Hasbún

RENTING A CAR

Although it might not be as fancy (or easy) as in other destinations, car rental is possible in Bolivia. In La Paz, there are local branches of several major companies, including Avis, Budget, Europcar, and Hertz. A small 4WD car is recommended. A good option for a local company is Barbol.
• **barbolsrl.com** •

WHEN TO GO

April to October (dry season).

PREPARE FOR YOUR TRIP

• **boliviaentusmanos.com** •
• **bolivia.com** •

GETTING THERE

Bolivia's largest airport, Viru Viru International Airport (VVI), is located in Santa Cruz de la Sierra—quite far from La Paz. El Alto International Airport (LPB) in the La Paz area receives flights from around South America.

LOCATION

In the state of Bahia, in the south of the Nordeste region of Brazil

ROUTE

Salvador da Bahia – Mangue Seco

LENGTH

125 mi (200 km)

TIME

Allow at least 4-5 days to fully enjoy the lively atmosphere of the cities and the sweet solitude of Brazilian beaches.

YOU'LL LOVE

The paradisiacal beaches, the warm welcome from Brazilians, the atmosphere that animates the streets.

BA-099

BA-099

SANTO ANTÔNIO

4 IMBASSAÍ

3 PRAIA DO FORTE

AREMBEPE 2

START
MI 0

1 SALVADOR
DA BAHIA

END
MI 125

MANGUE SECO
5

LINHA VERDE
AKA THE COCONUT HIGHWAY
FROM SALVADOR DA BAHIA ⟶ TO MANGUE SECO

Wild beaches, immense sand dunes, lush coconut groves, pristine rain forest, small fishing villages, sea turtles, sugarcane fields. . . . The Linha Verde explores a superb but little-known portion of the Brazilian coast: the stretch between Salvador da Bahia and Mangue Seco. It's a magnificent but fragile environment, where sustainable development offers a serious alternative to logging and pollution. Whether you are traveling by bus or car, the Linha Verde is a great getaway. The Atlantic coastline is covered with coconut groves. In the hinterlands is the Mata Atlântica, a piece of primitive forest, the same one that amazed Amerigo Vespucci when he first came upon these shores in 1500.

START/END OF ROAD TRIP	⬲
STOP	●
LANDMARK OR POINT OF INTEREST	★
ROAD	BA-099
ROAD TRIP	

125 MI

SALVADOR DA BAHIA: THE BIRTHPLACE OF MODERN BRAZIL

Salvador da Bahia de Todos os Santos! A mythical, legendary name! First of all, the site is astonishing: a vast bay nestled in the land for dozens of miles, like an immense maritime harbor with coasts dotted with islands and sandy or rocky coves. Protected from winds and storms, it makes for a magnificent natural shelter for sailors worn out by the perilous crossing of the Atlantic. It's easy to imagine the caravels of yesteryear dropping their anchors to cling to the coasts of Brazil, the ships' dark holds filled with enslaved people captured from Africa.

This is **Salvador da Bahia (1),** where the modern-day history of Brazil began in the 16th century; much of the country's development has its roots in the shores of this large bay. Therefore, it makes sense to start a trip to Brazil in Salvador and the

Nordeste. It's also the fourth most populous city in the country. Rio de Janeiro is a dream, with its natural wonders and splendid bay, but Salvador, the city with the most ties to Africa on the continent, fascinates travelers with its tropical and Afro-Brazilian character. It has been nicknamed "Black Rome" for its impressive number of churches (365, one for each day of the year, they say) and because a large percent of its population is made up of descendants of enslaved Africans.

The city has a historic center with a Portuguese feel. Walking up and down the streets to soak up the atmosphere is a must, especially on Tuesday and Saturday during the Brazilian summer, when Bahians always seem to be celebrating on the cobblestones, so much so that the *largos* are crowded and the streets often

blocked. A warm and human city, famous for its carnival and capoeira, Salvador seduces with its coastline, its majestic bay, the colonial and faded splendor of its old town (the Pelourinho), the richness of its gastronomy, and the energy of its inhabitants.

Had enough of parties, music, and capoeira demonstrations? Then it's time to hit the road to Praia do Forte. Along the way, make a stop in the coastal village of **Arembepe (2),** located 30 mi (45 km) north of Salvador. Far from mass tourism, this pocket village offers a small cobblestone square, a pretty church, and a handful of restaurants facing the sea. You can walk along the lagoon to reach Arembepe Beach, made famous in the 1970s as a hot spot for hippies—namely Mick Jagger and Janis Joplin.

FOCUS

Salvador da Bahia's Carnival

Salvador's carnival belongs to the people—the atmosphere is all about participation rather than spectacle. The important thing here is to *pular* (jump up and down)! The festivities celebrate the city's African roots, with Afro-Brazilian dance, folklore, and axé music, a fusion of Brazilian and Afro-Caribbean pop. The jubilation is absolute, the prohibitions fall away. It's a proverb come to life: "Bahia de todos os santos e de quase todos os pecados": Bahia of all saints and almost all sins.

PRAIA DO FORTE: FIESTA AND RELAXATION

Located about 50 mi (80 km) north of Salvador (only 36 mi/60 km from the airport), the old fishing village of **Praia do Forte (3)** has been transformed into popular tourist seaside resort, very popular with Bahians. A single road, perpendicular to the BR 99 (the Linha Verde) marks the entrance to the resort area. This holiday resort feels upscale and cut off from the world.

The city center is largely pedestrianized, so it's recommended that you leave your vehicle in one of the peripheral parking lots or at your hotel (if it has a parking lot). Here, everything is just a flip-flop walk away. Along the main street, the old fishermen's houses are home to scores of *pousadas,* restaurants, bars, and shops. In the evening, you'll find shopping and nightlife waiting for you.

Praia do Forte is home to the Projeto Tamar, temple of the sea turtle and symbol of the region, and the Sapiranga nature reserve, a vast coconut forest bordered by long sandy beaches, serving as a green setting for the town.

To take a swim, it's advisable to move away from the beach concentrated around the village's small church, on the Projeto Tamar side, where there is a lot of seaweed and there are rocky outcrops. A good option is to walk to the Tivoli Resort, or even farther to the southwest.

IMBASSAÍ AND DIOGO: SURF AND SUN

About 6 mi (10 km) north of Praia do Forte, **Imbassaí (4)** is a small tourist village in full swing that owes its name to the Río Imbassaí ("white water" in Tupi), which runs along white sand dunes before flowing into the ocean, forming a natural lagoon. It is a famous spot for surfers; non-surfers will be content to sip fruit juice under straw huts on the immense beach, or take a beautiful walk on the coast. There's no pavement in the village, just cobbled streets and sandy paths lined with palm trees.

About 3 mi (5 km) away, less developed than Imbassaí and a little more traditional, Diogo is a village stretched out between coconut groves. It is located a 20-minute walk from a beautiful wild beach. To get here, take a path that crosses blindingly white dunes, tempered by the green of the vegetation that clings to it. Be careful: At one point, you'll cross a bridge made of brick and mortar. Closer to the beach, the village of **Santo Antônio** is made up of a few colorful little houses.

In 1940, chased by the military dictatorship, the communist writer Jorge Amado took refuge in Mangue Seco. Inspired by the place, he wrote his novel *Tieta do Agreste,* a best-seller that was made into a movie. It was so successful that the mayor of Jandaira changed the name of the village of Coqueiros, where the film was shot, to Santana do Agreste, as it's called in the story. But the power of the book stops there: No one ever used this second name.

5

MANGUE SECO: THE ROAD ENDS ON THE BEACH

Mangue Seco (5) is close by. The last stop of the Linha Verde, it can be reached only by boat (about a 10-minute journey) from the small village of Pontal, 83 mi (133 km) north of Praia do Forte. Mangue Seco looks like an island; it is in fact a very long peninsula, bordered on the east by the Atlantic Ocean and on the west by the Río Real (which looks like a small sea). This is an exceptional natural site, preserved thanks to the efforts of some of its residents, who are proponents of sustainable development. They refused the construction of a major road intended to open up the tip of their peninsula. In order to protect the environment (dunes and beaches), a protected area has been established, which prevents the landscape from being disturbed by industries or real estate. Mangue Seco means "dry mangrove" or "dry wood"—not "dry mango," as someone who doesn't speak Portuguese might imagine.

Here you'll find a huge deserted sandy beach, 30 mi (45 km) long, mostly frequented by nesting turtles (protected by the Tamar Project,

which is dedicated to the preservation of marine turtles); a landscape of coconut trees planted in clusters or in entire forests; and high dunes of dazzling white sand that move under the effect of the northeasterly wind. The tropical climate is softened by the Atlantic breeze, and you'll see cashew trees, sandy streets, dirt roads, modest houses lapped by the waters of the río, no traffic lights, and minimal infrastructure—the nearest police station is on dry land. In short, it's a world apart and home to a way of life that the residents remain very attached to. It's quite a change of pace, after the dizzy parties and noise of Salvador, to find yourself in this earthly paradise that seems so far from everything.

NOT TO BE MISSED

The Mangue Seco dune, about 5 mi (8 km) long, divides the peninsula in two. A walk along the dune, especially at sunset, offers magnificent views between ocean and river, and the view at the foot of the lighthouse is particularly nice. It can get very hot during the day, so bring a hat, sunscreen, and water.

Historic Center of Salvador da Bahia

PLAYLIST

Antônio Carlos Jobim	Jorge Ben
THE GIRL FROM IPANEMA	**MAS QUE NADA**
Rodrigo Amarante	Chico Buarque
NADA EM VÃO	**ESSA MOÇA TA DIFERENTE**

PREPARE FOR YOUR TRIP

- **www.visitbrasil.com** • Brazil's official tourism website.
- **www.brazzil.com** • This site features articles about Brazilian political, economic, social, and cultural life, largely written by English-speaking Brazilian specialists and residents.

GETTING THERE

Salvador International Airport (SSA) mostly receives flights from around South America. You'll most likely fly into São Paulo or Rio de Janeiro and take a domestic flight to Salvador from there.

RENTING A CAR

Most rental agencies have a counter at Salvador's airport, and some have a second location in the city center. Note that traveling Linha Verde by bus is also possible (even though you lose a little autonomy): The Linha Verde company (aptly named) offers two buses per day that connect Salvador to Indiaroba. After that, a taxi or another bus will get you to Mangue Seco.

WHEN TO GO

Brazil's summer, from December to March, is punctuated by tropical showers and high temperatures. The weather is generally beautiful, and this time corresponds to the major school holidays (and is therefore more crowded). Overall, the best time to go is between September and late April.

WHERE TO STAY

Near Mangue Seco

- **Pousada O Forte:** *away from the village, on the way to the beach.* You'll fall in love with this pousada by the water, run by a French-Bahian couple. Twelve rooms for one to four people in bungalows, with terrace, hammock, and table available. Swimming pool, activities, and catering on site. A place that strives to respect both ethical and ecological rules.

In Praia do Forte

There are plenty of options, though many are expensive (you'll get a better deal if you book in advance).

- **Pousada Amanhecer:** *rua Aurora, s/n.* This modest *pousada* is located on one of the quietest streets in the village.

In Imbassaí

- **Pousada Capitù:** *rua Beira do Rio.* This charming *pousada* has 14 chalets with brick or raspberry walls, which stand out against the lush tropical garden. Stylish and elegant décor. Swimming pool nestled in a corner of the garden, spa and restaurant overlooking a quiet stretch of beach where deck chairs and umbrellas are installed. It is one of the few hotels in Imbassaí with direct access to the beach.

A BOOK FOR THE ROAD

Tieta by Jorge Amado

START
MI 0

1 PUERTO MONTT
2 RELONCAVÍ
HORNOPIRÉN
3 LEPTEPU
PUMALÍN
CHAITÉN
4

CHILOÉ ISLAND

7

6 PUERTO PUYUHUAPI
5 QUEULAT NATIONAL PARK
BOSQUE ENCANTADO

7 PUERTO CHACABUCO
8 COYHAIQUE

9 CERRO CASTILLO

Campo de Hielo Norte
Lago General Carrera

10 PUERTO RÍO TRANQUILO
PUERTO BERTRAND
11

Laguna San Rafael

12 TORTEL
7
PUERTO YUNGAY
13

END
MI 1,000

Campo de Hielo Sur
VILLA O'HIGGINS
14

LOCATION

Chilean Patagonia

ROUTE

Puerto Montt – Villa O'Higgins

LENGTH

1,000 mi (1,500 km)

TIME

7-10 days

YOU'LL LOVE

The feeling of rolling toward the edge of the world, the rain forests, the glaciers, the lakes, the condors in the sky, and the dolphins in the fjords.

110

CARRETERA AUSTRAL

FROM PUERTO MONTT ⟶ TO VILLA O'HIGGINS

A road that leads nowhere? Such is the Carretera Austral, inaugurated in 1986 to link the most isolated villages in Chile, through the almost uninhabited vastness of Patagonia (density: one inhabitant per square kilometer!). Leaving Puerto Montt, the route, alternating tar and track, forests and pampas, volcanoes and silence, crosses passes, spans fjords, and then ends up in Villa O'Higgins in an amphitheater of impassable mountains. At the end, a ferry is the only way to continue on.

Antofagasta

Santiago

CHILE

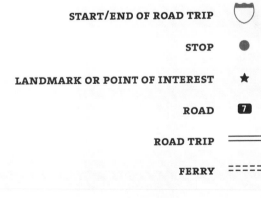

START/END OF ROAD TRIP ⬯

STOP ●

LANDMARK OR POINT OF INTEREST ★

ROAD 7

ROAD TRIP ═══

FERRY ┅┅┅

GLACIERS

IT ALL STARTS IN PUERTO MONTT

Santiago, the Chilean capital, shines under an almost Mediterranean sun 600 mi (1,000 km) to the north, while Punta Arenas, on the Strait of Magellan, shivers 1,200 mi (2,000 km) farther south in the winds blowing from Antarctica. Meanwhile, in **Puerto Montt (1),** it rains. A lot.

The headquarters of southern Chile and the Pacific salmon industry, Puerto Montt was founded in the mid-19th century by German settlers—the churches and old, almost Bavarian buildings in the area bear witness to this. Puerto Montt is a bit like the last frontier of civilization. The terminus of continental Chile and the beginning of island Chile, wedged between the ocean and the Andes, in a territorial strip that is narrower than ever. This is where Route 5 ends and Route 7 begins, the famous Carretera Austral, built

under the 1976-1988 military regime to connect the scattered villages of Chilean Patagonia to the world. The route has also earned the nickname "Senda General Pinochet." Before its construction, you could only reach this corner of Chile by boat—or by passing through neighboring Argentina, a challenge to national sovereignty.

It was the army that got it done. More than 10,000 soldiers, by means of blasting and bulldozing, patiently advanced the narrow ribbon of *ripio* (track) between wild valleys, passes, and glaciers. In some places, constrained by the geography, ferries took over, crossing or going up the fjords. The boat remains king in this land of water and mountains, where the continent bursts into a multitude of inhospitable islands covered in a cold rain forest.

Osorno Volcano and Llanquihue Lake

A FIERY VOLCANO AND PRIVATE RESERVE

Puerto Montt is only 25 mi (40 km) behind you, and already it's time for your first ferry ride. You'll need to cross the large estuary of **Reloncaví (2),** at the edge of the vast gulf of the same name, almost closed in on itself. On the port side and facing the bow, high wooded mountains glide toward the bay. On the starboard side—the sunset side—there are black islets and a distant coastline.

The road trip begins with a view of the immense Gulf of Ancud, separating the large island of Chiloé from the mainland. Fish pens bob on the water. Wooden boats await the hour of their departure to sea. Soon, the pavement loosens and the adventure really begins. In **Hornopirén,** wooden houses and tin shacks are scattered at the foot of snow-capped mountains. The Andes are just a stone's throw away, with their string of volcanoes aligned on a fault line.

The next jump is longer and more impressive: It takes 4 hours for the Agios ferry to bypass the islands of Pelada and Llancahue and reach **Leptepu (3)** by going up the Comau fjord, with its walls dotted with waterfalls and capped with blackish ridges. The road resumes, and it's just 6 mi (10 km) before another ride

on a ferry, this one with comfortable leather benches, and you'll soon find yourself face to face with a volcano that made headlines in 2008: **Chaitén (4).** That year, the cone, dormant for over 9,000 years, suddenly awoke, burying under a *lahar* (mudslide) much of the small town of Chaitén, located 7 mi (11 km) away—fortunately it was evacuated beforehand. The trees decapitated by the eruption still testify to the event, but the monster has gone back to sleep. It is now possible to climb the volcano without much difficulty (30 minutes) to observe the rhyolite dome that formed within the crater.

The new trail has been redeveloped thanks to the unfailing support of Douglas Tompkins, the wealthy founder of The North Face company. In the 1990s, he helped gradually bring back 700,000 acres (300,000 ha) of mountains, forests, and rivers that had been threatened by development in the area. It's now the largest private reserve in the world: **Pumalín.** Campsites, *cabañas,* information centers, and trails have been created for everyone to enjoy. And most of the territory was bequeathed to Chile after the death of the entrepreneur-benefactor in 2015. It is, to date, the largest donation of private land in history.

DETOUR TO CHILOÉ ISLAND

Instead of starting the trip south by Hornopirén, some people choose to first approach the large and beautiful Chiloé Island, before reaching Chaitén by crossing the Gulf of Ancud. Chiloé feels a world apart, with jagged coasts where colorful coastal villages rise up on stilts to ward off high tides. The island's wooden churches, dating back to the 17th and 18th centuries, blend local traditions with Jesuit influences—a feature that has earned them UNESCO World Heritage status. Many of them are charming, such as Chacao Viejo and Nercón. But Chiloé is also a national park that encompasses a large portion of the Pacific coastline, highlighted by dense forests draped in humidity. And on the opposite coast, in the summer, you can depart at Queilén toward Islote Conejos to meet the Magellanic penguins that nest there.

Chiloé Island

THE ENCHANTED FORESTS AND GLACIERS OF AYSÉN

After Villa Vanguardia, the Carretera Austral enters one of the most isolated regions of Chile: Aysén. The third largest region in the country (41,890 sq mi/108,494 sq km), it is home to just over 100,000 inhabitants, the majority of whom live in the city of Coyhaique.

Everywhere else, nature is evident. But at **Queulat National Park (5)**, it explodes. And when the clouds open up, you can see mountain peaks in the distance, and the Ventisquero Colgante ("hanging glacier") waterfall plunging from the peaks. You can approach it by crossing a stream on a long suspension bridge until you reach a jade-green lake. The generous cascades of the waterfall are above. Sometimes, a few coloumns of ice fall from the deluge in a deafening crash.

A few kilometers away, you have to leave your car on the side of the road and let yourself be drawn into the enchantment of **Bosque Encantado.** This "enchanted forest," dark and dense, lives up to its name. Dripping with humidity (11.5-13 ft/3.5-4 m of water falls here per year), a thick layer of moss covers decaying trunks, stumps, branches in clusters, and even the corpulent nothofagus trees reaching upward for light. We're talking about the *selva siempre verde,* "the evergreen forest." From the half-light, proud fuchsias emerge, showing off their purple corollas.

Nearby, the isolated village of **Puerto Puyuhuapi (6)** is located at the edge a well-carved fjord, with which it shares its name. Hostel Augusto Grosse, Casa Ludwig, Cabañas Rossbach: The names of the businesses here say a lot about the origin of the first settlers, who landed from the Sudetenland in the 1930s. After a craving for strudel, you can take a break at the nice Termas del Ventisquero, a few pools with warm water (95-105°F/35-40°C) situated on the side of the fjord, with views of the dolphins who sometimes swim around here.

Little by little, the forest spreads out to reveal pastures. They soon multiply in the long, narrow valley of the Simpson River, classified as a nature reserve, where large carpets of purple lupines extend in summer. The off-road Route 240 quickly leads to the fishing port of Puerto Aisén, and then to the pier of **Puerto Chacabuco (7).** It's a dead end, and from here you'll embark on one of the most memorable stretches of the trip, to Campo de Hielo Norte, the most northerly of the Patagonian ice caps (stretching over 1,600 sq mi/4,200 sq km). There, after 5 hours of navigation through the Estero Elefantes fjord and the maze of Patagonian canals, seven main glaciers descend toward the sea. On the west side, on the **Laguna San Rafael,** bordered by high black mountains, the *ventisquero* raises its colossal barrier of seracs of an intense blue, 200 ft (60 m) high and 2,600 ft (800 m) wide. Huge chunks of rock break away in spectacular collapses, forming high waves. The whole region is protected by a national park, classified as a World Biosphere Reserve.

FROM THE CHILEAN FAR WEST TO THE INLAND SEA OF LAGO GENERAL CARRERA

Coyhaique (8) is to Chile what Denver once was to the American West: a sort of frontier, where the *huasos* (local cowboys) go to do their shopping before returning to their ranches and vast pastures. Beef is king here and the lifestyle is rustic: Oftentimes, houses are heated only by a single stove. For entertainment, you can fly fish for trout or drink an artisanal beer at Mamma Gaucha restaurant.

Less than an hour south of the city, the barriers disappear. The Carretera Austral rises up and climbs along a river toward the old rocky ramparts of the aptly named **Cerro Castillo (9),** classified as a national reserve. It takes a few hours of walking to approach, after which you'll discover, as a reward, an exceptional panorama of black mountains, the (small) glacier coiled at their base, and the magnificent oval lake that stretches out below, with waters of intense jade-turquoise—sunny day required!

High misty mountains watch over the road, superb and wild, as the route goes up the wide valley of the Ibañez River, between sections of forest, lupines, and fireweed. Next stop: **Lago General Carrera,** the second largest lake in South America after Titicaca (714 sq mi/1,850 sq km), occupying a former glacial basin. In **Puerto Río Tranquilo (10),** you can set out via kayak or boat on its milky waters in the direction of Capilla de Mármol: large marble rocks polished by the waves, eroded into mushroom-like shapes at their base and pierced by passages and sculpted arches. Another excursion allows you to approach the isolated Laguna San Rafael National Park by another entrance: the Valle Exploradores and its glacier anchored to Campo de Hielo Norte, where the growing quantity of moraine debris covering the ice confirms the thesis of an ever-accelerating melting.

Cerro Castillo

(11) **(12)** **(13)** **(14)**

LAST VILLAGES BEFORE THE UNKNOWN

Little by little, the traffic diminishes. Rare buses venture as far as Cochrane, serving the charming hamlet of **Puerto Bertrand (11),** anchored on the sides of a rushing stream with showy turquoise waters: the Baker River. With wooden houses, hollyhocks, and white peaks on the horizon, the picture is perfect.

Cochrane is mostly of strategic interest: Fill up the gas tank and grab some cash at the ATM here. It is now time to re-launch south, in the wake of the Baker River. After days of progression on land, the Carretera Austral finally reaches the ocean—or, more precisely, the Gulf of Penas—in **Tortel (12).** It's an interesting village. Connected by road only since 2003, this town of nearly 500 inhabitants, without a telephone network, has no streets. Instead, stairs and high wooden footbridges connect it to the coast. Even the Plaza de Armas juts out onto the water on stilts.

A 30-minute boat ride away, the Isla de los Muertos is occupied only by a cemetery with old wooden crosses weathered by time, overgrown with ferns and gunnera—a monstrous cousin of rhubarb, which loves water and chilly climates. Who are the cemetery's occupants? Loggers, who died in 1906. No one knows their cause of death.

Tortel occupies a unique position at the junction of Campo de Hielo Norte and **Campo de Hielo Sur,** an ice cap four times larger than its neighbor. This frozen area—the third largest in the world (6,500

sq mi/16,800 sq km) after Antarctica and Greenland—stretches 220 mi (350 km) from north to south, to spill over into neighboring Argentina, where it feeds the famous Perito Moreno Glacier. Bernardo O'Higgins National Park, occupying a territory as large as the county of Belgium, protects most of this area, still partly unexplored. Governing a tangle of fjords, the Campo de Hielo Sur gives birth to 49 glaciers, tumbling down toward the sea in multiple tongues cracked with giant crevasses. From Tortel, it takes 3 hours of navigation to approach the Ventisquero Steffen (north side) and 5 hours to reach the sea of ice of Jorge Montt (south side)—at the end of a hike that just keeps getting longer thanks to climate change (the glacier has retreated 15 mi/25 km in 25 years).

Finally, the last (small) ferry and the last stage: From the pier of **Puerto Yungay (13)** to the dock of Río Bravo, crossing over the Mitchell fjord takes just 40 minutes. After another hundred kilometers, the end of the road is in sight: **Villa O'Higgins (14)** and its few gridded streets nestled in a grandiose amphitheater of high snow-capped peaks. End of the *camino*? Not really. Pedestrians and cyclists can continue by boat to Argentina for a new adventure. And motorists jump on the *Transbordadora Austral* ferry, which winds every 2-3 days from Puerto Yungay to Puerto Natales, for a 44-hour cruise in the heart of the wild Patagonia. A new challenge to take on, on the way to the edge of the South American continent.

PLAYLIST

Ben Harper
–
ONE ROAD TO FREEDOM

Red Hot Chili Peppers
–
ROAD TRIPPIN'

Nicola Cruz
–
CUMBIA DEL OVIDO

Eddie Vedder
–
NO CEILING

PREPARE FOR YOUR TRIP

• chile.travel •
• carretera-austral.net •
The "Barcazas" section gathers all ferry information
• conaf.cl • The website for Chile's national parks.
• rutadelosparques.org •
• tabsa.cl • The website for Transbordadora Austral Broom.

GETTING THERE

You can't reach Puerto Montt in flash. Fly into Santiago de Chile (Arturo Merino Benitez International Airport; SCL), and then take a connecting flight via LAN, the national carrier.

RENTING A CAR

After you explore the Carretera Austral via car, it's impossible to leave the car at the end of the road: You have to at least turn back to Coyhaique to return it to the rental company—that's a 350-mi (560-km) drive. With drop-off costs being higher than $1,000, it's advisable instead to go up to Puerto Montt from Puerto Chacabuco (near Coyhaique) via the Navimag ferry. It is much cheaper (about $180) and much more enjoyable—a real 24-hour cruise between the fjords and the islands of the Patagonian canals.

WHEN TO GO

December-March (during the Southern Hemisphere's summer).

WHERE TO STAY

Even if the weather is not always perfect, you can camp to enjoy the great outdoors. In cities and towns of a certain size, there are private youth hostels and cheap *hospedajes*. The hostels are generally more comfortable, and, for higher budgets, there are *cabañas* (mini-chalets), lodges in isolated regions, and even a few boutique hotels.

WHERE TO EAT

You will eat well in Chile. In this maritime region, seafood is in the spotlight, especially in *caldo de mariscos* (a thick soup). And what about the beef? Chileans swear by *churrasco*, a kind of big burger with steak, tomatoes, and avocado (not an easy bite!). For a meal that won't break the bank, there are *empanadas* (turnovers filled with cheese or meat). And for dessert: German-inspired cakes, exquisite *pie de limón*, and *manjar* (dulce de leche) ice cream.

A BOOK FOR THE ROAD

The Last Cowboys at the End of the World by Nick Reding

EUROPE

LOCATION

Southern Germany, in Bavaria

ROUTE

Lindau – Berchtesgaden

LENGTH

About 310 mi (500 km)

TIME

1 week

YOU'LL LOVE

The grandiose landscapes of lakes and mountains, the charm of painted houses, castles worthy of a fairy tale.

START
MI 0

1 LINDAU

`12`

`7`

2 FÜSSEN

`16`

`472`

3 OBERAMMERGAU

`23`

`2`

NEUSCHWANSTEIN CASTLE

LINDERHOF PALACE

START/END OF ROAD TRIP

STOP

LANDMARK OR POINT OF INTEREST

`308` ROAD

ROAD TRIP

Hamburg

Berlin

Cologne

GERMANY

Frankfurt

Munich

GERMAN ALPINE ROUTE
FROM LINDAU ➤➤➤ TO BERCHTESGDEN

The Deutsche Alpenstrasse stretches approximately 310 mi (500 km) south of Munich, from Lindau (near Lake Constance) to Berchtesgaden (on the Austrian border). Along the way, you'll pass forests, lakes, and snow-capped peaks. The dazzling green pastures, famous castles, and traditional houses adorned with flowers all make this an unmissable tour. Visitors here will find a romantic region strong in Bavarian traditions.

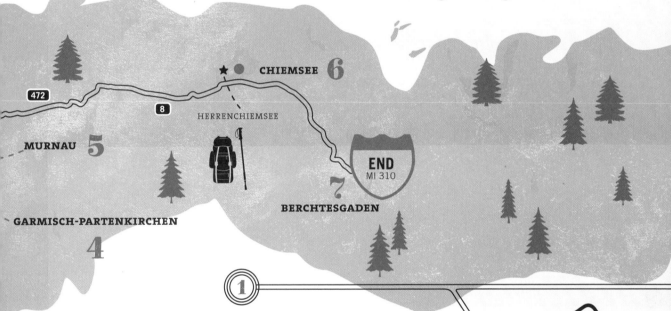

LINDAU: ON THE SHORES OF LAKE CONSTANCE

A small Bavarian enclave on Lake Constance, **Lindau (1)** is the starting point for the German Alpine Route. The medieval charm of this former imperial city attracts many tourists, yet despite its occasional crowds, Lindau remains a very pleasant place to visit. The city is home to an annual meeting of Nobel Prize winners, held since 1951, which is a testament to its popularity. In the Maximilianstrasse or on the port, you'll find people and cultures mingling on restaurant terraces, enjoying the Riviera-style atmosphere.

This side trip is a must for anyone craving German Baroque art. Start this 35 mi (56 km) trek in Weingarten, 22 mi (35 km) north of Lindau. This route is dotted with various Baroque churches, constructed and decorated by the biggest names in classic Baroque architecture. Highlights include Weingarten Abbey (rich in Italian influence), the beautiful Steinhausen Pilgrimage Church, works by Dominikus Zimmermann, and the exuberant Zwiefalten Abbey, built by Johann Michael Fischer. Marvel at the intricate paintings, stucco, and gilding of these fascinating structures.

DETOUR ALONG THE BAROQUE ROAD OF UPPER SWABIA

310 MI

FÜSSEN AND THE CASTLES OF LUDWIG II OF BAVARIA

For more than 700 years, **Füssen (2)** has stood the test of time without losing its authenticity. This small town lies in a prime location near the Austrian border, surrounded by numerous lakes and boasting a charming historic district perfect for strolling. Its proximity to two of King Ludwig II's famous castles makes it a perfect stop along the German Alpine Route.

The city's historic center can go completely unnoticed by those who cross the city by car. Take the time to stroll to discover its medieval alleys, imposing Gothic gables, painted houses, and shops decorated with old signs, all adding to its charm. The ascent to the Hohes Schloss castle also offers some surprises for those exploring on foot.

Füssen is home to two must-visit castles, **Neuschwanstein Castle,** which evokes images of Disney princesses and inspires thousands of tourists to snap selfies, and **Linderhof Palace.** Both have been classified as UNESCO World Heritage Sites since 2015. Most visitors also add a third castle to the circuit: Hohenschwangau Castle, located at the foot of Neuschwanstein. According to tradition, the castles should be visited in the chronological order of their construction, following the life of King Ludwig II: Hohenschwangau (where he spent his childhood), Neuschwanstein (his accession to power), then Linderhof (his rivalry with the kings of France), and Herrenchiemsee, visited later on this trip.

△ NOT TO BE MISSED

To visit the three castles in the same day, it's a good idea to start with Hohenschwangau, visiting the museum, and then climbing to Neuschwanstein (good luck!). Head to Linderhof in the middle of the afternoon, when there are fewer crowds. This also allows you to enjoy the park as it empties after the castle closes.

Neuschwanstein Castle;

OBERAMMERGAU

Oberammergau (3) is one of the most adorable Bavarian villages, surrounded by pastures and forests at the foot of the Alps, just 1 hour from Munich via the A 95. Its charm lies in the large number of painted facades that adorn farms, inns, and houses. Proud of its traditions, Oberammergau has also acquired inter-national fame for its wood craftsmanship (many of its inhabitants continue to make a living from it today). But the highlight of the village is its religious devotion, most notable in its represen-tation of the Passion of Christ. Since 1633, the villagers have kept a promise made after they were spared by the plague that decimated the surrounding region: Every 10 years, from May to October, residents reenact the mystery of the Passion, drawing large crowds and filling all sur-rounding hotels to capacity. The religious fervor here is so strong, in fact, that Judas even has a street named after him. While Oberammergau attracts lots of tourists, it is also an ideal base for exploring the highlights of the region, including Ettal Abbey and Wies Church.

LOVE AT FIRST SIGHT

PAINTED HOUSES

Painted houses can be found everywhere in Garmisch-Partenkirchen, but the most beautiful are in the historic part of the village. The best-known is the Pilatushaus (Ludwig-Thoma Str. 10), which is open for visits. It dates from the 13th century, when the art form known as Lüftlmalerei was first developed. The motifs, frequently featuring visual illusions and accompanied by say-ings or quotes, recall the Rococo style, but generally reflect a few com-mon themes: religious scenes, representations of trades, hunting scenes, and banquets. Fans of Grimm's fairy tales will want to visit the Hansel and Gretel House (Ettaler Str. 41). You'll feel like Little Red Riding Hood on her way to Grandma's, but rest assured, there is little risk of seeing the big bad wolf—the city is too civilized.

GARMISCH-PARTENKIRCHEN

The highlight of **Garmisch-Partenkirchen (4)** and all of the Bavarian Alps is the summit of Zugspitze. With its 9,718-ft (2,962-m) altitude on the German side, it is the highest point in Germany and offers the best view of Bavaria. The most practical (but expensive) way to get there is via the cogwheel train, followed by the cable car for the last 1,150 ft (350 m). Another faster route is to drive directly by car 6 mi (10 km) to Lake Eibsee (itself one of the highest points in Europe) to take the Eibsee cable car up to the summit.

Garmisch-Partenkirchen is also home to the best-known German ski resort, used in the 1936 Olympic Games, the 1978 World Championships, and again in the 2011 Olympics. The Olympic facilities are open to the public, and the surroundings are rich in hik-ing. Nature enthusiasts head to Partnachklamm, a gorge stretching 2,300 ft (700 m) across and more than 320 ft (100m) deep, offering a magnificent natural spectacle.

Despite the big local attraction of Zugspitze's summit, GaPa (as it is affectionately known) does not draw crowds to shop or enjoy its cozy hotels and spas. Garmisch is the heart of the new town, but roman-tics prefer to stroll along the Ludwigstrasse on the Partenkirchen side, famous for its old-style inns, local artisans, and traditional confection-ers. Both villages feature some fairly old houses with painted facades.

MURNAU

Murnau (5) is in the center of the "Blue Country," but this corner of Bavaria does not owe its name to its small lakes (Riegsee, Staffelsee, etc.) but instead to the artistic movement Der Blaue Reiter ("The Blue Rider"). Murnau has been home to many painters: Gabriele Münter and Wassily Kandinsky had a house here and received many artist visitors, including Franz Marc and Alexej von Jawlensky. An interesting collection of works from this period is visible in the Schlossmuseum. By car, by bike, on horseback, or on foot, you can follow in the footsteps of the "Blue Rider."

Another pilgrimage awaits lovers of German theater and literature. The giant red hat in the park, behind the tourist office, is a sculpture made in homage to the writer Ödön von Horváth, who lived in Murnau in the early 1930s. His pieces, which warned against the danger of National Socialism, were found among the books that the Nazis burned in 1933. He fled Berlin for Paris and died following an accident on the Champs-Élysées in 1938, at the age of 36. The sculpture has become the symbol of the "Murnauer Horváth-Tage" festival.

Murnau, Lake Riegsee

ON THE SHORES OF LAKE CHIEMSEE

Still following the German Alpine Road, head southeast of Munich, away from the Salzburg motorway. The small town of Prien is the main port of access to **Chiemsee (6),** the largest lake in Germany, known for its lovely islands. One of these islands is home to the third and last castle built by Ludwig II of Bavaria: the "little Versailles" **Herrenchiemsee.**

Visitors to the "Bavarian Sea" (as this lake is sometimes called) can enjoy the pleasure of a boat trip, a cycling tour, or even a picnic at the top of Kampenwand. There are many charming places to see, both in the countryside and at the water's edge, as well as on the islands. Two of the islands most worth visiting are Herreninsel and Fraueninsel (known as "Isle of Gentlemen" and "Isle of Ladies"). There are six ports around the lake, but Prien is the closest, operates year-round, and offers the most options.

Once you've had your fill of sunbathing, head toward the Austrian border, about 90 mi (150 km) southeast of Munich, toward **Berchtesgaden (7).** This last stop on the German Alpine Route is also an excellent stopover for those continuing onward to Salzburg. A small mountain town with a charming pedestrian center, Berchtesgaden is very pleasant, despite the summer crowds. Hikers will not be bored here. And in summer, traditional music and dances offer lots of fun. The city owes much of its fame to two very different locales, one natural, the other much less so: the beautiful Königssee lake and Hitler's infamous Eagle's Nest.

PREPARE FOR YOUR TRIP

• **germany.travel** • The website of the German National Tourist Board has information on Bavaria as well as the whole country.
• **deutsche-alpenstrasse.de** • Information on the German Alpine Route.

GETTING THERE

The simplest itinerary is to fly into Munich (Munich International Airport; MUC), and then reach Lindau by car (approximately 2.5 hours).

RENTING A CAR

Traveling from Munich, you will have no trouble finding a rental car. Sixt, Hertz, Europcar, Avis, and other rental companies all offer different types of cars for trips of various lengths. You'll also find rental agencies in cities and stations throughout Germany.

WHEN TO GO

Spring or early fall are best for traveling through Bavaria. The shores of Lake Constance become reminiscent of the Mediterranean. If the sun is out, you won't regret bringing your swimsuit! Try to avoid the month of November, when the region goes into hibernation, but come back in winter to enjoy the snow and the relatively mild weather.

WHERE TO STAY

Because this region is sometimes crowded due to trade shows, fairs, events, and the influx of tourists visiting the castles in summer, finding accommodations can be a real headache. Book hotel rooms or campsites as early as possible in advance of your trip. It can be safer to book by email than by phone.

A BOOK FOR THE ROAD

The Magic Mountain by Thomas Mann

Lake Chiemsee

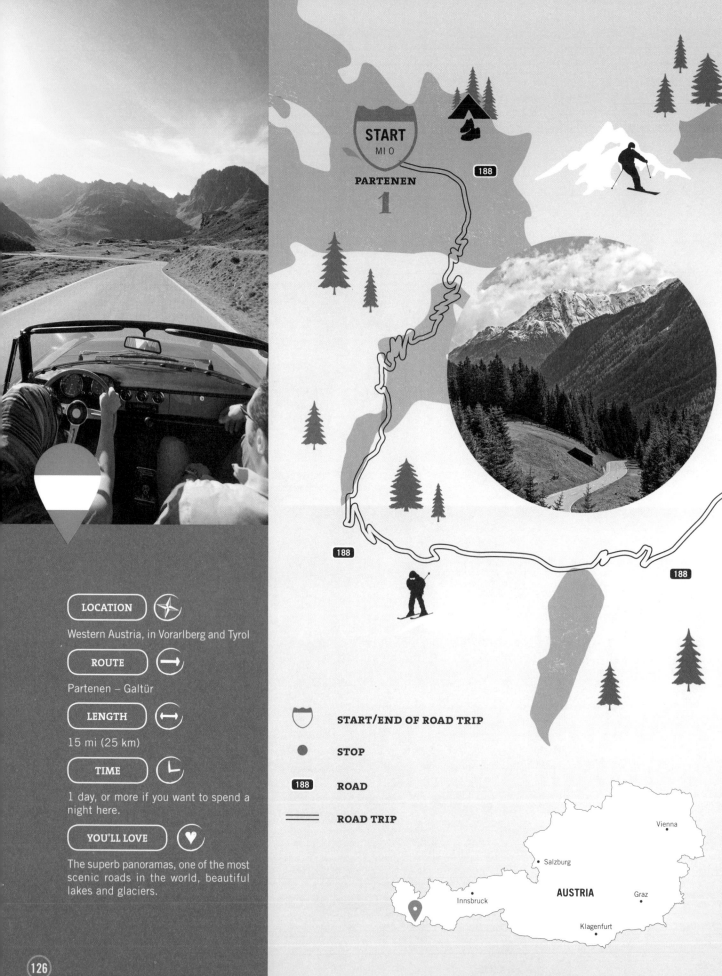

START
MI 0

PARTENEN

1

188

LOCATION

Western Austria, in Vorarlberg and Tyrol

ROUTE

Partenen – Galtür

LENGTH

15 mi (25 km)

TIME

1 day, or more if you want to spend a night here.

YOU'LL LOVE

The superb panoramas, one of the most scenic roads in the world, beautiful lakes and glaciers.

⬡ **START/END OF ROAD TRIP**

● **STOP**

188 **ROAD**

══ **ROAD TRIP**

Vienna

• Salzburg

AUSTRIA

Graz

Innsbruck •

Klagenfurt •

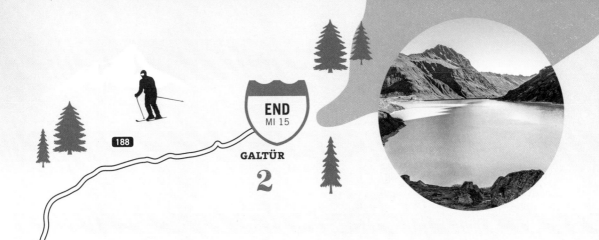

SILVRETTA HOCHALPENSTRASSE
IN THE HEART OF THE AUSTRIAN MONTAFON
FROM PARTENEN ➤➤➤ TO GALTÜR

The Montafon, the southernmost valley of Vorarlberg, stretches to one of Austria's most famous alpine routes: the Silvretta Road, which climbs in 30 switchbacks to 6,667 ft (2,032 m) at the Bielerhöhe Pass, right along the border between Tyrol and Vorarlberg. The road is not very long, but the natural beauty is plentiful—you will be amazed by the lakes, peaks, and glaciers! This is a great way to travel from one region to another while discovering unspoiled nature made up of forests, mountain pastures, and orchards, and where the local language and traditions are still preserved.

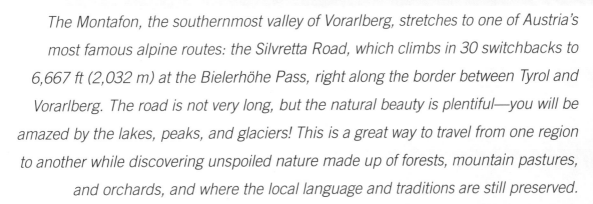

THE SILVRETTA, BETWEEN VORARLBERG AND TYROL

The famous Silvretta Hochalpenstrasse begins shortly after **Partenen (1).** The road is superb . . . and dizzying: No less than 32 switchbacks await you (those prone to carsickness may want to skip it!). Twelve miles (20 km) farther, across a beautiful amphitheater of mountains, lies the Bielerhöhe Pass, at an altitude of 6,667 ft (2,032 m), which marks the border between Vorarlberg and Tyrol. Take the opportunity to stop at Lake Stausee, which can be walked around in 1.5 hours. Cruises on the lake are also possible. The area offers many can't-miss hikes; be sure to take in a few. The road continues to **Galtür (2)** in Tyrol.

Silvretta Hochalpenstrasse

VORARLBERG

Almost equidistant from Paris and Vienna, Vorarlberg is the westernmost region of Austria and its second smallest (after Vienna), with a total area of 1,004 sq mi (2,601 sq km). With its mountains rising gently from the shores of Lake Constance, remarkable glaciers, and its renowned winter sports resorts, Vorarlberg is also one of the most touristed areas of the country. This land has always drawn visitors, starting with the Illyrians, followed by the Celts, the Romans, the Alemanni, and even the Swiss, who eventually left beautiful southern Switzerland to populate the region. Vorarlberg is also the most Swiss district of Austria: In 1919, when the Austrian Republic was created, part of the population wanted to be attached to Switzerland rather than to Austria.

TYROL

Tyrol is the symbol of Austria: its folklore, its traditions, its culture, and its typical architecture. Moreover, it is the region that most appeals to tourists, and many efforts are made here to best accommodate passing visitors.

Half of this region is made up of mountains (with 700 peaks over 9,840 ft/3,000 m!), glaciers, and mountain pastures; a third is covered with forests; and only a 10th is cultivated. It is no wonder travelers are so enthusiastic about Tyrol. Though it's home to many prestigious ski resorts in winter, the Alpine landscape has not been completely disturbed, and the villages maintain a welcoming charm in summer. In short, Tyrol offers superb landscapes that visitors of all ages can happily discover year-round.

PREPARE FOR YOUR TRIP

• **austria.info** • A thorough website on all there is to see and do in Austria. Provides practical information, covering topics such as architecture, design, sports, sustainable tourism, accessibility, and more. Also offers accommodation reservations.

GOOD TO KNOW

The Silvretta is a private road requiring paid toll (around €18).

GETTING THERE

If you fly into Salzburg Airport (SZG), Partenen is a 4-hour drive away. You can also fly into Zürich, Switzerland, and drive 2 hours to the start of the Silvretta Hochalpenstrasse.

RENTING A CAR

Finding a rental car in Austria is easy. The main rental companies are all available in Salzburg, or at other major airports in the region.. *Note:* Before entering an Austrian motorway, you will need to either buy a toll sticker to place on the windshield, or check that it is clearly visible on your rental car. These stickers can be purchased at gas stations near the border (and at the border itself). Otherwise, you can also buy them at some post offices or tobacco shops. They can also be purchased in advance online at tolltickets.com or on the Automobile Club Association website (**automobile-club.org**).

WHEN TO GO

The road is mainly closed November-June (dates vary depending on snow cover). Spring and fall are generally the optimal seasons to visit. Beware, the end of April and May (depending on the snow cover) are often dead months in the alpine valleys. Summer sometimes experiences violent thunderstorms, but the end of the season can be splendid, especially in the mountains. In winter, fog covers the valleys, but in high altitude, the snow fields sparkle under a generous sun.

WHERE TO STAY

- **Berggasthof Hotel Piz Buin:** *Bielerhöhe (Tyrol side).*
• **buin.at** • A large and modern building offering 20 cozy and stylish rooms and a beautiful, uncluttered lobby, all laid out unceremoniously at an altitude of 6,560 ft (2,000 m). Most of the rooms are equipped with patios and sliding glass doors, from which you can enjoy a view of the Silvretta Hochalpenstrasse. There is also a spa/sauna and shop on site. The restaurant features a traditional menu, with views of the lake and mountains.

- **Silvretta-Haus:** *Bielerhöhe (Vorarlberg side)*
• **silvretta-haus.at** • A fine example of contemporary architecture, typical of Vorarlberg. The interior features crisp and pleasant rooms, each with a view overlooking the lake and mountains. The panoramic café-restaurant is a great spot to sit and relax, even for a simple drink.

WHAT TO EAT

Austrian cuisine is lesser-known and too often compared to its German neighbor. This is an unfortunate mistake! Over the centuries, the country has been enriched by the culinary habits of its neighbors, to the point of offering a good hybrid of all the cuisines of Central Europe. Just don't count the calories! Foodies rejoice in this corner of Austria because "creative regional cuisine" has recently appeared in Vorarlberg. Ancestral recipes with enigmatic names (*Ofenkatze, Schmarollennockerl, Hafaloab,* etc.), formerly intended to feed mountain workers, have been reworked to appeal to the taste buds of visitors. It has obviously paid off: Today, Vorarlberg has the largest number of award-winning restaurants in Austria.

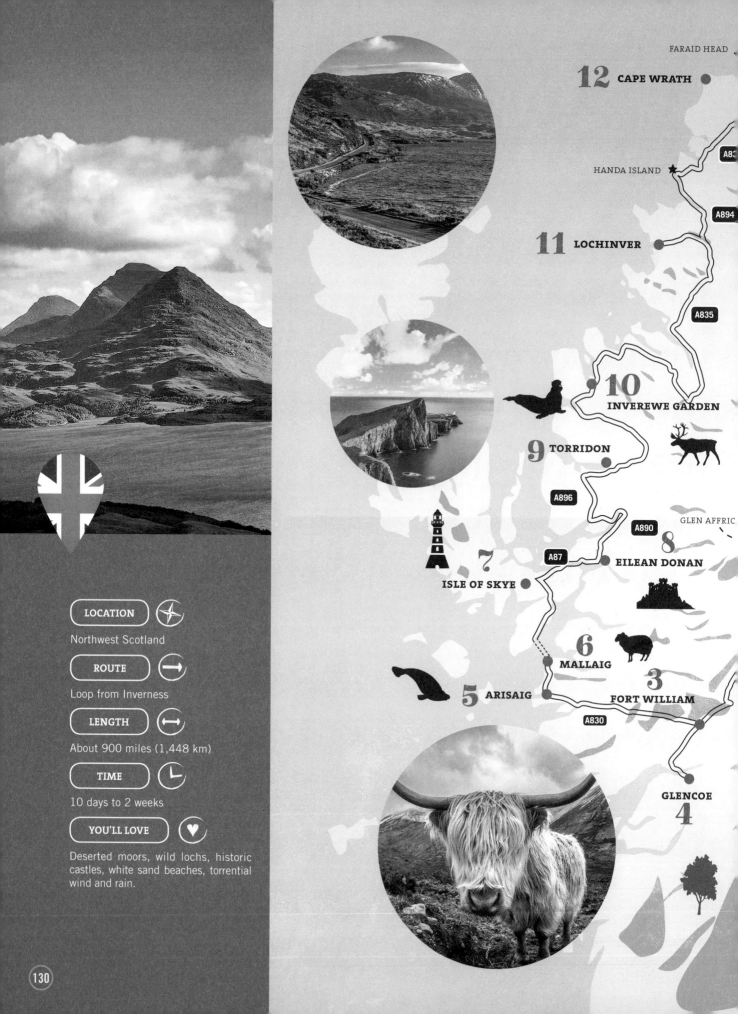

FARAID HEAD

12 CAPE WRATH

A83

HANDA ISLAND

A894

11 LOCHINVER

A835

10 INVEREWE GARDEN

9 TORRIDON

A896

GLEN AFFRIC

A890

8 EILEAN DONAN

A87

7 ISLE OF SKYE

6 MALLAIG

3 FORT WILLIAM

5 ARISAIG

A830

GLENCOE

4

LOCATION

Northwest Scotland

ROUTE

Loop from Inverness

LENGTH

About 900 miles (1,448 km)

TIME

10 days to 2 weeks

YOU'LL LOVE

Deserted moors, wild lochs, historic castles, white sand beaches, torrential wind and rain.

OF TONGUE **13** **DUNNET HEAD**

A836

★ **WICK**

★ **BADBEA**

A9

14
DUNROBIN

★ **GLENMORANGIE**

**START/
END**

INVERNESS 1

DRUMNADROCHIT

LOCH NESS 2

AROUND
THE HIGHLANDS
A TOUR OF SCOTLAND

Far north, hardly closer to London than the Arctic Circle, the Highlands form the spiritual heart of Scotland. This is where people still speak (a little) Gaelic, where sheep frolic in the scenic moors, and tales of monsters abound. Whisky is imbibed like beer and ghosts cheerfully haunt the castles. It's a land of legends, beauty, and adventure.

Inverness

Aberdeen

SCOTLAND

Dundee

Glasgow

Edinburgh

START/END OF ROAD TRIP	⬵
STOP	●
LANDMARK OR POINT OF INTEREST	★
ROAD	A830
ROAD TRIP	━━━
FERRY	-----

INVERNESS, CAPITAL OF THE HIGHLANDS

Its title of capital of the Highlands aside, **Inverness (1)** offers a slow introduction to this fabulous region. Capped by a castle built in 1836, the city center features red brick buildings lining the shores of the famous River Ness. It's home to many churches, but is most notable for its tartan shops and pubs.

Upon arrival, Shakespeare fans will want to head out to search for Macbeth's ghost at the picturesque Cawdor Castle. The building, backed by a lovely walled garden, dates from the 14th century and has remained in the same family for the past 600 years. As King Macbeth died in 1057, it's unlikely that he ever would have set foot here, but the folklore keeps business going. The castle grounds also offer a café, shops, and a 25-acre golf course.

To get to the castle, you'll partly cross the Culloden Battlefield. Prince Charles Edward Stuart (commonly known as "Bonnie Prince Charlie"), the heir to the royal Stuarts (and cousin of French King Louis XV), lost all hope of reconquering the throne of Scotland during one of the most historic battles here. In just one hour, his troop of Highlanders was wiped out. Tartan and bagpipes were banned and the English built nearby Fort George, in case of another uprising (which never came). Just a few yards away lies Chanonry Point, where you'll spot dolphins trawling the waters for salmon.

©Glen Affric

THE LOCH, THE MONSTER, AND THE GLEN

Visitors are drawn here to do the impossible: find the **Loch Ness (2)** monster. From Inverness, travel up along the Caledonian Canal, parallel to the A82 road, to reach this long ribbon of water. Tucked into the Great Glen Fault, which cuts across Scotland from the Atlantic to the North Sea, Loch Ness, stretching over 23 mi (37 km) long and 0.5-1.8 mi (1.2-3 km) wide, is the largest lake (in volume) among the British Isles. Definitely large enough to hide a monster!

Those searching for Nessie should start at the very commercial Drumnadrochit museum, where you can immerse yourself in the legends and inspect images of past sightings. Next, enjoy a pint or two at the Fiddler's Highland Restaurant to help convince yourself of her existence. Then, take a tour of the ruins of Urquhart Castle, placed above the loch, for the best lookout point. Hike along the paths of Glen Urquhart, with soft wood ground to the south and leafy green trees to the north.

On the last Saturday in August, visitors flock to **Drumnadrochit** to attend the famous Highland Games. The event features nonstop bagpipe music, running in kilts, and various athletic competitions, including stone put, weight throw, and hammer toss. Scots love to throw. And toast, too.

At the western end of the Great Glen sits the large market town of **Fort William (3),** famous for the waterways that flow into it year-round. Fort William is a former garrison town and still retains some of that charm to this day. Peering through the constant fog and drizzle, you'll spot the stony summit of Ben Nevis, the highest point in Great Britain at 4,410 ft (1,344 m), with its beautiful, marshy valley below. Hikers can scale this peak in 7-8 hours, but should remain cautious of the snow present most of the year.

Southeast of Fort William, **Glencoe (4)** is best remembered as the site of the famous 1692 massacre of the MacDonald clan, carried out by the Scottish henchmen of the King of England to silence any hint of rebellion. More than three centuries later, the valley is known instead for the pure grandeur of its landscape of moors, surrounded by rocky pyramids.

DETOUR VIA GLEN AFFRIC

The landscape of Glen Affric is marked by rolling moors and low mountains, winding lochs and lush waterfalls. The gray skies, windblown trees, and fresh air are invigorating to most visitors. Others enjoy driving the one-lane road, meandering along the sometimes-blue waters of Loch Beinn a'Mheadhoin, between pines and birches, moss mats, and lush heather fields. In the distance, snow-capped peaks will have visitors basking in Scottish beauty.

Neist Point, Isle of Skye

THE ISLAND ROUTE

Continuing from Fort William, this photogenic route forages along the A830 for 50 mi (80 km). The land meets with Loch Eil, an arm of the sea reaching inland. Here you'll find Glenfinnan, known as the place where Bonnie Prince Charlie launched the 1745 Jacobite uprising, before moving on to Culloden and later fleeing to the Isle of Skye (where he disguised himself as an Irishwoman).

The village of **Arisaig (5),** at the outpost of the Strait of Sleat, is a great place to admire the sea for what it is: beautiful and wild. Here you'll find moors full of sheep but devoid of humans, while the more populated coastal areas boast rocky barricades on clear sandy beaches with views of numerous islands where seals congregate.

From **Mallaig (6),** take a short 30-minute ride on the *Caledonian MacBrayne* ferry to the **Isle of Skye (7),** the largest of the Inner Hebrides islands. Skye's vast expanse of 636 sq mi (1,656 sq km) is quite rugged, marked by the Cuillin Mountains with a peak of 3,258 ft (993 m) and various cliffs along its peninsulas. Most of the roads and paths lead to peaks, lighthouses, and other scenic viewpoints. Venture to Neist Point Lighthouse or Rubha nam Brathairean ("Brother's Point") to enjoy panoramic views of the gray ocean billowing with foam, rocky cliffs jutting into the water, and green valleys strewn with sheep. A little farther out lies the Old Man of Storr, a steep hill also worth a visit.

Skye remains tied to its Gaelic culture, evident in the cottages of Kilmuir, a restored village once populated with farmers. This is also home to many castle ruins, as well as the still-inhabited Dunvegan castle, home to the MacLeod clan. Connoisseurs of Talisker whisky can also visit their distillery here. Tastings are offered at the beginning of the visit rather than the end, to prevent accidents on the isle's single-track roads.

DETOUR TO THE "ISLANDS BEYOND THE SEA"

When traveling via ferry from the village of Uig on the Isle of Skye, be prepared for extreme conditions. Crossing the Shiant Strait can sometimes be stormy. Sail 3 hours on the open waters to discover Na h-Eileanan Siar (the "Western Isles")—otherwise known as the Outer Hebrides. This archipelago of 70 barren islands has a rich history: This is where the descendants of Celtic and Viking settlers became sheep breeders, fishermen, and weavers. On Lewis and Harris, the largest island, more than two-thirds of the people still speak Gaelic—evidenced by the numerous bilingual signs. These islands offer a mix of tar landscape and white sand beaches, with turquoise waters. The ocean breeze is perfect for walking, so keep alert when driving these narrow roads and pass courteously.

THE NORTHWEST COAST: FROM THE MOUNTAINS TO THE SEA

Made famous by the film *Highlander,* **Eilean Donan (8)** projects an austere and iconic silhouette above the salty waters of Loch Duich. Home to one of the most beautiful fortified castles in Scotland, this tiny island can only be accessed by a single stone bridge.

From here, leave the A87 and head down the single-lane winding roads toward the beautiful fjord of **Loch Torridon (9).** Visit the former hunting lodge turned luxury hotel, and settle down into a leather armchair to enjoy some local whisky. The area is rife with mountain summits, proving that this part of Britain, at least, is anything but flat.

In Poolewe, **Inverewe Garden (10)** offers a vast expanse of greenery from all corners of the world. About an hour away, the pleasant fishing village of Ullapool is an important embarkation port for the surrounding Outer Hebrides.

The farther north you travel, the more jagged the west coast of the Highlands becomes. The waters are dotted with entire fleets of islands, known as the Summer Isles. The roads become narrower and more winding, linking the small and pretty towns and scattered ports. In **Lochinver (11),** wildlife-watchers will delight in the view of seals along the bay and deer grazing in fields. From here, you have a choice of which to explore next: the white sands of dreamy Achmelvich Beach, or the well-framed ruins of Ardvreck Castle along the austere Loch Assynt— you can't go wrong either way.

Later in the day, as the traffic lessens, the largely unpopulated lochs and fjords provide a quiet solitude. The offshore wind, the fresh air, and the warm light all evoke the feeling of the North. On the slippery edges of the cliffs of **Handa Island** and **Faraid Head,** puffins nest and take flight. The cliffs of **Cape Wrath (12)** stand out in the distance, marking the "end of Scotland," the mythical end of the world. But this area is not as harsh as it sounds— it's full of sublime beaches and tempting waters. Don't be fooled: The water temperature is only 55°F (13°C) in summer!

Glenmorangie distillery

13

BACK TO INVERNESS

14

The northern coast of Scotland is perfectly isolated. The human population is sparse, concentrated mostly along the coast of Loch Eriboll, on the sides of the alluring **Kyle of Tongue,** where the ruins of Caisteal ("castle") Bharraich overlook vast sandbanks. In the background, Ben Hope shyly peeks out above the clouds, at 3,041 ft (927 m).

The land's end is a little farther, at **Dunnet Head (13),** at 58°40' north latitude, near the Castle of Mey, where the Queen Mother spent all her summers in a large neo-Gothic mansion flanked by a pretty vegetable garden. From here, London can be seen 620 mi (1,100 km) away, but a much closer view is the offshore archipelago of the Orkney Islands. All that remains of their long-ago

lords of the Sinclair clan are the name of a bay and, at Noss Head, the ruins of a castle still braced on the promontory where it has stood for six centuries.

The northeastern coast of the Highlands is not quite as cheerful, and its towns even less so. Thurso and **Wick** are a bit drab, though the latter hosts a fascinating museum dedicated to the golden age of herring fishing. Continuing along the coast, look for the remains of **Badbea,** a village built on an unstable foundation atop a sloping cliff. This was once known as a "clearance village," where farmers and fishermen resettled in the 19th century after being driven from the Highlands to make way for more profitable sheep farms. The wind here is so

violent that the inhabitants, it is said, had to tie up both their chickens and their children! Meanwhile, in **Dunrobin (14),** 20 mi (30 km) to the south, the Earls and Dukes of Sutherland, enriched by wool, built their castle. Its furniture, library, and canvases by great portrait painters all evoke a sense of cultured elitism. In the gardens, the trophy room is stocked with giraffe heads and elephant feet, souvenirs of their many safaris in Sudan.

Inverness is almost in sight. Continue on past the Dornoch Firth, then that of Cromarty, but celebrate Scottish whisky one last time at the **Glenmorangie** distillery. This benchmark of single malt is certainly enough to justify a final stopover.

Eilean Donan Castle

PREPARE FOR YOUR TRIP

- visitscotland.com •
- westscotland.com •
- venture-north.co.uk •
- northcoast500.com •
- walkhighlands.co.uk •

GETTING THERE

Fly to London, Aberdeen, Glasgow, or Edinburgh, and then head north by car.

RENTING A CAR

Rent a car to explore the Highlands, but don't forget to drive on the left side of the road! Be careful on small single-lane roads and be courteous when passing: The closest vehicle stops first to let the oncoming one pass.

WHERE TO STAY

Most travelers prefer B&Bs, where a hearty breakfast (often Scottish style, with blood sausage), is served, and the owners are very welcoming. If you're on a tight budget and not afraid of getting wet, campsites (generally open April-September) are a great option. The weather and quality of the grounds may vary, but most campgrounds also offer small bungalows. Youth hostels are another popular option, especially in Inverness. Avoid the hotels here—most are expensive and not always great quality.

WHAT TO EAT

Scots truly appreciate seafood. Haggis (stuffed sheep's stomach) is also a must-try favorite dish. Restaurants offer affordable lunchtime menus, and it's easy to find options at fast food eateries, fish-and-chips joints, and take-aways (take-out spots). Also popular are tearooms (which serve sandwiches, hot dishes, and much more than tea), and pubs (where you can enjoy local dishes like steak and kidney pie or bangers and mash). In more isolated areas, dinner reservations are highly recommended. Grocery stores are also available, but may have limited operating hours.

A BOOK FOR THE ROAD

The Highland Witch by Susan Fletcher

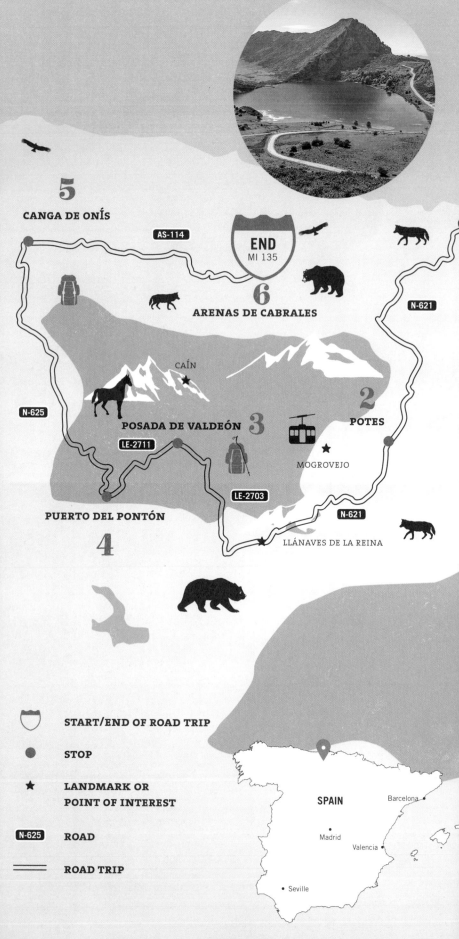

5
CANGA DE ONÍS

AS-114

END
MI 135

6
ARENAS DE CABRALES

N-621

CAÍN

2
POTES

N-625

POSADA DE VALDEÓN

3

MOGROVEJO

LE-2711

LE-2703

N-621

PUERTO DEL PONTÓN

4

LLÁNAVES DE LA REINA

LOCATION

Northern Spain, Cantabria, Castilla y León, Asturias

ROUTE

San Vicente de la Barquera – Arenas de Cabrales

LENGTH

135 mi (220 km) without detours

TIME

3 days without excursions

YOU'LL LOVE

The waterways filled with fish, the snow-capped peaks, the mountain hikes, the granaries, the scent of martagon lilies, and the golden eagles flying overhead.

⬡ **START/END OF ROAD TRIP**

● **STOP**

★ **LANDMARK OR POINT OF INTEREST**

N-625 **ROAD**

═══ **ROAD TRIP**

SPAIN

Barcelona

Madrid

Valencia

Seville

START
MI 0

1 SAN VICENTE
DE LA
BARQUERA

A TOUR OF THE
PICOS DE EUROPA
FROM SAN VICENTE ➤➤➤ TO LAS ARENAS

In the north of Spain, the snowcapped peaks of the Picos de Europa rise up among the Cantabrian mountain range. The golden eagle flies overhead, while the wolf's howl echoes through the canyons. High in altitude, with many switchbacks, these roads feature spectacular views and wild landscapes. Here in Spain, everything feels mystical. In the prairies and the gorges, it's easy to imagine the shouts of the Knights of the Reconquista. Roman bridges and churches evoke the region's religious history. The traditional haylofts, or hórreos, *recount the difficult life of the shepherd, while the coal mining past can be seen at dark entrances hidden in the folds of the valleys. With its rich history and numerous hikes, a road trip under the incredible silhouette of the Naranjo de Bulnes is well-worth the journey. ¡Olé!*

A TRIP ON THE HORIZON

The Picos de Europa stretch along a 25-mi (40-km) strip over the mountain regions of Asturias, Cantabria, and León, about 18 mi (30 km) south of the Costa Verde. The highest peak among them is Torre de Cerredo, which stands at 8,690 ft (2,650 m) tall. The Picos de Europa are protected by the Picos de Europa National Park and are classified as a UNESCO biosphere reserve. Historically, these snowcapped mountains served as a landmark for sailors who saw them from afar while navigating the ocean. Wild and very jagged, the Picos de Europa are divided into three massifs: El Cornión in the east, Los Urrieles in the center, and Andara in the east. These peaks are not served by any through roads—travelers through the valleys should be aware of dead ends.

The region also features three tumultuous rivers—Deva, Cares, and Stella—where salmon and trout fishers make their living. Mineral deposits and livestock are the main resources of this austere massif, where hunting is strictly regulated.

135 MI

Mogrovejo

PICOS DE EUROPA IN CANTABRIA (EAST)

From **San Vicente de la Barquera (1)** on the Cantabrian Coast, head southwest on the N 621. The Desfiladero de Hermida gorge juts into your path, with 330-ft-high (100-high) walls offering just a sample of the true majesty you can see here. The gorge is so narrow that the sun only penetrates through seven months out of the year. This road leads to the Church of Santa Maria de Lebeña, a 10th-century Mozarabic church surrounded by walnut and cherry trees and highlighted by some Romanesque features that were added on over the years. The park's information center in Tama will tell you all you need to know about the flora and fauna that surrounds you.

Not far away, the small Cantabrian town of **Potes (2),** dominated by the Torre del Infantado tower, is the center of excursions in the Liébana region. Commercial and very lively in summer, it is a good starting point for visiting the Cantabrian mountains. Potes is known for its *orujo*, a type of potent pomace brandy, often mixed with herbs, coffee,

honey, or cream. Continuing on 1 mi (2 km) west, the CA 185 leads to the Santo Toribio de Liébana monastery. Known throughout Europe since the 8th century for the wonderful illuminations done by the monk Beatus of Liébana, this austere monastery houses a piece of the True Cross (believed to be a piece of the actual cross used in the crucifixion of Jesus). A pilgrimage to honor the cross is held here every year on April 16, the patronal feast day.

The Rio Deva now accompanies you for 15 mi (25 km), in the valley of Camaleño, which ends in a dead end. Ample and green, the road crosses very nice little villages. The village of **Mogrovejo,** at the foot of a medieval watchtower, has a squat, unpretentious church that has kept its original character. Half a mile (1 km) away, you'll come across the impressive glacial cirque of Fuente Dé, where the Deva river has its source. For an extraordinary view over Los Picos, take a 4-minute ride on a funicular up 2,950 ft (900 m) to the Mirador del Cable.

HIKING

The Puertos de Áliva walk from the Mirador del Cable is a great option. You'll reach the Hotel Áliva in 2 mi (4 km). If you wish to continue, look on the right, near the pass, for a path leading down for 6 mi (10 km) to the village of Espinama in the valley. Those who venture down here often hitchhike to return back up to the funicular parking lot.

Another hike available from the Mirador del Cable is the daylong descent (on the Asturias side) to Sotres. Admire the tiled roofs, while skirting the famous Naranjo de Bulnes, one of the most impressive mountains in this range. Its west face, surrounded by peaks of 8,200 ft (2,500 m), is a dream for climbers. Be sure to bring water and supplies.

PICOS DE EUROPA IN LEÓN (CENTER)

Ready to keep going? Take the N 621 southwest at Potes, along the Liébana Valley. Here, as the road twists and turns, you'll find a Mediterranean climate where vineyards mix with oak trees. This juxtaposes the arid landscape of the San Glorio pass, at an altitude of 5,279 ft (1,609 m). Just before, the Mirador de Liesba offers a glance of the peaks of the mountain range, which are often drowned in the mist. The descent passes through the province of León, starting with the village of **Llánaves de la Reina.**

Those who wish to enter the heart of the Picos de Europa will follow the route north on the LE 243 to **Posada de Valdeón (3),** via the Pandetrave Pass at 5,125 ft (1,562 m). Located on the Rio Cares, the panoramic views from this town are stunning. This quiet little village makes a great base camp for the many hiking trails offered by the Picos de Europa information center.

Much like Switzerland and Portugal, this region is full of *hórreos* (granaries mounted on stilts and slate to protect crops from rodents and other predators). Farm tools are often hung on the facades of these buildings, which are protected by the national park.

Sitting down to a plate of *huevos fritos* in the restored hamlet of Caín, 5 mi (9 km) north of Posada, facing the summit of Cerredo, is the perfect way to admire your surroundings. Be careful: The road to Caín is very steep and narrow. Bridges, sheep pens, narrow passes, and torrential weather all add to the experience here! The descent toward easier roads is via Posada de Valdéon and Puerto del Pontón at 4,200 ft (1,280 m).

LOVE AT FIRST SIGHT

"THE DIVINE THROAT"
The Cares Trail, or Ruta del Cares, (6 hours round-trip), winding along the Garganta Divina ("Divine Throat" in Spanish), is one of the most spectacular hikes in northern Spain. It's a relatively easy and popular trail, but with some passages overhanging 650 ft (200 m), it is not recommended for those with vertigo or a fear of heights.

Sentier de Cares

PICOS DE EUROPA IN ASTURIAS (NORTH)

From **Puerto del Pontón (4),** head north on the N 625, via the Miradores de Piedrafitas and Oseja. The fantastic Los Beyos road weaves its way through enclosed gorges here. This beautiful route leads to the crossroads of several valleys with green landscapes year-round.

As the region changes, so does the landscape. The town of **Canga de Onís (5)** is worth a stop to see its beautiful medieval bridge. Continue east on the AS 262 to the sanctuary of Covadonga, a symbol of the Spanish Christian resistance against the Moors in 718. It is from here that the Reconquista began. Covadonga is recognized as a national pilgrimage site, and therefore is populated with plenty of shops and restaurants. Don't miss visiting the beautiful Santa Cueva de Covadonga sanctuary, tucked into a cave and waterfall along a hillside cliff. A statue of the Virgin stands next to the tomb of Don Pelayo, hero of the famous battle of Covadonga.

The enormous basilica houses a museum of sacred art.

Next, take the AS 114 at Covadonga to reach **Arenas de Cabrales (6),** 20 mi (32 km) east. Famously made here, Cabrales cheese is an interesting blue cheese that resembles Roquefort. Its flavors differ according to the cows and where they grazed, and how long the cheese was aged—the cheese can range from mild to very, very strong! It can be made strictly from cow's milk, or a mix of cow's, sheep's, and goat's milk, according to preference. From Arenas, the wide and comfortable AS 264 road leads you along the Rio Cares to Poncebos after 4 mi (6 km), where you can take the funicular to Bulnes (2,123 ft/647 m). You can also link up to the famous Cares Trail that leads to Cain, in León, after 3 hours of walking.

LOVE AT FIRST SIGHT

THE LAKES OF COVADONGA

The tour (about 2 hours on foot) of the superb small glacial lakes of Enol and La Ercina will relax anyone after driving 7 mi (12 km) of switchback roads from Covadonga. These lakes are home to the Feast Day of Saint James, celebrated on July 25. Beware, the roads are closed from 8:30am to 7pm on holidays, during Holy Week, and in summer—catching a shuttle is mandatory. The Pedro Pidal information center can answer any questions about the fantastic crags and karst peaks of this mountain range dominated by the Peña Santa de Castilla (8,517 ft/2,596 m).

FOCUS

WOLVES IN THEIR HOME

The last of the Iberian wolves protected by the national park frequent the upper alpine floors. At Covadonga Mountain, the park has restored a wolf trap once used by locals. It is a round wall pierced by a tunnel and with a platform on top. Asturians and their dogs would chase the wolf into an opening that led to the tunnel. The wolf was then isolated on the platform and could thus be easily approached.

Here, you'll also observe other wildlife: Learn to recognize the flights of the griffon vulture (always in pairs), versus the flight of the solitary golden eagle. There's also the bearded vulture, whose Spanish name, *quebrantahuesos,* meaning "bone breaker," illustrates its way of feeding. Wildcats, desmans (an animal similar to a mole), chamois, and brown bears are all among the emblematic species of the area.

The parks are also home to various flora, including the martagon lily, yellow and blue gentian, edelweiss, wild geranium, columbine, houseleek, saxifrage, and silene (do not pick these—they are protected!).

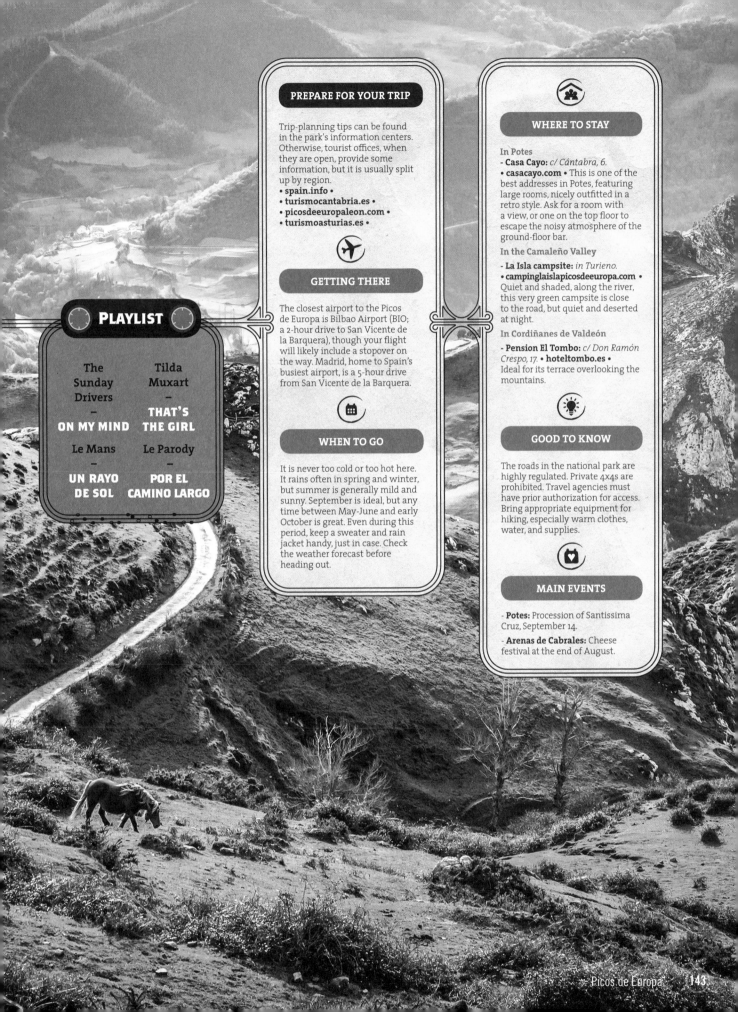

PLAYLIST

The Sunday Drivers	Tilda Muxart
–	–
ON MY MIND	**THAT'S THE GIRL**
Le Mans	Le Parody
–	–
UN RAYO DE SOL	**POR EL CAMINO LARGO**

PREPARE FOR YOUR TRIP

Trip-planning tips can be found in the park's information centers. Otherwise, tourist offices, when they are open, provide some information, but it is usually split up by region.
• **spain.info** •
• **turismocantabria.es** •
• **picosdeeuropaleon.com** •
• **turismoasturias.es** •

GETTING THERE

The closest airport to the Picos de Europa is Bilbao Airport (BIO; a 2-hour drive to San Vicente de la Barquera), though your flight will likely include a stopover on the way. Madrid, home to Spain's busiest airport, is a 5-hour drive from San Vicente de la Barquera.

WHEN TO GO

It is never too cold or too hot here. It rains often in spring and winter, but summer is generally mild and sunny. September is ideal, but any time between May-June and early October is great. Even during this period, keep a sweater and rain jacket handy, just in case. Check the weather forecast before heading out.

WHERE TO STAY

In Potes
- **Casa Cayo:** *c/ Cántabra, 6.*
• **casacayo.com** • This is one of the best addresses in Potes, featuring large rooms, nicely outfitted in a retro style. Ask for a room with a view, or one on the top floor to escape the noisy atmosphere of the ground-floor bar.

In the Camaleño Valley
- **La Isla campsite:** *in Turieno.*
• **campinglaislapicosdeeuropa.com** • Quiet and shaded, along the river, this very green campsite is close to the road, but quiet and deserted at night.

In Cordiñanes de Valdeón
- **Pension El Tombo:** *c/ Don Ramón Crespo, 17.* • **hoteltombo.es** • Ideal for its terrace overlooking the mountains.

GOOD TO KNOW

The roads in the national park are highly regulated. Private 4x4s are prohibited. Travel agencies must have prior authorization for access. Bring appropriate equipment for hiking, especially warm clothes, water, and supplies.

MAIN EVENTS

- **Potes:** Procession of Santissima Cruz, September 14.
- **Arenas de Cabrales:** Cheese festival at the end of August.

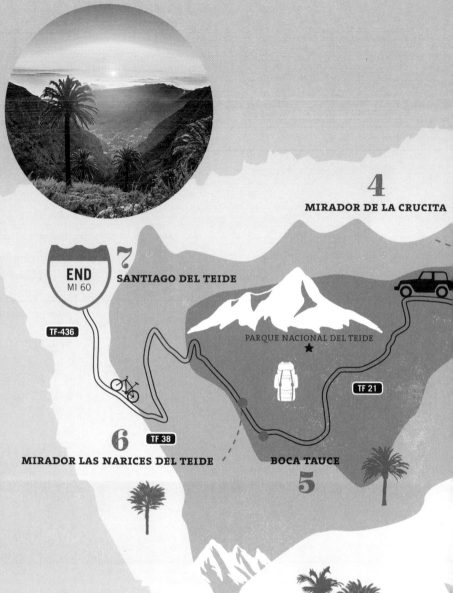

4
MIRADOR DE LA CRUCITA

END
MI 60

7
SANTIAGO DEL TEIDE

TF-436

PARQUE NACIONAL DEL TEIDE

TF 21

6
TF 38

MIRADOR LAS NARICES DEL TEIDE

BOCA TAUCE

5

 LOCATION

Canary Islands, Tenerife Island

 ROUTE

La Laguna – Santiago del Teide

LENGTH

60 mi (96 km)

TIME

You'll need at least a day to explore the park by car, but 2 days is more reasonable.

 YOU'LL LOVE

The volcanic landscapes and their incredible colors, the subtropical flora, the canyons, the ascent to the top—on foot or by funicular.

 START/END OF ROAD TRIP

 STOP

★ **LANDMARK OR POINT OF INTEREST**

TF 38 **ROAD**

 ROAD TRIP

 VOLCANIC ZONE

START
MI 0

LA LAGUNA 1

★ TEIDE OBSERVATORY

2
MIRADOR DE ORTUÑO

MIRADOR DE CHIMAGUE
3

TF 24

MOUNT TEIDE
VOLCANIC ROUTE
FROM LA LAGUNA ➤ TO SANTIAGO DEL TEIDE

This volcanic road takes you to the center of the island of Tenerife in the Canary Islands. The slopes of the Teide, the world's third largest volcano, offer the most unusual landscapes in the heart of a national park classified as a UNESCO World Heritage Site. Culminating at 12,198 ft (3,718 m), the snowcapped summit of Teide overlooks sumptuous subtropical flora and black and red lava landscapes, under an eternal spring at 72°F (22°C) on average. With more than 3 million annual visitors, the Teide is a truly unmissable sight.

CANARY ISLANDS

Puerto del Carmen

• Santa Cruz de Tenerife

Las Palmas
de Gran Canaria

Costa Adeje

LA LAGUNA: AN ELEGANT, HISTORIC CITY

Once you arrive, you might feel like you're in city in the heart of Latin America! And for good reason: **La Laguna** (1) served as an architectural model for Havana in Cuba and Cartagena in Colombia. Formerly called "San Cristóbal de La Laguna," it later simply became La Laguna. A sign of its prestigious past, the city retains several dozen palaces with Baroque or Mannerist facades, ornate wooden balconies, and elegant patios. Its classification as a UNESCO World Heritage Site in 1999 definitively protected the historic city center.

Home to nearly 30,000 students, the city leads the way in Tenerife, culturally and intellectually. The local nightlife truly thrives as well—it's not just for tourists. More than a gateway to the famous volcano, La Laguna is a refreshing and vibrant stopover.

VOLCANO IN VIEW

From La Laguna, take the TF 24 road, which climbs toward the ridge of the volcano. Listed as a UNESCO World Heritage Site, the **Parque Nacional del Teide** is a true marvel. It receives 3 million visitors each year, the most of any Spanish national park. It is a unique subtropical high mountain area in Europe. While the Teide volcano is the true highlight, known for its status as the highest point of the Iberian Peninsula, the entire park is incredible. At first seeming like a desert, the landscape transforms into a pine forest, and the panorama changes completely. From rocky chaos, the land becomes a dark sea of lava, giving way to layers of various colors and textures: yellow-green reflections and shades of brown, sometimes smooth and shiny like silk, other times rough and matte like sandpaper. Farther on, a few canyons recall the landscapes of the American West. And a few miles after that, the desert landscape meets with the meager vegetation of groves, punctuated here and there by other volcanic rock formations. Finally, a forest appears, followed by the huge, jaw-dropping crater.

A LEGENDARY VOLCANO

During a big volcanic eruption, dust blocks the horizon and swallows up the sun. The Guanches, original inhabitants of the Canary Islands, lacking a scientific explanation, turned to their gods. They accused Guayota (god of evil, living inside the volcano) of kidnapping Magec (god of light) and taking him to the bottom of the crater. But Achamán, the god of the gods, got the better of Guayota and freed the sun, which resumed its place in the sky, while blocking the volcano where he imprisoned the villainous Guyota. Apparently, he is still locked inside.

Several watchtowers offer remarkable views from the entrance to the Esperanza pine forests, such as the Mirador de Montaña Grande on the northern part of the island.

Going past Forestal Park, you'll reach **Mirador de Ortuño (2)**. If you can stop at only one viewpoint, make it this one, at an altitude of 5,315 ft (1,620 m). You'll enjoy a wide panorama over an immense and dense forest of Canarian pines, with the Teide and the coast as a backdrop. An informative panel shows the evolution of the forest, marking periods of fires and deforestation. Stop at **Mirador de Chimague (3)** after crossing the road that goes down to Güímar. This spot provides a unique perspective of a young pine forest, partly replanted in the middle

of the 20th century to add greenery to these bare hills after centuries of erosion. A little farther, the Mirador de Ayosa viewpoint provides a nice lookout toward Puerto de la Cruz, La Orotava, and the Teide.

Finally, the **Mirador de la Crucita (4)** marks the entrance to Teide National Park and its diverse landscape. Tropical ferns, pine forest and succulents give way to a lava desert with a thousand colors. The earth is black, the rock volcanic, the vegetation sparser.

Continue on the TF 21 road from the El Portillo Pass at 6,627 ft (2,020 m). Stop at the visitor center, 500 ft (150 m) away, to learn about the volcano and the surrounding hikes. You can also check the weather and funicular departure times here.

TEIDE NATIONAL PARK HIKES

Among the many hikes in the park, the top choices are the Fortaleza Trail (easy, 3 mi/5 km), the Arenas Negras Trail (a 4.7-mi/7.6-km loop, with a vertical drop), the Los Roques de García Trail (easy, 1 mi/2 km from the parador), and the Montaña Blanca-Pico del Teide Trail, which reaches almost to the summit of Teide, via the Mirador de la Fortaleza along the TF 21 road (2.2 mi/3.5 km, 6 hours, with a drop of 4,429 ft/1,350 m).

Continue on the ridge of the volcano through rugged lava fields varying from green to yellow, from brown to black, from orange to gray. Here, the stems of the Tajinastes, a type of viperina plant with flamboyant flowers in spring, become white plumes in winter. The song of Teide chaffinch birds brings the eroded hills to life. The air is cold because of the altitude, but the sun often appears above the clouds.

Up next is the funicular, which climbs almost to the top of Teide. Only 200 people per day are allowed to access the summit. Access to the crater itself requires making a reservation two months in advance. From the funicular, the ascent to the summit takes an hour on foot. But the view is extraordinary: Marvel at the crater, measuring 10 mi (17 km) in diameter; the vast field of dried lava; and the wide ocean.

Still on the TF 21 road, from the parking lot opposite the Parador de Cañadas del Teid hotel, the lava columns of Roques de García, Finger of God, and Cathedral frame the slopes of Mount Teide, with its snowcapped summit like a majestic Olympus. Eerie fairy chimneys and sharp peaks rise to the sky, changing with the colors of the sun.

Continue toward **Boca Tauce (5).** The **Mirador Las Narices del Teide (6)** brings together the silhouette of Pico Viejo at Teide and the panorama of the two gaping craters. Observe the last lava flow, now a solidified dark sea, dating back to 1798.

Roques de García

The volcanic landscape continues down toward the village of **Santiago del Teide (7),** a worthwhile stopover. Like a calm and flat island, surrounded by fields and wooded mountains, it is a good base camp for exploring the region, but you can also make do with just a short stop along the way.

Returning to La Laguna, visit the world-famous **Teide Observatory** on the C 824 road. It is one of the largest solar observatories in the world,

located at the top of this barren mountain at 7,840 ft (2,390 m) altitude. Along with Chile and Hawaii, the Canary Islands are one of the best places in the world for sky- and stargazing. Their position in the southern part of the northern hemisphere allows a reading of the sky on both parts of the globe. The observatory is located 4 mi (7 km) from the El Portillo Visitor Center, on the TF 24 toward La Laguna. Visits to the observatory are allowed during the day (not at night), and only when accompanied by specialized guides.

Playa de Las Americas

FORTUNATE ISLANDS

Don't look for canaries here. The name of the Canary Islands comes from *Canariae Insulae* ("Dog Islands"). Was this a reference to wild dogs or seals that look like dogs? No one knows. The Greeks called them the "Fortunate Islands." The Guanches, of Berber origin, were the first inhabitants. They lived happily until the beginning of the 15th century, when Jean de Bethencourt convinced to the king of France to finance an expedition to evangelize the Canaries. He was dazzled by their natural riches, notably the red dye of the Orseille lichen, roccella tinctoria (today it's

protected). These first explorers gave way to the Portuguese and the Spanish, who claimed the islands as their territory in 1479. Needless to say, the poor Guanches paid the price. Between 1492 and 1498, Christopher Columbus took advantage of these islands as a stopover on his voyages to America.

Tenerife has the highest peak in Spain with the Teide volcano to the north and immense beaches to the south. To the east is the capital Santa Cruz, next to the old town of La Laguna. On the west coast, two superb botanical gar-

dens, including the Sitio Litre Garden, which inspired Agatha Christie, brighten up the entrances to the attractive Puerto de la Cruz. Colonial balconies, sandy shores, and hotels draw many tourists. To the south of the island, Los Cristianos and its modern hotel infrastructure are aimed at lovers of nightlife and beautiful beaches such as Playa de Las Americas. In spite of its development as an industrial port, the Canary Islands' economy depends on 12 million annual tourists.

FOCUS

A Brief Glossary of Vulcanology

Andesite: viscous lava with a porphyritic structure

Basaltic: fluid lava based on basalt

Volcanic bomb: lava projected during an eruption and cooled in different forms

Caldera: circular depression several kilometers in diameter, caused by the central collapse of a volcano

Crater: exit point of volcanic rocks rising from a volcano's chimney

Dike: blade of igneous rock

Lahar: mud flow formed by water, tephras, and volcanic ash

Lapilli: volcanic fragments similar to gravel

Magma: molten rock

Burning Cloud: deadly fumes from volcanic gas

Tephra: ash and slag

Volcano types: Explosive or gray volcanoes erupt of vapor, and effusive or red volcanoes erupt of liquid magma. A shield volcano has a diameter greater than its height. A stratovolcano has a diameter balanced at its height. A fissure volcano is formed by a linear opening.

PREPARE FOR YOUR TRIP

- spain.info •
- turismodecanarias.com •
- volcanoteide.com •
- reservasparquesnacionales.es •

GETTING THERE

There are two airports on Tenerife, Tenerife South Airport (TFS) and Tenerife North Airport (TFN).

WHEN TO GO

To avoid the influx of tourist who arrive on cruise ships—and can triple the island's population in one day—choose February-March for Carnival celebrations, spring for flora, or winter to avoid the crowds of both international visitors and Spanish mainlanders.

GOOD TO KNOW

Bring a guidebook to identify exotic plants. Do not pick or collect anything in Teide National Park, and do not leave the marked trails. Bring hiking equipment to the mountains to climb up the foot of Mount Teide.

MAIN EVENTS

The February-March Carnival celebrations are famous for lively folk music performances by such internationally renowned musicians as Los Sabandeños ensemble.

- Santa Cruz de Tenerife Carnaval
• carnavaldetenerife.es •
- Holy week in La Laguna
• aytolalaguna.com •
- The San Marcos de Tegueste, and multiple festivals all over the island until November.

WHERE TO STAY

The best accommodations are in hostels or guest houses.

In Santiago del Teide

- Hotel Casona del Patio:
avda de la Iglesia, 72.
This superb place combines charm, modernity, luxury, and intimacy all at the same time. This old but updated building, standing on a base of large volcanic stone, has large bay windows and offers some rooms with views of the Teide mountains and volcano.

In the Parque Nacional del Teide

- Parador Nacional Las Cañadas del Teide: *at the foot of the magical Teide.*
• parador.es • This hotel offers 40 classic and comfortable rooms with AC. Most rooms feature views of the hills, lava fields, or the volcano. People come here for the special atmosphere, a result of being almost alone in the park.

- Refugio Altavista: *on the Montaña Blanca-pico del Teide hiking trail.*
• volcanoteide.com •
Only hikers sleep here, at the highest refuge in Spain. Indeed, because there is no road! Located at an altitude of 10,696 ft (3,260 m), this beautiful stone refuge was built in 1892 but has modern renovations. The purity of the air offers incredible views of the night sky.

SIGHTS

- Museums in Arrecife
- Colonial district of La Laguna
- Hilltop village of Masca
- Giant rocks in Puerto de Santiago
- Geological routes of the Anaga Mountains

A BOOK FOR THE ROAD

More Ketchup Than Salsa: Confessions of a Tenerife Barman
by Joe Cawley

LOCATION

Alsace, Bas-Rhin, Haut-Rhin

ROUTE →

Marlenheim – Thann, with an optional stopover in Wissembourg

LENGTH

105 mi (170 km)

YOU'LL LOVE ♥

The famous blue ridgeline of the Vosges, the chain of castles, the half-timbered houses and their flowered balconies, fabulous gastronomy and wine-tasting opportunities, and the Alsatian hospitality.

START
MI 0

1 MARLENHEIM

2 DANGOLSHEIM

D422

3 BŒRSCH

D35

4 HEILIGENSTEIN

5 MITTELBERGHEIM

6 ANDLAU

7 DAMBACH-LA-VILLE

D35

HAUT-KŒNIGSBOURG CASTLE

9 SAINT-HIPPOLYTE

8 KINTZHEIM

10 RIBEAUVILLÉ

D1B

11 KAYSERSBERG

D415

★ COLMAR

12 ROUFFACH

D83

END
MI 105

THANN 13

WISSEMBOURG ★

THE ALSACE
WINE ROUTE
FROM MARLENHEIM ➤➤➤ TO THANN

STRASBOURG
★

Beautiful surroundings enhance this famous wine route that crosses Alsace from north to south. Geraniums cover balconies throughout splendid wine-growing villages. Castles are tucked into the bluish mist of the Vosges, overlooking the vineyards. Storks nest on steeples and watchtowers. Red sandstone crosses mark intersections of roads. From April to October, popular festivals and wine abound. Inaugurated in 1953 during a car rally, the Alsace Wine Route is one of the oldest tourist routes in France.It follows the old Roman road of the Vosges.

Paris

Nantes

FRANCE

Montpellier

Toulouse

START/END OF ROAD TRIP

STOP ●

LANDMARK OR POINT OF INTEREST ★

ROAD D422

ROAD TRIP ══

Strasbourg

WINE ROUTE IN THE LAND OF WISSEMBOURG

North of the Bas-Rhin region and the classic wine route, the vineyards of **Wissembourg** produce quality wines. In Cleebourg, all the grands crus are represented on 220 acres (89 hectares), with some 200 winegrowers grouped together in a wine cooperative. Pinot gris and riesling are also famous here.

Traditions are preserved in this region, rich in medieval castles, vestiges of the Maginot Line, and pottery workshops in Betschdorf and Soufflenheim. The abbey church of Wissembourg, founded by monks and dating back to the origins of these vineyards, is worth a visit.

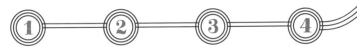

STRASBOURG VINEYARD ROUTE

Twelve mi (20 km) west of Strasbourg, the grape varieties of the Marlenberg grand cru mark the start of the Alsace Wine Route in **Marlenheim (1).** Every year on August 15, riesling and pinot noir are also spotlighted during the celebration of *L'Ami Fritz,* an event commemorating Erckmann-Chatrian's novel of the same name. The event features a reenactment of a peasant wedding, complete with Alsatian costumes, traditional music and dance, flowery floats, and a firework-show finale.

On the Wine Route, the fortified villages of Westhoffen, Traenheim, and **Dangolsheim (2)** are home to some opulent houses where winegrowers' symbols can be seen, carved into the thresholds and windows. These symbols include bunches of grapes, vine leaves, barrels, and allegorical monsters devouring vines. Wine presses and fountains decorate the region's eateries—be sure to stop and enjoy a *flambée flamekueche* tart (an Alsace specialty) with a glass of wine. Next, visit the tiny Romanesque Saint-Ulrich chapel in Avolsheim to admire its restored ocher and green frescoes. The miniature town of **Bœrsch (3),** featuring typical construction of the Alsace region, seems frozen behind its walls and towers. **Heiligenstein (4)** offers tastings of pinot noir, as well as Klevener de Heiligenstein, made from an Austrian variety of grape that was brought back from Italy by the town's mayor in 1742. The town hall even features a tribute to this local wine. Whichever variety you choose, these tastings make for the perfect kickoff to a visit to the nearby castles of Ottrott.

STRASBOURG, CAPITAL OF EUROPE

The European capital since 1949, **Strasbourg** has lots of sightseeing to offer. The historic city center of the "Grande Île" of Strasbourg, classified by UNESCO, is worth a day in itself and can be visited on foot or by tram. Start with the cathedral and its astronomical clock. Then, stop for a meal to restore your strength before taking a boat trip around the Petite-France district and enjoying the many museums. If you have time, don't forget the German imperial quarter of Neustadt, which is currently also being classified by UNESCO. A visit to Strasbourg is well worth your time.

If time permits, make a zigzagging detour toward the beautiful neighboring towns of Obernai and Barr. They reflect the richness of wine-growing Alsace, sumptuous and a bit scornful toward their Lorraine neighbors. An old local legend claims that Alsatians have big ears because Alsatian mothers lift their children by the ears to show them the other side of the Vosges and make fun of the neighbors.

On a hill south of Barr, **Mittelbergheim (5)** bears the label of "Most Beautiful Village of France," as it opens onto the sunny basin of the Zotzenberg grand cru vineyard. Toward the south, the austere **Andlau (6)** is nestled at the exit of a rocky gorge. In addition to its Kastelberg and Moenchberg grand crus, the village is known for the miracle of the bear. The legend, dating back to the 9th century, tells of Saint Richardis, who in fleeing her abusive husband, was visited by an angel

who told her to build a convent in a certain spot, which would be indicated by a bear. She later encountered a bear on the banks of the river, scratching at a spot in the dirt. It was here that Richardis built her convent, which attracts many pilgrims to this day. Saint Richardis and her bear are immortalized throughout Andlau, as evidenced by the wonderful friezes and sculptures on building facades.

Continue toward the largest Alsatian vineyard (1,160 acres/470 hectares) in **Dambach-la-Ville (7),** whose ramparts hide a superb flower-filled village. The village square is known for its quality wines and atmospheric *winstubs* (wine lounge-restaurants). Not far away, the bell tower of Saint-Sébastien chapel seduces with its charm in the middle of the vineyards. Passing Sélestat, visitors of all ages will enjoy a stop at **Kintzheim (8)**

and its castle, "the king's home." While parents can learn about the grand cru Classé Praelatenberg wines from the bishops of the Ebersmunster Abbey, children will enjoy the bird sanctuary exhibit, where you can see the world's largest bird species circle above the castle. The nearby Montagne des Singes animal park on the route to Haut-Kœnigsbourg castle is also a worthwhile stop.

Above the vineyards, the fragrant fir forests cover the Vosges slopes all the way up the famous Route des Crêtes. The road is frequented by wild boars, deer, and many motorcyclists on weekend getaways.

LOVE AT FIRST SIGHT

HAUT-KŒNIGSBOURG

Enjoy a stop in the center of the Alsatian vineyards, under the verdigris roofs and the red walls of the formidable Haut-Kœnigsbourg, camped on a panoramic ridge at an altitude of 2,484 ft (757 m). Donated by the city of Sélestat to German Kaiser Guillaume II and restored at his expense, the enormous fortress became French again 10 years later as part of the Treaty of Versailles. The historic weapons, wardrobes, signs, and tapestries here will make you feel like you've stepped back in time.

WINE ROUTE OF THE COLMAR REGION

After a stop for tastings in Scherwiller and **Saint-Hippolyte (9),** you'll approach "Les Perles du Vignoble," a string of beautiful wine-growing villages, linked together by the old vineyard path. It's hard to decide where to go or which winery to visit—but you really can't go wrong here.

Ribeauvillé (10), under its three castles, offers white wine for tasting in one of the oldest cellars in France. Hunawihr is famous for the Rosacker grand cru. The cellars of Riquewihr and **Kaysersberg (11)** harken back to a prestigious medieval heritage. Crémant d'Alsace, a sparkling wine resembling champagne, can be found in the cellars of Beblenheim and Bestheim. And to learn more about the history of these wines, the Alsace Vineyard and Wines Museum at the Château de la Confrérie Saint-Étienne de Kientzheim will quench your thirst for knowledge.

HIKING

From the Alsace Wine Route, about 50 wine trails are signposted for walking. Of course, they all end at a cellar! Each path is unique and offers different themes on viticulture, heritage, landscape, and local history. A word of advice: Save the tasting for the end of the route. A favorite is the Grands Crus wine trail, which connects Les Perles du Vignoble around Kaysersberg, Riquewihr, Hunawihr, and Ribeauvillé.

LOVE AT FIRST SIGHT

COLMAR
If there is one must-visit city near the wine route, it's Colmar, city of art and history and "capital of Alsatian wine." Commercial and popular, the city center can be reached on foot. Be sure to check out the glazed roof of the Customs House, the striking Isenheim Altarpiece at the Unterlinden Museum, and the sculpted faces of the House of the Heads . . . and then stop for charcuterie and foie gras. You'll need something to pair with the wines you've chosen along the way!

Kaysersberg

SOUTH ALSACE WINE ROUTE

The road continues, slowly calming down after so many stops and tourists. The Vosges plains and mountains follow each other around churches and abbeys. Vineyards spread out around the noble Turckheim, flower-filled Eguisheim, Husseren-les-Châteaux, and the beautiful houses of **Rouffach (12).** The Alsatian hills are more natural—the road becomes peaceful under the foothills, protected by the regional natural park.

Between the water sources of Soultzmatt and **Thann (13),** famous for its late harvests, the vineyard is steeper. It is cultivated in terraces at Guebwiller and above the Tour des Sorcières in Thann, with slopes so steep that the grape pickers often must secure themselves to the rails with carabiner clips. The Wuenheim Winegrower's Museum and the South Gate of the Alsace Wine Route in Thann are both great ways to end this epic wine journey. Prost! Raise a toast to health and a good trip!

FOCUS

THE 7 ALSATIAN GRAPES

The wines here bear the name of their grape variety—and all pair perfectly with various gourmet offerings.

sylvaner: dry, light, and fruity; ideal for seafood

pinot blanc auxerrois: fruity; goes well with all dishes

riesling: elegant and delicate; recommended for fish and sauerkraut

pinot noir: imported from Burgundy; pairs well with meat

pinot gris: heady, full-bodied, fresh, and rich; good with foie gras and roasts

dry muscat: fruity with a musky taste; best as an aperitif or with asparagus

gewürztraminer: full-bodied and well-structured; good with international cuisine, cheeses, and desserts or as an aperitif

There's also **edelzwicker,** a blend of several grape varieties. This light and slightly sparkling white wine is served inexpensively in a pitcher in all taverns.

And **crémant d'Alsace** is a sparkling wine, similar to champagne.

In addition to the **AOC Alsace, AOC Alsace Grand Cru** (51 terroirs), and **AOC Crémant d'Alsace appellations,** other labels include **Vendanges Tardives** and **Sélection de Grains Nobles.**

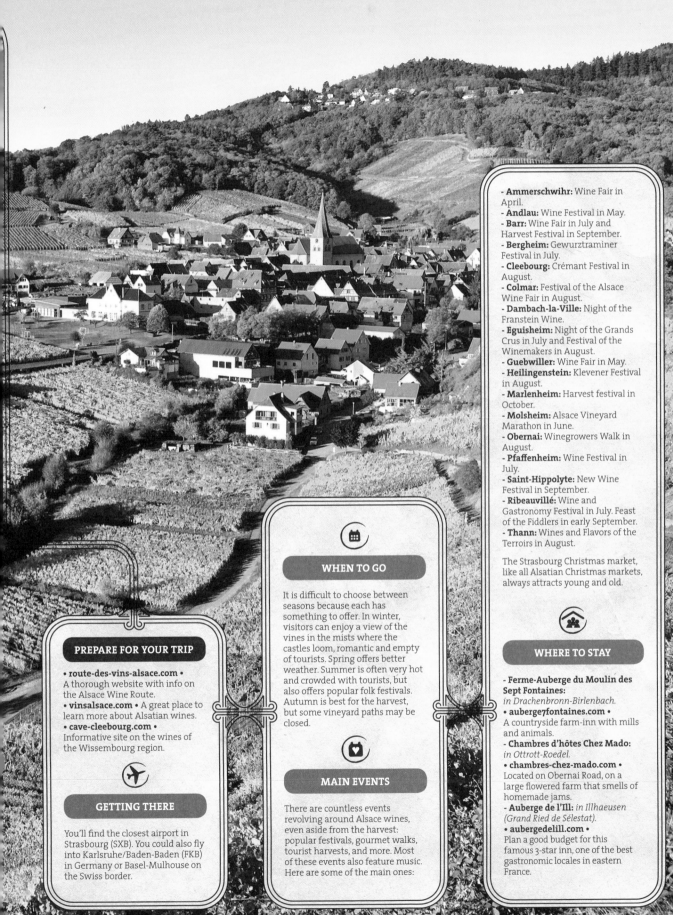

- **Ammerschwihr:** Wine Fair in April.
- **Andlau:** Wine Festival in May.
- **Barr:** Wine Fair in July and Harvest Festival in September.
- **Bergheim:** Gewurztraminer Festival in July.
- **Cleebourg:** Crémant Festival in August.
- **Colmar:** Festival of the Alsace Wine Fair in August.
- **Dambach-la-Ville:** Night of the Franstein Wine.
- **Eguisheim:** Night of the Grands Crus in July and Festival of the Winemakers in August.
- **Guebwiller:** Wine Fair in May.
- **Heilingenstein:** Klevener Festival in August.
- **Marlenheim:** Harvest festival in October.
- **Molsheim:** Alsace Vineyard Marathon in June.
- **Obernai:** Winegrowers Walk in August.
- **Pfaffenheim:** Wine Festival in July.
- **Saint-Hippolyte:** New Wine Festival in September.
- **Ribeauvillé:** Wine and Gastronomy Festival in July. Feast of the Fiddlers in early September.
- **Thann:** Wines and Flavors of the Terroirs in August.

The Strasbourg Christmas market, like all Alsatian Christmas markets, always attracts young and old.

WHEN TO GO

It is difficult to choose between seasons because each has something to offer. In winter, visitors can enjoy a view of the vines in the mists where the castles loom, romantic and empty of tourists. Spring offers better weather. Summer is often very hot and crowded with tourists, but also offers popular folk festivals. Autumn is best for the harvest, but some vineyard paths may be closed.

MAIN EVENTS

There are countless events revolving around Alsace wines, even aside from the harvest: popular festivals, gourmet walks, tourist harvests, and more. Most of these events also feature music. Here are some of the main ones:

PREPARE FOR YOUR TRIP

- • route-des-vins-alsace.com • A thorough website with info on the Alsace Wine Route.
- • vinsalsace.com • A great place to learn more about Alsatian wines.
- • cave-cleebourg.com • Informative site on the wines of the Wissembourg region.

GETTING THERE

You'll find the closest airport in Strasbourg (SXB). You could also fly into Karlsruhe/Baden-Baden (FKB) in Germany or Basel-Mulhouse on the Swiss border.

WHERE TO STAY

- **Ferme-Auberge du Moulin des Sept Fontaines:** *in Drachenbronn-Birlenbach.*
- • auberge7fontaines.com • A countryside farm-inn with mills and animals.
- **Chambres d'hôtes Chez Mado:** *in Ottrott-Roedel.*
- • chambres-chez-mado.com • Located on Obernai Road, on a large flowered farm that smells of homemade jams.
- **Auberge de l'Ill:** *in Illhaeusen (Grand Ried de Sélestat).*
- • aubergedelill.com • Plan a good budget for this famous 3-star inn, one of the best gastronomic locales in eastern France.

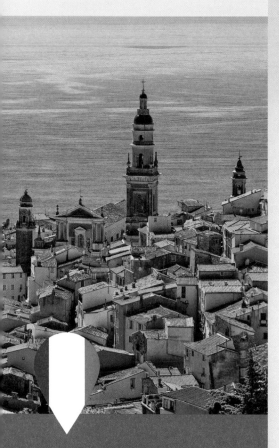

LOCATION

Southeast of France, French Riviera (Alpes-Maritimes)

ROUTE

Nice – Menton

LENGTH

15 mi (24 km), 13 mi (21 km), or 17 mi (30 km) depending on the route you choose

TIME

Plan at least one full day.

YOU'LL LOVE

Magnificent panoramas from the Alps of the Mercantour to Corsica, the silvery wake of boats on the water, exotic flowers in the gardens, the views of fortified castles.

M 2564

FORT DE LA REVÈRE ★

2 ÈZE

M 6007

BEAULIEU-SUR-MER ★

START
MI 0

VILLEFRANCHE-SUR-MER

1 NICE

M 6098

★ CAP FERRAT

🛡 **START/END OF ROAD TRIP**

● **STOP**

★ **LANDMARK OR POINT OF INTEREST**

M 6098 **ROAD**

—— **ROAD TRIP**

Paris

• Nantes

FRANCE

Montpellier

Toulouse

160

STOP
MI 17

5 MENTON

D 6007

ROQUEBRUNE-CAP-MARTIN 4

M 2564

LA TURBIE
3

MONACO

M 6007

M 6098

CAP D'AIL

ÈZE-SUR-MER

THE CORNICHES OF THE
FRENCH RIVIERA
FROM NICE ➤ TO MENTON

*The three corniches are three roads with three different views along the
French Riviera, each connecting Nice to Menton, near the Italian border.
The Grande Corniche, the most panoramic, reaches an altitude of 1,640 ft
(500 m) at the Col d'Èze. The Moyenne Corniche, the classic route, rises
980 ft (300 m) above Villefranche. The Basse Corniche is the prettiest,
but also the most urbanized and crowded. It runs along the coast to Italy
and does not exceed 330 ft (100 m) in altitude. Each corniche has its
own personality, varying according to the surrounding light, the altitude,
and the traffic. It's up to you to choose the one that's right for you.*

The Corniches of the French Riviera

THE GRANDE CORNICHE

Built on the orders of Napoleon and cut at very steep heights, the Grande Corniche winds between Nice and La Turbie and offers sumptuous panoramas on the coast of the French Riviera.

From **Nice (1),** follow the M 2564 along the chic Cimiez district via Boulevard Bischoffsheim, then via Boulevard de l'Observatoire. If the light pollution of Nice makes it hard to see the stars, head toward the white dome of the observatory (visible from all over the city), built by architect Charles Garnier and designed by Gustave Eiffel. It houses a computing center and a large 59-ft (18-m) telescope, which was once the largest refracting telescope in the world.

The Grande Corniche heads east and over the Col des Quatre Chemins (1,053 ft/321 m), climbing to the belvedere of the Col d'Èze (1,680 ft/512 m), the endpoint of the Paris-Nice cycling race. On the right is the fortified silhouette of the old village of **Èze (2)** (1,407 ft/429 m). As French Romantic author George Sand once wrote, "The sinuous coast provides a magical backdrop at every step. The ruins of Èze, planted on a cone of rock, with a

picturesque sugar loaf village, inevitably catch the eye. It is the most beautiful point of view of the road, the most complete, the best composed." To the north, the snowcapped peaks of the Alps highlight the sky, while to the south, the turquoise waters of the bay of Villefranche stretch out indefinitely. Take a detour through the **Fort de la Revère** (2,300 ft/700 m) preservation. The fort itself is closed to visitors, but the surrounding park offers an exceptional 360-degree panorama from Corsica to the Mercantour.

Soon you'll discover the looming Roman ruins of **La Turbie (3),** famous for the Trophy of Augustus monument. The Grande Corniche then runs along the A8 motorway, with magnificent views over **Monaco,** its cliffs, and its harbor. The corniche crosses a small road heading toward Peillon, Sospel, and other picturesque villages near Menton. Next, you'll head to **Roquebrune-Cap-Martin (4),** topped by a medieval castle, to join the Moyen and Basse Corniches on the D 6007, where the three roads become one.

NICE, AN ECLECTIC CITY

From downtown Nice, it takes about 5 minutes to reach the beach via the Promenade des Anglais. In addition to its squares and churches, highlights include the Lascaris Palace, the Museum of Modern and Contemporary Art, and the Masséna, Beaux-Arts, Chagall, and Matisse museums. The surrounding gardens as well as the flower, fruit, and vegetable markets add to the pleasures of Nice. Enjoy a lavender ice cream at Fenocchio in Old Nice, or buy some candied fruit at Auer, in front of the opera house. There's plenty to do and see here.

FOCUS

A MONUMENTAL TROPHY

Don't be surprised by the white Roman columns that stand next to the tiled roofs of the small church of La Turbie. This national monument was built to honor Emperor Augustus's victory over the surrounding tribes. Built from stone from the nearby Roman quarry, the monument is partially restored, standing at 115 ft (35 m) high.

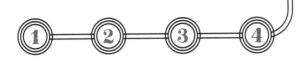

THE MOYENNE CORNICHE

"Joyful love is here, it makes us smile. . . . We are happy on Nationale 7," French singer Charles Trenet sang about this drive in 1955. The Moyenne Corniche follows the route of the former N 7 along the D 6007. Because a large part of this road is four lanes, it is the easiest corniche to use if you want to travel quickly.

To the right of the start of the Grande Corniche in **Nice (1),** take the D 6007 toward Avenue Bella Vista (which keeps the promise of its name: a beautiful view!). Along the northern part of Mont Boron and its fort, it crosses the beautiful Col de Villefranche with a breathtaking view of **Cap Ferrat** and the bay of **Villefranche-sur-Mer.**

You'll soon reach the old village of **Èze (2)** via the Fragonard perfumery, above the Nietzsche Trail. Pass under the monument of **La Turbie (3)** and its panorama over **Cap d'Ail.** The Moyenne Corniche avoids crossing Monaco and only passes through the exotic garden above the city and its cliffs, offering a spectacular view below. It overlooks Monaco Station, crosses the heights of the Beausoleil district, and meets up with the Grande Corniche before arriving in **Roquebrune-Cap-Martin (4).** Here you can visit famed architect Le Corbusier's hut, classified by UNESCO and reachable via the Customs Trail. It took three years to build this "architectural manifesto for athletic bachelors," as his designer Eileen Gray called it; her home Villa E-1027 is next door. Le Corbusier also designed the frescoes and units for the neighboring campsite. The site is closed to children under seven years old.

ÈZE, AN INSPIRATIONAL EAGLE'S NEST

Beyond the double fortified door that gives access to the old village of Èze, medieval houses with tiled roofs, narrow streets, stairways, and old stones await you. Historical signs guide visitors through the village, while old cellars are transformed into souvenir shops. Afficionados of Baroque art will love visiting the nave of the magnificent 18th-century Church of Our Lady of the Assumption and the Chapel of the White Penitents.

The botanical garden, seemingly suspended between sky and sea, offers a bird's-eye-view of castle ruins, the French Riviera, Saint-Tropez, Italy, and even Corsica. Succulents, aloes, euphorbias, and gigantic cacti adorn this remarkable garden, dotted with waterfalls, caves, and terra cotta sculptures.

Enjoy the fragrances of the Fragonard and Gallimard perfumeries before descending the Friedrich Nietzsche path toward Èze-Bord-de-Mer, hidden among olive and oak trees. This peaceful setting is where the philosopher conceived the third part of *Thus Spoke Zarathustra*. The area has become very touristy, so it's best to start your visit early in the morning. Otherwise, sleep in and wait to explore the old village in the evening, when crowds are lighter.

Menton

THE WONDERFUL VILLAS OF CAP FERRAT

On Cap Ferrat, the Villa Ephrussi de Rothschild is like a perfect dream. The half-Italian, half-Moorish palazzo, all in pink and white, is adorned with collector's paintings, while the surrounding 17-acre (7-hectare) park plunges into a deep blue sea. The legend of the Baroness Ephrussi, dressed in pink, equals the magnificence of the gardens. Imagine an aviary in which some 50 multicolored parrots frolic and magnolias and bougainvillea are animated by musical water features. Continue to Villa Santo Sospir, at the end of the cape, which artist Jean Cocteau decorated with frescoes during his long stays in the company of his patron and friend, Francine Weisweiller. It's all gathered here to create a picture of paradise.

THE BASSE CORNICHE

The Basse Corniche twists and turns along the coastal strip, serving every town and beach from Villefranche-sur-Mer to Menton.

From the center of **Nice (1),** head toward the M 6098 (ex N 98), and bypass Mont Boron along the coast. Cross the heights of **Villefranche-sur-Mer,** where the road peaks at 330 ft (100 m). The old town is nestled in a romantic bay above the port of Darse. Many of the buildings date back to the 17th century. The only downside here: The beaches are mainly pebbles. Continuing along, the road passes by the dark vaults of the astonishing Rue Obscure, and the impressive frescoes of the Cocteau Chapel. To the south of the city, the pine forests of the **Cap Ferrat** peninsula have long attracted celebrities, from the king of Belgium to Charlie Chaplin.

The Basse Corniche returns to sea level at the port of **Beaulieu-sur-Mer,** a charming, somewhat-retro seaside resort with a mild climate. In 1902, archaeologist Théodore Reinach built Villa Kérylos, a marvelous Greek villa, here at the tip of the Baie des Fourmis. Today it's property of the Institut de France, a popular stop for architecture aficionados.

Cross **Èze-sur-Mer** and its garden on the Gulf of Saint-Hospice, and then go up to **Cap d'Ail.** Travel down through the tunnels and then back up to **Monaco** and its remarkable Oceanographic Museum, and enjoy an inexpensive snack on the terrace.

Tradition and modernity coexist in Monaco, between skyscrapers, luxury hotels, and casinos. The area is easily explored on foot, but if traveling by car, drive alongside the castle and the racing circuit before passing under the Larvotto Tunnel. Continue through the La Condamine and Monte-Carlo districts toward Beausoleil, via Boulevard du Larvotto and Avenue de la Princesse-Grace.

Here you'll join up with the two other corniches before arriving in **Roquebrune-Cap-Martin (4),** where the Baie du Soleil stretches out. The medieval castle of this perched village and the stairs around its thousand-year-old olive tree provide the opportunity to take superb photos.

Now united on the D 6007, the three corniches form a single road to the Italian border, 2 mi (3 km) east of **Menton (5),** famous for its sweet variety of lemons. With its fragrant morning markets, popular annual Lemon Festival, and charming spots to enjoy a drink, Menton is worth enduring the traffic jams that block its access during rush hour. Visit the Cocteau Museum, the chapels, the basilica, and the many gardens that make this city a peaceful stopover.

PREPARE FOR YOUR TRIP

- en.nicetourisme.com •
- france-voyage.com •
- cotedazur-tourisme.com •

GETTING THERE

Nice is easily reached via its international airport (NCE) or train station.

GOOD TO KNOW

For the easiest, most direct route, take the Moyenne Corniche up and return via the Grande Corniche. Or, if driving directly toward Italy, take the Moyenne Corniche at nightfall when the boats anchor in the bay of Villefranche—it's magical! The Basse Corniche allows you to stop more often to enjoy the views along the beaches and capes.

WHEN TO GO

Plan to visit mid-season or in winter to avoid the massive tourist crowds.

WHERE TO STAY

In Nice

- Villa Saint-Hubert:
26, rue Michel-Ange.
• **villasainthubert.com** •
A cute 20th-century villa nestled in Nord, a quiet, out-of-the way, residential area of Nice.

In Villefranche-sur-Mer

- Hôtel Provençal:
4, av. du Maréchal-Joffre.
• **hotelleprovencal.fr** • An impressive building with three towers, offering pleasant views of the garden and the sea, as well as superb hospitality.

In Beaulieu-sur-Mer

- Hôtel Sélect: *1, rue André-Cane.*
• **hotelselect-beaulieu.com** •
A beautiful hotel with a perfectly central location.

In Èze Village

- Èze Hemitage Hôtel-Restaurant:
1941, av. des Diables-Bleus.
• **ezeermitage.com** •
A quiet hotel with swimming pool and easy access to long-distance hiking trails.

A BOOK FOR THE ROAD

Tender is the Night by
F. Scott Fitzgerald

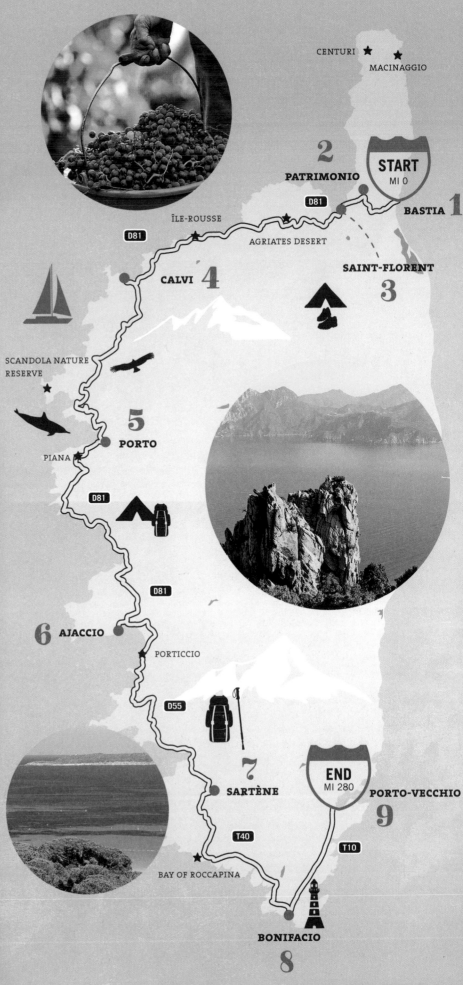

CENTURI ★ ★ MACINAGGIO

2

START
MI 0

PATRIMONIO

D81

BASTIA

1

ÎLE-ROUSSE

D81

AGRIATES DESERT

SAINT-FLORENT

3

CALVI

4

SCANDOLA NATURE
RESERVE

5

PORTO

PIANA

D81

D81

6 AJACCIO

PORTICCIO

D55

7

SARTÈNE

END
MI 280

PORTO-VECCHIO

9

T40

T10

BAY OF ROCCAPINA

BONIFACIO

8

LOCATION

West coast of Corsica

ROUTE

Bastia – Porto-Vecchio

LENGTH

About 280 mi (450 km)

TIME

At least 8 days. Those in a hurry can complete each step in less than a day, but there is so much to see that it's best to take your time.

YOU'LL LOVE

Grandiose landscapes, paradisiacal beaches, mountains, history, activities, nature, gastronomy.

CORSICA
BETWEEN SEA AND MOUNTAIN
FROM BASTIA ➤——➤ TO PORTO-VECCHIO

"By the scent of its maquis, from afar, with my eyes closed, I would recognize Corsica," said Napoleon of his native land. Wild, spectacular, mysterious, unforgettable. From the mountainous Cap Corse to the idyllic beachesof the south, it is your turn to explore one of the most beautiful playgrounds for a road trip. Close your eyes and take in the scent of the Corsican maquis.

START/END OF ROAD TRIP

STOP

LANDMARK OR POINT OF INTEREST ★

ROAD

ROAD TRIP

Paris

Nantes

FRANCE

Montpellier

Toulouse

CAP CORSE

Starting from **Bastia (1),** drive up toward Cap Corse: an ideal first step to get an overview of all the riches of the island. The narrow and windy roads pass a string of perched villages to discover at your leisure: **Centuri,** Barcaggio, Nonza, Luri, Pino . . . not to mention **Patrimonio (2),** with its breathtaking view over the bay of Saint-Florent and the mountains of Nebbio. Throughout your journey, there are valleys leading to the sea on the east side, steep mountainous landscapes on the west side, superb hikes (a favorite is the Sentier des Douaniers in **Macinaggio,** to the north), and gorgeous beaches that punctuate your route. Make sure to pick up some of your favorite regional wines and muscat to bring home with you.

To reach Calvi, take the D81 west. Consider a stopover in **Saint-Florent (3),** renowned for its relaxed lifestyle and its pretty port at the end of a magnificent bay. Have a bit more time? Explore the coves of the wild coast of the **Agriates Desert** by boat, where a change of scenery is guaranteed. Also check out the **Île-Rousse,** a very popular seaside resort in summer, and its three beautiful sandy beaches.

Centuri, Cap Corse

CALVI

You have arrived in **Calvi (4),** capital of Balagne and one of the most popular tourist destinations in Corsica. The town has a Mediterranean atmosphere with 4 mi (6 km) of beaches, port restaurants, and a 15th-century citadel overlooking the bay. Discover the Saint-Jean-Baptiste cathedral, the Saint-Antoine oratory, the Sampiero barracks (former palace of the governors), and the Christopher Columbus house. Every year in June, the city hosts a large electro-pop festival called Calvi on the Rocks, when revelers from all over Europe and beyond meet to party. For diving enthusiasts, great spots for all skill levels can be found near the city. One top pick features the wreckage of a B17 plane, an American bomber from World War II.

Continue your route south, via the D81 toward Ajaccio. Picturesque landscapes unfold before your eyes, delighting all lovers of breathtaking natural settings. Definitely consider a stop in **Porto (5)** and the Scandola Nature Reserve (a UNESCO World Heritage Site), to discover its Genoese tower and enjoy magnificent sunsets over the entire bay. Don't forget **Piana,** where you'll find an unspoiled village with a population of less than 500, which offers a great view. On the sea side, do not miss the famous calanques of Piana—indescribably beautiful—and the magnificent beach of Arone (village 8 mi/12 km from Piana).

LOVE AT FIRST SIGHT

SCANDOLA NATURE RESERVE, THE JEWEL OF CORSICA

This highlight of your trip to Corsica is simply unmissable. Welcome to the first site in France dedicated to the preservation of natural heritage. This marine and land reserve was listed as a UNESCO World Heritage Site in 1975. It's a small, well-preserved paradise located on volcanic cliffs with rich and diverse flora and fauna—around 30 native plant species (arbutus, tree heathers, myrtles, holm oaks, and more), eagles, peregrine falcons, crested cormorants, dolphins, and gray shearwaters. Located in the town of Orsani in southern Corsica, the Scandola peninsula can be reached by boat from Porto, Calvi, and Ajaccio (many agencies organize boat trips). You can also hike from the Col de la Croix (between Calvi and Porto) to reach the village of Girolata (around 4 hours round-trip).

Calvi

Bonifacio

○ 6 ○ ○ 7 ○ ○ 8 ○ ○ 9 ○

AJACCIO:
BEAUTIFUL AND REBELLIOUS

Deeply Mediterranean, **Ajaccio (6)** has character: an old town with colorful houses where the citadel watches over the Sanguinaires Islands and a superb natural setting at the foot of the mountains. Here you are, in the native lands of Napoleon. For a dose of history, go to the Bonaparte house, which his family lived in at the end of the 17th century. Place d'Austerlitz (to the west of the city) was erected as a monument to the glory of the emperor. And don't forget to take a little tour of the lively market in César, Campinchi square.

There are many hiking options in the surrounding area. Around the Gulf of Ajaccio, there are more than 20 beaches (the most scenic are located on the Route des Sanguinaires). There are great spots for swimming on the other side of the bay in **Porticcio.** Then, head to Sartène, where you can explore the southwest part of the island: a rustic and authentic region, with contrasts between the calm and unspoiled beaches of the Gulf of Valinco and the mountainous Alta Rocca.

SARTÈNE:
"THE MOST CORSICAN OF TOWNS"

The writer Prosper Mérimée described **Sartène (7)** as a magnificent city with a lot of character. The labyrinthine streets of old Sartène take you along cobbled paths, secret passages, and granite ramparts, and houses with gray and brown facades. Get off the beaten track and discover the Sartenais, which is full of prehistoric sites (in Tizzano and on the Cauria plateau in particular).

Fourteen miles (22 km) south of Sartène is the magnificent **bay of Roccapina,** where the turquoise sea invites you to dive. Even farther south at the end of the island, from **Bonifacio (8),** you can see the Lavezzi Islands from the top of its chalky, sculpted cliffs. This picturesque, fortified town is an essential stopover. Try the walk from the Saint-Roch pass to the Pertusato lighthouse, or one of the many excursions to cliffs, creeks, and caves. Finally, those who have a little more time can go as far as **Porto-Vecchio (9).** The east coast has some of the most beautiful beaches on the island (Santa Giulia and Palombaggia among them).

PLAYLIST

The Velvet Underground
–
WHO LOVES THE SUN

Quiet Island
–
EDGE OF THE WORLD

Yolanda Lisi
–
LA PLAGE (LA PLAYA)

Arcade Fire
–
DEEP BLUE

PREPARE FOR YOUR TRIP

• **visit-corsica.com** • The website of the Corsica tourist office.

GETTING THERE

There are several airports on Corsica: Bastia–Poretta Airport (BIA), Calvi–Sainte-Catherine Airport (CLY), Ajaccio Napoleon Bonaparte Airport (AJA), and Figari–Sud Corse Airport (FSC). It's also possible to take a ferry from mainland France. From Marseille, Toulon, and Nice, ferries travel to Bastia, Ajaccio, Île-Rousse, and Porto-Vecchio.

WHEN TO GO

Go in March-June or September-October to avoid crowds.

RENTING A CAR

Travel by car, motorcycle, or even bike: Corsica is a paradise for all kinds of road trip fans. Car rental is possible in large cities (Bastia, Ajaccio, Porto-Vecchio, etc.), but remember to book in advance during the summer. The ferry allows you to bring your own vehicle from the mainland. Whatever your means of transport, make sure to be extremely cautious on the roads of the island.

WHERE TO STAY

- **La Villa Calvi:** *chemin Notre Dame de la Serda, Calvi*. • **hotel-lavilla.com** • A superb location in a green setting overlooking the citadel. Swimming pools (five in total!), spa, and impressive rooms for an exceptional stay.
- **U Capu Biancu:** *Lieu Dit Ricetti, Pozzoniello, Bonifacio*. • **capubiancu.com** • Incredible décor of stone and wood, crowned by a breathtaking view of the sea and the scrubland. Private beach and restaurant offering authentic cuisine.

WHERE TO EAT

- **La Vela d'Oro:** *pedestrian lane parallel to the port road, Macinaggio (Cap Corse).* A restaurant run for several generations by the same family, specializing in seafood. Menus from €16-22.
- **A Merendella Citadina:** *19, rue Conventionnel Chiappe, Ajaccio.* You'll get a warm welcome and refined dishes from this restaurant, which offers top-notch Corsican and Mediterranean cuisine. It's tasty and authentic.

A BOOK FOR THE ROAD

The Sermon on the Fall of Rome by Jérôme Ferrari

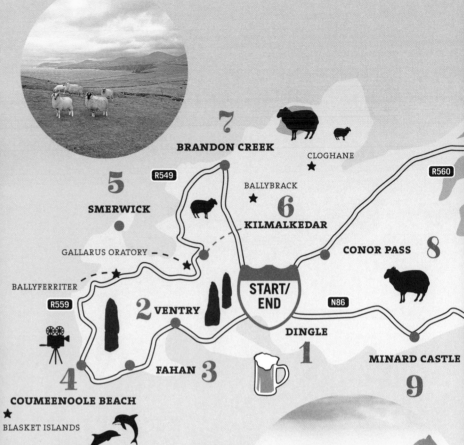

BRANDON CREEK

7

CLOGHANE

R549

R560

BALLYBRACK

5

SMERWICK

6

KILMALKEDAR

CONOR PASS

8

GALLARUS ORATORY

BALLYFERRITER

R559

2 VENTRY

START/
END

N86

DINGLE

1

MINARD CASTLE

FAHAN 3

4

COUMEENOOLE BEACH

9

BLASKET ISLANDS

SKELLIG ISLANDS

LOCATION

Ireland, County Kerry, Dingle Peninsula

ROUTE

Loop from Dingle

LENGTH

About 80 mi (130 km)

TIME

About a day

YOU'LL LOVE

Taking photos of the stone huts, clouds, heather, raging ocean, and black-headed lambs in the spring.

N86

★
INCH

SLEA HEAD DRIVE
LOOP FROM DINGLE

The rugged beauty of this wild landscape will have you following in the footsteps of Irish history. This coastal road, west of Dingle, is Ireland's most photographed region, and it's also part of the famous Wild Atlantic Way. The wind blows, mist wraps around huts and ring forts, and suddenly the sun appears, magically revealing spectacular cliffs. The Atlantic Ocean turns from gray to green, from silver to dark blue around the Blasket Islands and white sand dunes. In the evening, traditional music in local pubs will warm you up.

IRELAND

Galway

Dublin

Limerick

Cork

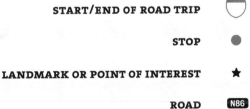

START/END OF ROAD TRIP	⬲
STOP	●
LANDMARK OR POINT OF INTEREST	★
ROAD	N86
ROAD TRIP	━━

DINGLE: A FESTIVE ATMOSPHERE

"That made me love Mary, the Rose of Tralee . . ." Rhythmic notes of Celtic music escape from the colorful facades of pubs in the fishing port of **Dingle (1).** This is one of the best spots in all of Ireland to listen to traditional music, better known as just trad. So clap your hands, stomp your feet, and tour the harbor pubs, where you'll discover trad as well as country, jazz, and blues. Some of the pubs are more touristy, but it's easy to find authentic spots where locals drink, eat, and enjoy the music, too.

The next day, awake and refreshed, take the R 559 running along the Dingle Peninsula, where some people still speak the Irish language. Have a solid breakfast, as you'll probably be nibbling Irish-style tea and cakes throughout the day—the main meal here takes place in the evening. As you drive, standing stones and rocks, often engraved with the medieval ogham alphabet, are not uncommon sights in open fields. The plume of King Arthur and the Knights of the Round Table hangs over **Ventry (2).** A long beach wraps around the bay, lined with dunes and wildflowers. About 2 mi (4 km) southwest, the Celtic and Prehistoric Museum houses fossils. Between Ventry and Slea Head, more than 400 drystone huts have been found. Difficult to date, they were probably used as shelters for shepherds. The best ones to visit are indicated by signs. From **Fahan (3),** a path leads to the prehistoric Dunbeg Fort, half collapsed in the sea and located on a steep, narrow strip of land over the ocean. The road then rises very quickly and winds up the side of Mount Eagle.

THE DINGLE WAY

Irish people definitely love a good walk! The Dingle Way, noted on signposts by the silhouette of a yellow man, circles the Dingle Peninsula for 38 mi (162 km). Do not miss the gateways, interesting wooden passages spanning fences to avoid letting cattle out. Plan out your stops and pub visits in advance, and try for mid-season. Hiking equipment with a compass recommended.

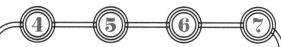
ISLANDS FOR HERMITS

Ten miles (17 km) from Dingle, at the western end of the peninsula, the spectacular view from Slea Head stretches to **Skellig** and **Blasket Islands.** The formidable dark rocks of the two Skellig Islands, classified by UNESCO, stand out toward the south. Seals and puffins inhabit the smaller of the two. Skellig Michael—the largest—was the site of a 6th-century monastery where the monks, isolated most of the year, cut 500 steps out of the rock. Between the cliffs of the coast, the vast **Coumeenoole Beach (4)** tells the romantic scenes of the 1970 film *Ryan's Daughter,* directed by David Lean.

A little farther on, the ogham stone of Dunmore Head—superbly planted in this ancient panorama—bears a long inscription. You might feel like you've come to the end of the world . . . or at least very close. On the Blasket Islands, the long-ago inhabitants led an unchanged lives there for centuries. Their oral traditions and ancestral customs are collected and displayed at the interesting Great Blasket Visitor Center in Dunquin. The last of them left in 1953; some emigrated to the Americas. In **Ballyferriter,** the ruins of a castle evoke Pierce Ferriter, the Irish poet and insurgent who was executed in 1653, a story told at the Chorca Dhuibhne Museum, opposite the village church. From here, a path leads to Dún an Óir Fort, whose grasses cover another place of resistance.

Nearby, the bay of **Smerwick (5)** is bordered by beaches and cliffs all the way to Sybil Head. Small donkey bridges and a narrow road lead to the monastic remains of Reask and its standing stone. Farther east, a wonderful rustic chapel shaped like an overturned boat, the **Gallarus Oratory,** has remained intact since the 7th century. From the flat stones without mortar to the fine sculpted cross, the atmosphere is captivating. Check out the church in **Kilmalkedar (6),** one of the most significant religious sites on the peninsula. Engraved tombstones, ogham stones, and the Hermitage of Saint Brendan complete this oceanfront tour. Some say this tireless navigator left the beach of **Brandon Creek (7)** to reach Newfoundland five centuries before Christopher Columbus.

NOT TO BE MISSED

*From **Ballybrack,** The Saint's Road ascends to Mount Brandon (about half a mile), Ireland's second highest peak. Very popular with pilgrims in the Middle Ages (especially on his feast day on May 16), this path is once again popular with hikers. At the top, be careful of the steep cliffs on the north side. Avoid the hike in foggy weather.*

FILM

IN THE FOOTSTEPS OF
RYAN'S DAUGHTER

A walk (about 1 hour) leaves from the center of Dunquin and leads to the ruins that served as a setting for the 1970 film *Ryan's Daughter,* starring Robert Mitchum. You'll love the view, a spectacular panorama as far as Clogherhead where storm waves crash against the reefs.

Skellig Islands

NORTHEAST OF THE PENINSULA

This detour from Dingle is worth adding day for its grand panoramas. Head for the magnificent **Conor Pass (8),** toward Kilcummin, in the northeast of the peninsula. The road is very narrow and not recommended for RVs and prohibited for vehicles over 2 tons. On the north side, along the bays of Tralee and Brandon, long meadows covered with white cottongrass and dark lakes descend to the sea. On the south side—slightly warmed by the Gulf Stream—the mist and the sun play hide and seek on the beaches. There are more birds than tourists in the villages of **Cloghane** and Brandon, facing the Magharee Islands, and you'll find many campsites on the coast. **Inch** beach has over 2 mi (4 km) of clear sand and good surfing. Six miles (10 km) from Annascaul on the return route to Dingle, you'll discover the remains of **Minard Castle (9)** and the miraculous Holy Well. Between rocks, meadows, and waves, this romantic landscape will entice you.

IF YOU WANT TO GO FARTHER

THE WILD ATLANTIC WAY

As the name suggests, this wild road trip along the Atlantic Ocean is one of the longest coastal roads in the world. On the west coast of Ireland between Cork and Donegal, these 1,550 miles (2,500 km) are dotted with beaches, ports, capes, dizzying cliffs, and over 150 spectacular viewpoints. As soon as you get out of your car, ocean spray lashes your face, and you hear terns and northern gannets calling from the beaches.

From **West Cork,** the towns of **Clonakilty** and **Baltimore** attract whales and dolphins who frolic there in summer. From here, a boat trip to the **Roaring Water Islands** is tempting. The fishing villages of **Mizen, Sheep's Head,** and **Barea** have kept their old ways, evidenced by abandoned mines and milk collection. Don't miss the delicious seafood in **Iveragh.** Through **Kerry** and its purple rhododendrons and then the **Dingle Peninsula,** the WAW makes its way along the north coast and crosses the Shannon into County Clare. The architecture of the surf-swept cape of **Loop Head** fascinates, with its lighthouses and towers isolated in cliffs carved into natural arches. Golf courses and beaches soften the landscape around **Spanish Point** and **Lahinch.**

After crossing the **Cliffs of Moher,** the WAW enters **Burren National Park,** which is riddled with limestones and sinkholes. The changing light also reveals white and pink saxifrage. Bypassing Galway Bay and its famous oysters, consider a stopover in **Galway,** a bustling city with ample shopping and dining opportunities. Continue along the coast of Connemara toward **Spiddal,** the beaches of **Dog's Bay,** and the imposing **Kylemore** Abbey, dominated by the summit of Croagh Patrick. Bays follow one another through Mayo and Sligo to the village of **Strandhill** and the **Mullaghmore** Peninsula.

Finally, the WAW ends in **Donegal,** where we cross the highest accessible cliffs in Europe at **Slieve League.** Various hikes and walks punctuate this last part of the journey. In spring, the fuchsia hedges light up the embankments and paths with red and purple bells that the Irish call "the tears of God."

Cliffs of Moher

PREPARE FOR YOUR TRIP

- ireland.com •
- discoverireland.ie •

GETTING THERE

Your best bet is to fly into Dublin (DUB), Ireland's biggest airport. From there, it's a 4-hour drive across the country to reach Dingle.

RENTING A CAR

At the Dublin Airport, rental agencies are served by shuttle buses. When you return, allow extra time to take the shuttle back to the airport.
It is also possible to cycle Slea Head Drive (rentals in Dingle).

WHEN TO GO

The best time is May to October. In winter, you risk stormy conditions, fog, and many B&Bs and other services being closed. And watch out for the wind near the cliffs. No matter the season, it's always windy!

GOOD TO KNOW

Take the route clockwise; otherwise, buses on the narrow roads will block you.
The roads are winding and very, very narrow, and don't forget, they drive on the left side of the road here! Irish drivers tend to travel at full speed in the middle of the road. The 50 mph (80 km/h) speed limit is greatly overestimated; instead, expect an average of 30 mph (50 km/h). The road signs are in Irish and in English.

WHERE TO STAY AND EAT

For accommodations, good options are available in youth hostels (many also offer private rooms) and campsites. For food, pubs are the most economical option.

- **B&B Russell's:** *The Mall, Dingle.* • **russellsdingle.com** • A quiet, family-friendly location.
- **Greenmount House:** *Gortonora, Dingle.* • **greenmounthouse,ie** • Ask for a room with a view of the bay for an unforgettable stay.
- **O'Sullivan's Courthouse Pub** and **O'Flaherty** in Dingle: Perfect pubs for atmosphere and concerts.
- **Paidi o Se's:** *Church Cross, Ventry.* A pub full of atmosphere.
- **O'Connor's Guesthouse:** *Main Street, Cloghane.* • **cloghane.com** • Music, accommodations, and a restaurant.
- **Beenoskee B&B:** *Cappateige, Connor Pass Road, Castlegregory.* • **beenoskee.com** • For the hospitality and the perfect atmosphere.
- **Dingle Gate Hostel:** *The Mall, Annascaul.* • **dinglegatehostel. com** • A modern, simple, and inexpensive hostel.

A BOOK FOR THE ROAD

McCarthy's Bar: A Journey of Discovery In Ireland by Pete McCarthy

PLAYLIST

The Pogues
–
DIRTY OLD TOWN

Doolin'
–
WHEN WE WILL BE MARRIED

The Corrs
–
BREATHLESS

The Dubliners
–
ROCKY ROAD TO DUBLIN

TROLLS PENINSULA

HÚSAVÍK

12

DETTIFOSS

14 AKUREYRI

864

15

HÉRAÐSVÖTN RIVER

LAKE MÝVATN

13

1

4

ÞINGVELLIR

3

VATNAJÖKULL

9

GEYSIR

37

START/
END

35

REYKJAVÍK

5

SELJALANDSFOSS

1

8

KIRKJUBÆJARKLAUSTUR

1

1

HVERAGERÐI

2

VÍK **7**

VESTMANNAEYJAR ISLANDS

SÓLHEIMASANDUR

SKÓGAR

6

LOCATION

Around Iceland

ROUTE

Loop from Reykjavík

LENGTH

828 mi (1,332 km)

TIME

10 days to 2 weeks

YOU'LL LOVE

The untouched landscapes, swimming
in hot springs, fjords, whales.

START/END OF ROAD TRIP

● STOP

★ LANDMARK OR POINT OF INTEREST

1 ROAD

══ ROAD TRIP

GLACIER

RING ROAD
AND BEYOND
ALL AROUND ICELAND

11
FÁSKRÚÐSFJÖRÐUR

1

1

● HÖFN **10**

Touring an entire country on one road? It's possible in Iceland. Driving the Ring Road (Route 1, Þjóðvegurinn in Icelandic) between crumpled lava fields and horse-grazing valleys connects you to a multitude of adventures. To the south, it even skims a few fjords, touches wild black-sand beaches, and nears the largest glacier in Europe, the Vatnajökull. This country road promises the best of Iceland in one trip.

1

REYKJAVÍK:
ENERGY TO SPARE

Icelanders, two-thirds of whom live in here, are proud of their vibrant capital city. Some visitors say Reykjavík feels a little more like a large and friendly provincial town, with a tight core of old wooden houses painted with tar and bright colors. See its plethora of museums, murals, and emblematic modern buildings such as the Hallgrímskirkja church, with a concrete design and basalt-style columns, and the futuristic Harpa concert hall, which sparkles like the northern lights at night. **Reykjavík (1)** is an increasingly iconic European nightlife destination—especially in summer, when there are nearly 24 hours of daylight!

SPLASH
CONTEST

The temperature is 45°F (7°C). The sky is gray, weeping in bursts of rain. This is the best time to put on your swimsuit! The water of the Blue Lagoon, turquoise and slightly milky, is pumped from a depth of more than 3,280 ft (1 km), raising the thermometer to 102°F (39°C). It's like a huge sauna, with clouds high above as the only ceiling. (It's also very popular; remember to book ahead!) You'll find more thermal waters along the Golden Circle, including Laugarvatn Fontana and the vast Secret Lagoon in Flúðir. In the winter, you might be able to take a swim while observing the northern lights. Or go wild with a swim in the Reykjadalur hot river, near Hveragerði, reached via a 2-mi (3-km) hike.

Ísafjörður

Akureyri

ICELAND

Reykjavík

Vík í Mýrdal

THE GOLDEN CIRCLE IN SIGHT

As soon as the city fades away, lava appears, covering the ground with a blackish layer. After your first 30 minutes on the Ring Road, you'll find **Hveragerði (2),** the Icelandic gardening capital. Tomatoes and bananas grow in its greenhouses, heated by geothermal energy! Branch off toward the heart of the Golden Circle, en route to **Geysir (3),** the site that gave its name to all the geysers in the world. Here, the superheated water of Strokkur spurts out every 5 to 10 minutes in a spray of up to 65 ft (20 m) high, showering spectators when the wind blows in. Its neighbor, the Grand Geysir, wakes up sporadically, depending on seismic activity. In 2000, it sprang up for two days, reaching 400 ft (122 m) high! Around it, the powerful Hvítá River flows into a fault-canyon, forming the magnificent Gullfoss, its "golden falls" often enveloped in a rainbow born from its spray. The Golden Circle tour ends in the **Þingvellir** National Park **(4),** where the Icelandic Parliament met from the year 930 until its transfer to Reykjavík in 1798. The site is located precisely on the mid-Atlantic rift line, formed by a large fault that continues to grow at an average rate of 0.1 in (3 mm) per year, tearing Iceland between two continents. On one side is the Eurasian plate, on the other the American plate.

DETOUR TO THE VESTMANNAEYJAR ISLANDS

About 6 mi (10 km) from the coast, the very active fishing port of Heimaey nestles at the foot of the Eldfell volcano, which emerged from a pasture one night in January 1973. The massive eruption lasted five months and enlarged the area of the island by 15 percent. As soon as you get off the ferry, you spot Eldfell and its imposing sulfur yellow dome. From the easily reached summit, the 360-degree panorama embraces the perfect cone of the sleeping Helgafell, and, on the opposite side, grassy cliffs nibbled on by sheep. Offshore, islets protected by rock walls dot the steel of the ocean. Some are topped by the solitary hut of a puffin hunter.

RISE AND FALL

Back on the Ring Road, Hekla, the most active of Icelandic volcanoes, is hidden under its cap of clouds in the distance. The first stop is at **Seljalandsfoss (5):** pretty falls tumbling 210 ft (65 m) down a rocky ridge, with a path running behind. Twenty minutes later, the Skógafoss (200 ft/60 m) plays its own thundering score, projecting its wide veil behind a rocky fold. Here you'll discover a church, an old school, small houses with peat roofs topped with grass (ideal for protection from the cold), and a folk museum in **Skógar (6)** (pop. 25)—a perfect picture of Iceland.

You will start to see more *Einbreið brú* ("single-lane bridge") signs as the Ring Road approaches **Vík (7),** a pretty village stuck near an almost closed-off bay. On the east side, the high cliffs of Dyrhólaey, partly made of basalt, navigate their own field of volcanic pebbles and black sand. The basalt sea stacks of Reynisdrangar wade through the icy water. A lighthouse and nature reserve populated by arctic terns, fulmars, skuas, and puffins complete the panorama.

The next step is a bit difficult to pronounce: **Kirkjubæjarklaustur (8).** Legend says that a sermon once saved this village from an eruption of dangerous Katla. This volcano is indeed the "kettle" that its name evokes: Invisible to the eye, it hides under the skullcap of Mýrdalsjökull, which overflows the caldera in tongues of ice. Explosive and unpredictable, Katla is at the origin of many *jökulhlaup,* floods as destructive as they are sudden, caused by the partial melting of a glacier during eruptions. They shaped the dismal plain of Mýrdalssandur, where the extremely fine sand flies around in such abrasive winds that car rental companies refuse to cover any damage. Sheared by torrents, the Eldgjárhraun lava field, which follows, is one of the largest in history: It covers nearly 440 mi (700 km). In the distant desert of gravel and rock of Skeidarársandur, the metallic mass of a large bridge bears witness to the devastating power of the *jökulhlaup.*

THE MYSTIQUE OF THE TROLL

Twenty percent of Icelanders believe in the existence of trolls and elves, known as the *huldufólk* ("hidden people"). Linked to the forces of nature, these beings are sometimes presented as giants, sometimes as children. They would hide within clusters of rocks and hate to be disturbed, to the point of causing all kinds of catastrophes for their human neighbors. With each new section of road, there is a study considering its impact on trolls. Some have even proposed a national park to ensure their protection!

LOVE AT FIRST SIGHT

AIRPLANE HUNTING
About 1 mi (2 km) east of the Sólheimajökull junction, a lonely road leads to the black sand beach of Sólheimasandur, where a U.S. Army DC-3 crashed in 1973. Today it's a very photogenic wreck, which requires a little effort to see: Access is on foot and the walk is over 2 mi (4 km) in the wind.

Seljalandsfoss

FROM THE LARGEST GLACIER IN EUROPE TO THE EASTERN FJORDS

As you travel southeast on the Ring Road, you approach a colossus: **Vatnajökull (9)** occupies an area almost equal to that of Puerto Rico (8 percent of Iceland!), half a mile thick in places. It's the largest glacier in Europe outside the Arctic and is fully protected by the largest national park on the continent. At its foot, the Jökulsárlón lagoon is filled with icebergs, some lacerated with blackish streaks of ash, others an intense blue or translucent, shining like ice cubes in a glass. Water flows into the ocean through a single gully encumbered with monoliths of ice.

Past the large port of **Höfn (10),** the Ring Road grazes some wild black-sand beaches, perfect for a pebble hunt. Clinging to the coast, the road continues from cape to cape toward the pretty port of Djúpivogur and the Berufjörður fjord, which is enclosed by peaks and often covered with snowfields until midsummer. The main road soon veers away from the coast and heads straight toward Egilsstaðir. From this point, take Route 96, which walks quietly along the sides of Stöðvarfjördur, **Fáskrúðsfjörður (11),** and Reyðarfjörður.

Lake Mývatn

LAND OF VOLCANOES AND SMOKE

Now you'll reach the long crossing across the eastern plateau. Bad weather always seems to be the order of the day on these lunar lands, where you can sometimes spot the ghostly silhouettes of reindeer emerging from the fog. After an hour and a half, a junction appears in the middle of this no man's land. To the right, Route 864 bumps up to Jökulsargljúfur, a canyon 15 mi (25 km) long and almost 140 ft (120 m) deep, probably sculpted by a glacial flood (*jökul-hlaup*). At the bottom flows the wild river Jökulsá á Fjöllum, interspersed with **Dettifoss (12),** the most powerful waterfall in Europe, dumping over 52,000 gallons (200 cubic m) per second. The falls, about 144 ft (44 m) high, descend in a deafening crash in a small amphitheater of basalt. Just upstream, the torrent crosses another rocky bar at the beautiful Selfoss Falls, accessible by a 25-minute hike.

Then comes **Lake Mývatn (13).** Spread over 14 sq mi (36 sq km), this very shallow lake (8 ft/2.5 m on average) is surrounded by hills and a multitude of micro-craters formed by steam eruptions. Those who camp on its shores quickly understand the origin of its name: *Mý-vatn,* the "lake of flies." In nice weather, millions of insects fill the air with their annoying whirring. Attracted by the sustenance, 15 species of ducks nest here, not to mention loons, grebes, stilts, and swans. Sheep and cows graze in the green pastures. But vulcanism is not far; it manifests itself in many forms in the area. First are the "black castles" of Dimmuborgir, sculpted in lava. In Höfði, the flow is half-submerged in the lake. The Hverfjall volcano stands nearby with its perfect cone of brown and red. In Hverir, 4 mi (6 km) to the east, fumaroles rise from the earth next to pools of burning mud. Behind the nearby geothermal power station of Krafla, Leirhnjúkur is a vast expanse of frozen magma still warm beneath the surface. But most extraordinary is the small crater Viti (literally translated as "hell"). Also formed by the Krafla volcano, this crater contains a lake of milky jade and its shores are sprinkled with sulfur puddles. Finish with a bath in the 95-104°F (35-40°C) waters of the Mývatn Nature Baths, spread out against the austere immensity of Iceland.

DETOUR TO HÚSAVÍK

North of Lake Mývatn, the port of Húsavík wakes up in summer with the return of whales—and tourists. From May to October, you can go whale-watching on board old wooden trawlers or reconditioned sailboats. Patience is often rewarded: 9 times out of 10, you will spot at least one whale, and if you're lucky, a breaching humpback. Offshore is the island of Lundy, named for the puffins that inhabit it, where the arctic swells and winds reign supreme.

AKUREYRI: AND THE CIRCLE IS COMPLETE

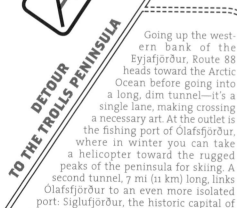

DETOUR
TO THE TROLLS PENINSULA

Going up the western bank of the Eyjafjörður, Route 88 heads toward the Arctic Ocean before going into a long, dim tunnel—it's a single lane, making crossing a necessary art. At the outlet is the fishing port of Ólafsfjörður, where in winter you can take a helicopter toward the rugged peaks of the peninsula for skiing. A second tunnel, 7 mi (11 km) long, links Ólafsfjörður to an even more isolated port: Siglufjörður, the historic capital of herring. In summer, a museum like no other sells live fish in reconstructed 19th-century warehouses—a nice little trip back in time.

Planted on the side of the Ring Road, the Goðafoss waterfall, almost 40 ft (12 m) high, has a symbolic value: In the year 1000, the lawspeaker Þorgeir Þorkelsson Ljósvetningagoði is said to have thrown the idols of his ancient gods into the falls, anchoring Iceland to the Christian world. Half an hour later is **Akureyri (14),** the second-largest city in Iceland with 18,000 inhabitants, located in the notch of the very long fjord of Eyja, where whales can often be seen at the gates of the city. There is a beautiful public swimming pool and an array of unexpected museums (notably celebrating industry, motorcycles, and aviation), but Akureyri is not strictly a tourist spot. Its supermarkets and row of lively bars make it an essential and comfortable stopover.

The drive back to the capital takes at least a day—more if you plan to treat yourself to extra stops. The banks of the **Héraðsvötn river (15)** saw the establishment of some of the first Viking settlements 1,000 years ago. This area has rafting, Icelandic horses (they're very furry with short legs), and historic sites like the venerable Viðimýrarkirkja (a church from 1834) and the Glaumbær farm, both with peat walls and grass roofs. Then comes one last fjord with soggy watercolor landscapes, and the hinterland, leaving the Northwest fjords and the Snæfellsnes Peninsula for another trip.

COLD FEVER

Released in 1998, this film features a young Japanese man who goes to Iceland to memorialize his parents, the pretext for an endearing and sometimes surreal road trip movie, linking sublime landscapes and wacky situations born from the clash between cultures.

RENTING A CAR

Car rentals are expensive in Iceland. If you stick to the Ring Road, there's no need for 4WD drive. A standard car is sufficient almost everywhere, except in the wild heart of the island.
• **bluecarrental.is** •
• **kukucampers.is** •

WHEN TO GO

From late May-early June to August.

WHERE TO STAY

You can find accommodations in Iceland without breaking the bank thanks to the many campsites, many of them free, and some with mini bungalows. There are also quite a few welcoming and affordable youth hostels. Guesthouses (often with shared bathroom), farmhouses, B&Bs, and hotels are more expensive, unless they offer the sleeping bag formula: no sheets provided, so bring your own bedding. Book in advance for high season (particularly July).

WHERE TO EAT

Restaurants are expensive in Iceland, but you can find cozy cafés, bakeries, and fast-food restaurants everywhere. The best budget option is doing your shopping at the supermarket (Bónus is the cheapest).

A BOOK FOR THE ROAD

Independent People by Halldór Laxness

PREPARE FOR YOUR TRIP

• **visiticeland.com** •
• **icelandreview.com** •

GETTING THERE

Keflavík International Airport (KEF), about 50 minutes west of Reykjavík, frequently gets kudos for being one of the best airports in Europe, and the plaudits are well deserved. Flying into Iceland is a pretty seamless experience. The country's main carrier, Icelandair • **icelandair.com** • serves more than 30 destinations in the United States, Canada, and Europe.

PLAYLIST

Björk
–
IT'S OH SO QUIET

Ásgeir
–
KING AND CROSS

Of Monsters and Men
–
LITTLE TALKS

Sigur Rós
–
HOPPÍPOLLA

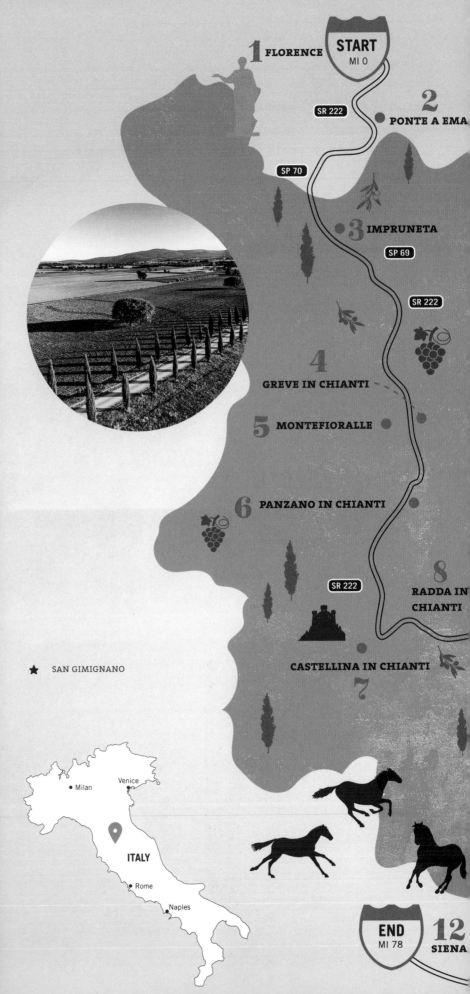

LOCATION
Central Italy, Tuscany

ROUTE
Florence – Siena

LENGTH
About 78 mi (125 km)

YOU'LL LOVE
Local gastronomy, vineyards and wine-tastings, fortified villages, green hills.

1 FLORENCE START MI 0

SR 222

2 PONTE A EMA

SP 70

3 IMPRUNETA

SP 69

SR 222

4 GREVE IN CHIANTI

5 MONTEFIORALLE

6 PANZANO IN CHIANTI

SR 222

8 RADDA IN CHIANTI

CASTELLINA IN CHIANTI

7

★ SAN GIMIGNANO

Venice
Milan

ITALY

Rome

Naples

END MI 78 12 SIENA

CHIANTI ROUTE
FROM FLORENCE ➤ TO SIENA

Two great cities of northern Italy, Florence and Siena, frame the most beautiful landscapes of Tuscany on the 78-mi (125-km) route to Chianti. Alleys of cypress trees lead to sun-drenched farms and wineries. Vineyards, olive groves, and rural, rustic houses dot the landscape. You'll pass fortified ruins, hermitages, and abbeys, and walk through the sublime settings of Italian Renaissance paintings.

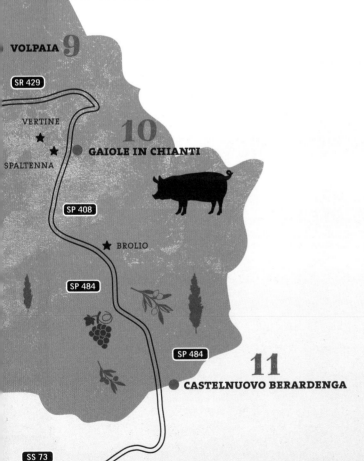

VOLPAIA 9

SR 429

VERTINE

10

SPALTENNA · GAIOLE IN CHIANTI

SP 408

BROLIO

SP 484

SP 484

11
CASTELNUOVO BERARDENGA

SS 73

START/END OF ROAD TRIP	⬚
STOP	●
LANDMARK OR POINT OF INTEREST	★
ROAD	A1
ROAD TRIP	=
CHIANTI CLASSICO REGION	▪

FLORENCE: CITY OF THE ARTS

Florence (1), the capital of Tuscany, is undoubtedly one of the most beautiful cities in Italy and holds over half of the country's works of art. Before hitting the road, treat yourself to one or two days (at the very least) to visit its treasures and wonders.

The relatively small historic center, around the green waters of the Arno, can be visited on foot. Early risers will be rewarded with smaller lines in front of the museums: the Uffizi galleries, the Accademia, the Museum of San Marco, the Duomo, and the Bargello National Museum. A few minutes from the Bargello, cross the famous Ponte Vecchio bridge and shop the stalls for art, jewelry, and souvenirs. Prepare to do a lot of walking. Fra Angelico, Botticelli, Piero della Francesca, Michelangelo, Leonardo da Vinci, Donatello, Filippo Lippi, have mercy on our feet!

You'll find some breathing room away from the crowds as you go north toward the Opificio delle Pietre Dure and the Church of Santa Croce, adorned with frescoes collected by Giotto. To the south is the astonishing naked sculpture of Christ on the cross in the Basilica di Santo Spirito. On the other side of the Arno River, the districts of antique dealers and craftsmen are also quieter. If you have time, check out the collections of the Pitti Palace and the baroque Boboli Gardens. At the end of the day, sunset is the perfect time to hike up to the Basilica San Miniato al Monte.

Take a walk in the evening at aperitivo time (around 7pm-9pm), in Oltrarno near San Frediano and Piazza Santo Spirito. The bars and enoteche (Italian wine shops) are fun and friendly.

LA CHIANTIGIANA AND ITS VINEYARDS

Take the **Chiantigiana (SR 222)** to exit Florence from the south of the city in the direction of **Ponte a Ema (2).** Travel between the beautiful hills, covered with vines that were once so dear to Leonardo da Vinci. They are entangled with olive groves and paths lined with cypress trees leading to old farms or *casa colonica*.

To fully appreciate this route, take the time to enjoy the superb panoramas, visit its villages and their surrounding vineyards, and stop in the many estates for a few wine-tastings (in moderation of course).

After Grassina, a detour to the west to **Impruneta (3),** famous for its terracotta objects, allows you to admire the treasure of the Basilica of Santa Maria. Returning to the Chiantigiana, don't miss a stopover in the village of **Greve in Chianti (4).** The triangular Market Square is lined with palaces and arcades leading to the Santa Croce Church. Take a last look west toward the hilltop village and the fortifications of **Montefioralle (5)** before setting off on the winding hill roads, where you'll find many estates that produce their own wine. Halfway along the Chianti road, the silhou-

ette of the castle and the church of **Panzano in Chianti (6)** stands out.

Crossing the Pesa River, the Chiantigiana continues south to **Castellina in Chianti (7).** The ramparts and defenses of the town bear witness to the frenzied struggle for its possession, waged for centuries between Florence and Siena. Stroll the Via delle Volte, which runs alongside the surrounding wall of the town. The panorama extends over a quintessential Tuscan landscape: lines of vineyards, silver olive groves, cypresses, and a maze of small roads. A small archaeological museum and an Etruscan tomb will take you back in time.

DETOUR TO SAN GIMIGNANO

From Chianti, you are only 15 mi (25 km) from **San Gimignano.** Treat yourself to a side trip to one of the most stunning towns in Tuscany, listed as a UNESCO World Heritage Site. This remarkable city, with its 14 medieval towers, stands atop a hill like a lookout. The city has remained almost identical to what it was in the year 1300! To make the most of it, spend the night, and make sure to taste the Vernaccia, an old, white wine that was popular during the Renaissance.

Another possible escape is Monteriggioni, a magnificent town surrounded by towers and linked together by walls that are still intact.

It was in Panzano that butcher Dario Cecchini became famous for reciting Dante's verses while cutting slices of his ham. A stopover in his butcher's shop or one of his two restaurants is highly recommended.

• dariocecchini.com •

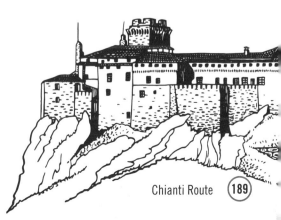

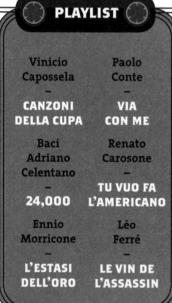

PLAYLIST

Vinicio Capossela	Paolo Conte
–	–
CANZONI DELLA CUPA	**VIA CON ME**
Baci Adriano Celentano	Renato Carosone
–	–
24,000	**TU VUO FA L'AMERICANO**
Ennio Morricone	Léo Ferré
–	–
L'ESTASI DELL'ORO	**LE VIN DE L'ASSASSIN**

⑧ ⑨ ⑩ ⑪

CHIANTI MOUNTAINS AND FORTIFIED VILLAGES

After leaving the Chiantigiana behind and heading east toward the isolated Chianti Mountains, the SS 429 takes you to the perched village of **Radda in Chianti (8)**, between the valleys of Pesa and Arbia. All the elegance of the 15th century appears on the Palace of Podesta, surrounded by pedestrian streets. In the southern suburbs of Radda, the restored Romanesque Church of San Gusto in Salaio is located at the foot of a large cedar in a lush conch of vineyards.

Four miles (7 km) to the north, the fortified hamlet of **Volpaia (9)** has remained authentic. This stronghold, once a refuge for pilgrims, now shelters hikers and produces a renowned organic wine. Continue to **Gaiole in Chianti (10),** the last village of the Chianti League, famous for its wild boars who feed on acorns from the surrounding wooded hills.

Get to Siena via **Castelnuovo Berardenga (11),** at the southeastern edge of the Chianti mountains. This outpost of the Republic of Siena never completed its defenses. Taken by the Florentines in 1555, the village has since been devoted to the production of wine and oil, offering a quiet stopover before approaching the city of Palio, through Barca.

NOT TO BE MISSED

*The fortified church of **Spaltenna** and the hilltop village of **Vertine** to the west, the magnificent Romanesque abbey of **Coltibuono** to the northwest, and the impressive pentagonal fortress of **Brolio** to the south.*

SIENA: LAND OF THE PALIO

The Crete Senesi, lunar-looking hills in the
colors of clay, surround **Siena (12).** It's a
grandiose landscape for a city that still
vibrates with history.

Like Florence, Siena unleashes dizzying
artistic wealth, while at the same time
exuding a sweet Tuscan atmosphere. To
experience this, sit on a terrace in Piazza
del Campo, one of the most beautiful in
the world, when the sun shapes the coat
of arms of the facades and the curved
brick paving. This is the place where various clans challenge each other during the
Palio, a famous horse race that takes place
twice a year. The 17 districts of the city,
or *contrade,* bear the names of animals
and compete in front of the enthusiastic
Sienese. Following a traditional pageant,
there is a lightning race of about a minute
when the horses are ridden bareback, all
accompanied by plentiful traditions.

Siena established its own style through
its architects, sculptors, and painters. Its Civico and dell'Opera museums,
Pinacoteca, Duomo, and the Piccolomini
library are all examples of medieval architecture like no other. Explore the maze of
interlocking alleys, some leading to a small
square, some to a secret fountain, or even
to an old pink palace with walls studded
with coats of arms. The always-crowded
shopping street should be experienced
during *passeggiata* (the late afternoon
stroll, beloved by Italians). Siena marks the
end of your journey.

CHIANTI CLASSICO
MUST-TRY TUSCAN WINES

Everyone knows chianti, the most famous
of Tuscan wines. Chianti classico (normal
or Riserva) is a geographical nod to the surrounding Chianti route.

Traditionally, "normal" Chianti is drunk
young and in a flask, and Chianti Riserva
must age at least 15 months and should be
drunk in Bordeaux bottles. Gran Selezione,
another cut above, is made with the
best grapes. The historic Chianti Classico
DOCG—identifiable by the black rooster
on the bottle—corresponds to a delimited
terroir. It involves nearly 600 winegrowers
who share over 17,000 acres, making their
wines from 80 percent Sangiovese, the
flagship grape variety. Just make sure to
choose a designated driver before tastings.

GETTING THERE

Florence's Aeroporto di Firenze-
Peretola (FLR) is a small airport,
with no direct flights to the United
States. Delays and cancellations
due to inclement weather are
common. Tuscany's busiest airport,
Aeroporto di Pisa-San Giusto in
Pisa, is less than an hour and a half
away from Florence by bus, train,
or car. There are direct flights from
JFK to Pisa during the summer.

WINE ESTATES

- **Castello di Verrazzano:**
2.5 mi (4 km) north of Greve.
• verrazzano.com •
Renaissance gardens and
accommodations in old
farmhouses.

- **Azienda Agricola San Donatino:**
(Castellina in Chianti).
• sandonatino.com •
Taste Chianti among vineyards and
olive groves.

- **Castello di Volpaia:**
• volpaia.com •
Organic wine sales in the castle
tower.

- **Fattoria di Corsignano:**
(Vagliagli).
• tenutacorsignano.it •
After visiting the cellars, sleep
peacefully between cypress trees
and a luxurious swimming pool.

- **Château, spa, and farmhouse of
Baron Ricasoli:** *(Gaiole-in-Chianti).*
• ricasoli.it •
Chic stays and tastings at the
Selezione of Chianti Castello di
Brolio, in the Chianti mountains.

START
MI O

SORRENTO
1

TERMINI
2

CAPRI

 LOCATION

Southern Italy, Campania

 ROUTE

Sorrento – Vietri sul Mare (Salerno)

 LENGTH

15 mi (25 km) for the classified road;
47 mi (75 km) from Sorrento to Salerno

 TIME

Half a day or more, depending on
your preferences and accommodation
options.

 YOU'LL LOVE

The hazy and changing light along the
road, the vibrant colors of the facades,
the fragrant gardens, the little niches
with Madonna statues that light up in
the evening in the crevices of the rocks,
the spaghetti with sea urchins.

START/END OF ROAD TRIP

STOP

LANDMARK OR POINT OF INTEREST ★

ROAD TRIP

UNESCO-CLASSIFIED ROAD

8 **VIETRI SUL MARE**

END
MI 47

6

RAVELLO

ATRANI

MINORI

7

AMALFI

5

BOMERANO DI AGEROLA

NOCELLE

FURORE

POSITANO

3

PRAIANO

4

THE AMALFI
COAST
FROM SORRENTO ⟶ TO VIETRI SUL MARE

★ LI GALLI ISLANDS

Suspended between sky and sea, the Amalfi Coast Road wraps around small pastel-colored fishing ports and chic resorts in southern Italy. Fifteen mi (25 km) of this road is listed by UNESCO, traveling around villages of the Lattari Mountains, steep coves, and terraced gardens that smell of jasmine and lemon. Visit during low season for unforgettable landscapes and fewer crowds.

Milan

Venice

ITALY

Rome

Naples

47 MI

CAPRI IN THE DISTANCE

Start your trip with a stop at the large beach of **Sorrento (1),** located 31 mi (50 km) south of Naples, famous for both its stunning views and its lemons. Hike along the Sorrentine Peninsula (facing the island of Capri), which blooms in spring. This is a relaxing way to discover exuberant wild flora, dominated by the scarlet flowers of wild pelargonium. Stop at the peaceful Giardini di Cataldo for a glass of limoncello, a lemon liqueur renowned as the best in Italy.

From the top of Monte San Costanzo, accessible by car from **Termini (2),** marvel at the view of the rocks of Capri, lost in the haze.

DETOUR TO THE ISLAND OF CAPRI

The 7 square miles (11 sq km) of the island of Capri seem to magically float on the blue waters of the Mediterranean. Despite successive waves of tourists, the harmony of the maritime vibes, the cool caves, and the almost tropical vegetation cascading over the sea still make Capri a backdrop for the gods. If you want a break from the crowds in Piazza Umberto, nature lovers can take refuge on the plateau at Anacapri, preferably in the evening to inhale the intoxicating scents of pines and fruit trees along the whitewashed walls.

Cars are prohibited on the island from mid-March to early November. Airboat, ferry, or speedboat trips to the Isle of Capri are provided year-round, primarily from Sorrento. You can also explore the island on foot or funicular.

NOT TO BE MISSED

The gardens of Augustus. Mount Tiberius. The neoclassical Villa San Michele, celebrated by Axel Munthe for its gardens and panoramic views. Take a chairlift to the Mount Solaro Belvedere, 1,932 ft (589 m) above vineyards and olive trees. From Marina Grande, speedboats tour the famous Blue Grotto and the island's many other caves.

IN THE FOOTSTEPS OF ODYSSEUS

This UNESCO-listed route actually begins at Colle di San Pietro, west of Positano. From the golf course of Salerno, the view of the three craggy **Li Galli Islands** stands out. Formerly the private property of dancer Rudolf Nureyev, these islands were known for the mythological sirens whose songs attracted sailors, only to strand them on the reefs. This was where Odysseus is said to have tied himself to the mast of his ship while his sailors covered their ears as they passed through this deadly cape.

The pastel harmony of the houses of **Positano (3)** soon emerge on the cliff. You'll definitely want to get out the camera here! Once a commercial port, Positano has become a popular spot for jet-setting business travelers and tourists. Drop off your car in one of three parking lots near the flour mill, or in one of the more expensive parking lots along Viale Pasitea. Leave the city center to stroll through the alleys and see domed roofs that evoke Asian architecture and the trade of Amalfi ships to Tunisia. The small beaches below are very tempting, but remember, you'll have to climb a few hundred steps back up to the city center!

Try a 3-hour hike on the Path of the Gods, which links the beautiful village of **Nocelle** to **Bomerano di Agerola** (bring your hiking gear). The plateau is peppered with meadows and chestnut woods. Despite its splendid view of the Gulf of Salerno, it is not recommended for people prone to vertigo.

As you pass through the village of **Praiano (4),** it's almost impossible not to stop. For now, just admire the cove below and the tiny port of **Furore,** nestled within a crack in the rock 2.2 mi (3.5 km) away.

Positano

AMALFI, THE JET-SET COAST

Finally, you'll reach **Amalfi (5),** formerly accessible only by sea. In fact, the old part of the city is now under the ocean. Maritime trade and fishing made this area lively before the construction of the coastal road in the 19th century.

In Piazza Flavio Gioia, tourism is in full swing at the cafés and souvenir shops overflowing with ceramics. Overlooking a monumental staircase, the Duomo, which has been remodeled several times, houses interesting Baroque features. Visit the treasures of the Diocesan Museum and the palm-shaded Paradiso cloister. To fully appreciate the square, leave the center and to go beyond the Duomo to the small alleys and squares, where the fountains and the vaulted passages have equal charm with fewer tourists. The charm of Amalfi is evident no matter what part of the city you're in.

> **P**
>
> To find a place to park in Amalfi, go to the enclosed parking lot Luna Rossa, between Amalfi and **Atrani.** This tiny fishing village, closed to cars, is worth a visit, too.

About 10 mi (16 km) away, a narrow and winding road leads to the hilltop village of **Ravello (6),** overlooking the Valley of the Dragon. Palm trees, umbrella pines, and lemon trees intertwine, illuminated by mauve and pink bougainvilleas, white jasmines, and crimson pelargoniums. You will not be the first to be seduced by Ravello! Wagner, Garbo, and Bogart have all settled here. Pay a visit to the Duomo and its museum, and don't forget the magnificent terraced gardens of Villa Rufolo, the source of inspiration for Richard Wagner's *Parsifal.* A little farther on, the romantic Villa Cimbrone (where a suite is named after its frequent guest, Greta Garbo) leans against the mountain. Opposite, the old villages of Scala and Pontone stretch out on the hill.

> **P**
>
> Good to know: The center of Ravello is closed to traffic, but parking is reasonably priced for the area. Avoid parking in Pontone; the village is a dead end.

The road continues to twist and turn toward Maiori, from where the majolica dome of the church rises. It then descends toward the quiet port of **Minori (7),** the last haven of peace before the industrial port of Salerno. Here, you'll find three districts: the commercial port and its quays, the *lungomare* waterfront, and finally the winding web of alleys in the historic center, difficult to reach by car. Stop for a *passeggiata* (stroll) in the evening, visit the 11th-century Duomo, or imagine the Crusades at the Castello di Arechi.

The route ends almost 2 mi (3 km) to the west, on the heights of **Vietri sul Mare (8),** a friendly and colorful village. Vietri sul Mare is renowned for its ceramics; peruse the town's many ceramics shops to bring home a souvenir to help you commemorate this trip of a lifetime.

Ravello

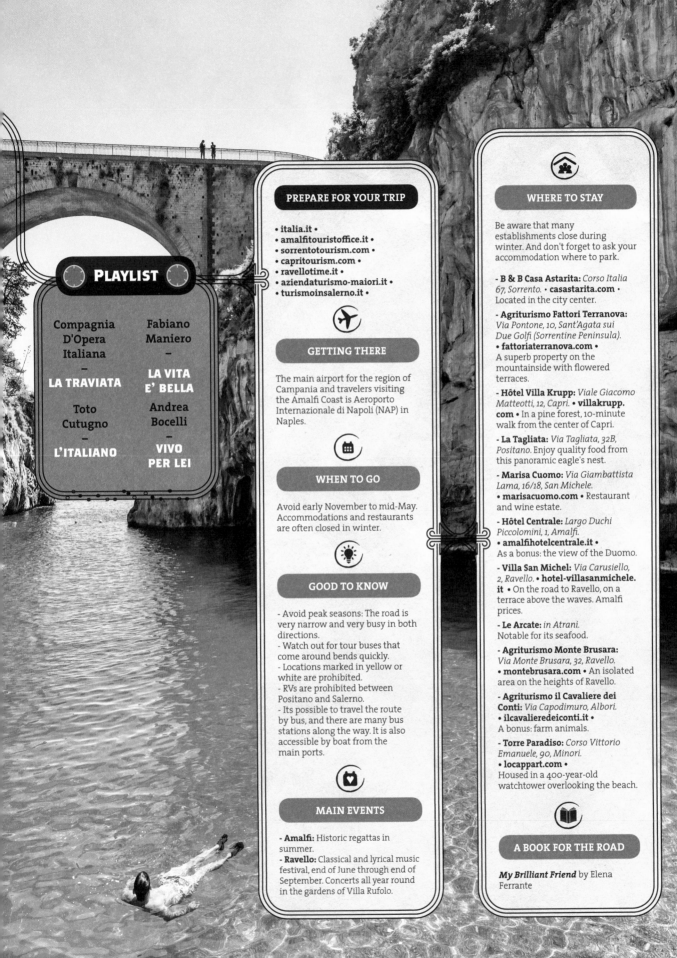

PLAYLIST

Compagnia D'Opera Italiana
–
LA TRAVIATA

Fabiano Maniero
–
LA VITA E' BELLA

Toto Cutugno
–
L'ITALIANO

Andrea Bocelli
–
VIVO PER LEI

PREPARE FOR YOUR TRIP

• italia.it •
• amalfitouristoffice.it •
• sorrentotourism.com •
• capritourism.com •
• ravellotime.it •
• aziendaturismo-maiori.it •
• turismoinsalerno.it •

GETTING THERE

The main airport for the region of Campania and travelers visiting the Amalfi Coast is Aeroporto Internazionale di Napoli (NAP) in Naples.

WHEN TO GO

Avoid early November to mid-May. Accommodations and restaurants are often closed in winter.

GOOD TO KNOW

- Avoid peak seasons: The road is very narrow and very busy in both directions.
- Watch out for tour buses that come around bends quickly.
- Locations marked in yellow or white are prohibited.
- RVs are prohibited between Positano and Salerno.
- Its possible to travel the route by bus, and there are many bus stations along the way. It is also accessible by boat from the main ports.

MAIN EVENTS

- **Amalfi:** Historic regattas in summer.
- **Ravello:** Classical and lyrical music festival, end of June through end of September. Concerts all year round in the gardens of Villa Rufolo.

WHERE TO STAY

Be aware that many establishments close during winter. And don't forget to ask your accommodation where to park.

- **B & B Casa Astarita:** *Corso Italia 67, Sorrento.* • **casastarita.com** • Located in the city center.

- **Agriturismo Fattori Terranova:** *Via Pontone, 10, Sant'Agata sui Due Golfi (Sorrentine Peninsula).* • **fattoriaterranova.com** • A superb property on the mountainside with flowered terraces.

- **Hôtel Villa Krupp:** *Viale Giacomo Matteotti, 12, Capri.* • **villakrupp. com** • In a pine forest, 10-minute walk from the center of Capri.

- **La Tagliata:** *Via Tagliata, 32B, Positano.* Enjoy quality food from this panoramic eagle's nest.

- **Marisa Cuomo:** *Via Giambattista Lama, 16/18, San Michele.* • **marisacuomo.com** • Restaurant and wine estate.

- **Hôtel Centrale:** *Largo Duchi Piccolomini, 1, Amalfi.* • **amalfihotelcentrale.it** • As a bonus: the view of the Duomo.

- **Villa San Michel:** *Via Carusiello, 2, Ravello.* • **hotel-villasanmichele. it** • On the road to Ravello, on a terrace above the waves. Amalfi prices.

- **Le Arcate:** *in Atrani.* Notable for its seafood.

- **Agriturismo Monte Brusara:** *Via Monte Brusara, 32, Ravello.* • **montebrusara.com** • An isolated area on the heights of Ravello.

- **Agriturismo il Cavaliere dei Conti:** *Via Capodimuro, Albori.* • **ilcavalieredeiconti.it** • A bonus: farm animals.

- **Torre Paradiso:** *Corso Vittorio Emanuele, 90, Minori.* • **locappart.com** • Housed in a 400-year-old watchtower overlooking the beach.

A BOOK FOR THE ROAD

My Brilliant Friend by Elena Ferrante

OTHER ROAD TRIPS IN ITALY

★1 ★2

★3

LAKE COMO TOUR

At the foot of the Alps, Lake Como is one of the largest Italian lakes, 87 mi (140 km) in circumference, accessible along winding roads. Seen from the sky, the lake forms an upside-down Y, with a large city at each of its branches: Colico to the north, Lecco to the east, and Como to the west. Its peaceful shores have long been a holiday destination.

Since ancient times, sumptuous villas have sprung up on these coasts: Villa d'Este, Villa Melzi d'Eril, and Villa Carlotta, which especially deserves a visit. It is the work of the Marquis Giorgio Clerici, who erected the majestic building in front of the village of Bellagio. Its park stands out for its impressive collection of botanical species: camellias, sequoias, cedars, and plane trees.

Do not miss a trip to the Sacro Monte di Ossuccio, at an altitude of 1,375 ft (419 m) on the west shore of the lake. Its 15 chapels were erected between 1635 and 1710, facing Isola Comacina, the only piece of land in the middle of the lake. They belong to the group of Sacri Monti of Piedmont and Lombardy, listed as a World Heritage Site by UNESCO. These 15th- and 16th-century chapels were created to be places of prayer in Europe as an alternative to holy places like Jerusalem.

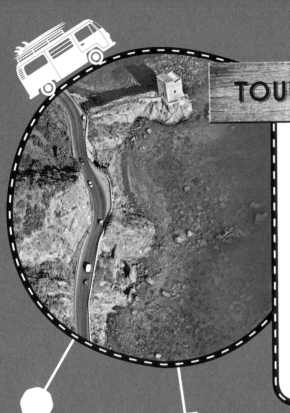

TOUR OF SICILY

Seen from above, Sicily, the largest island in the Mediterranean Sea, looks like a triangle at the foot of the Italian boot. Each side has its own road, exceptional landscapes, and unique histories, evident in archaeological remains from Greek and Roman antiquity. On the east coast, the S114 links Medina to Syracuse. It runs along Etna, the largest active volcano in Europe, and serves Taormina, a village perched on a cliff.

To the west, the S115, from Syracuse to Trapani via Marsala, crosses rural countryside. On the coast, it passes through Agrigento and its Valley of the Temples archaeological park, where temples, agoras, necropolises, and underground aqueducts cover over 3,200 acres. The S113, from Trapani to Medina through Palermo, runs along the north coast and below a mountainous area. Several places along here are worth a stop, such as the village of Cefalù and the Greco-Roman archaeological site of Tindari.

Described as "the most beautiful natural architecture in the world" by Le Corbusier, the Dolomites stretch out in the north of the Italian Alps. This large mountain range with steep cliffs is made up of pale rocks that turn red during sunset. Although impressive, this jagged massif is relatively young: "only" 70 million years old. Listed as a World Heritage Site, the Dolomites continue to fascinate painters, geologists, mountaineers, and cyclists.

From Bolzano to Cortina d'Ampezzo, the great road of the Dolomites runs for almost 68 mi (110 km) through breathtaking landscapes. Allow about a day for the journey by car, taking the time to stop for photos. Bolzano, steeped in both Italian and Austrian culture, features the Museo Archeologico dell'Alto Adige, built in order to present Ötzi "the iceman," the naturally mummified body of a man from around 3300 BC, discovered by chance in 1991.

The great road of the Dolomites runs through a series of passes and valleys, connecting several exceptional sites. Lake Carezza in particular is an emerald-green jewel with crystal clear waters, in the middle of woods and rocks. The star of the show is the Tre Cime di Lavaredo, at 9,839 ft (2,999 m) high, three sharp mountain peaks pointed toward the sky.

GREAT ROUTE OF THE DOLOMITES

LOCATION

Vestlandet, southwestern Norway

ROUTE

Stavanger – Åndalsnes

LENGTH

About 600 mi (970 km)

TIME

Allow 15 days minimum. The mountain roads, the fjords to cross, and the reduced speed limits make the trip longer.

YOU'LL LOVE

The wild grandeur of the fjords, the iconic landscapes of Norway, the many hikes.

END
MI 600
E39

10 ÅNDALSNES
E136

ÅLESUND
11

63
9
Geirangerfjord GEIRANGER
DALSNIBBA
15

Breheimen
LOM 8
55
Jotunheimen
7
LUSTER
Lustrafjorden
6 SOGNDALSFJØRA
E16
Sognefjorden LÆRDAL 5
Nærøyfjord
AURLAND
4
13

EIDFJORD 3
BERGEN
7
Sørfjorden
13
Hardangervidda
TROLLTUNGA National Park
2 ODDA
Folgefonna SKARE

13

START
MI 0

Lysefjord
KJERAGBOLTEN
STAVANGER
1 PREIKESTOLEN

THE ROUTE OF FJORDS

FROM STAVANGER ➤➤➤ TO ÅNDALSNES

Vestlandet ("the west of the country") is probably the most touristy region in Norway, and for good reason. Its famous fjords (including the Geirangerfjord and the Nærøyfjord, both listed as UNESCO World Heritage Sites) and its mountains dominated by glaciers (including the largest in Europe, the Jostedalsbreen) offer landscapes of unparalleled majesty. As you make your way through this trip, you will understand why these lands are so magical.

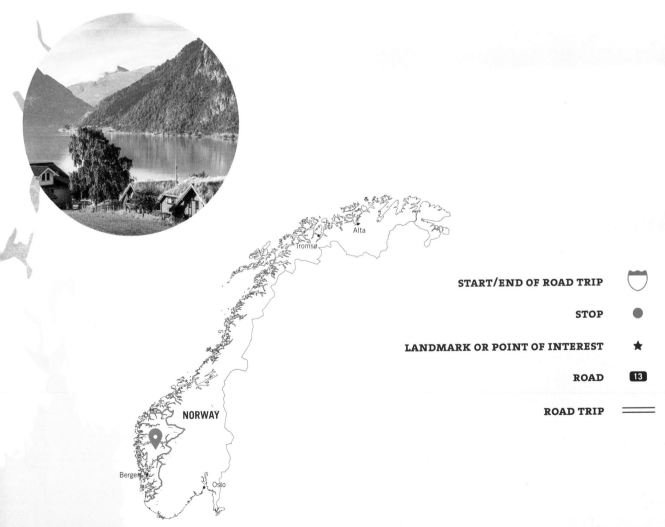

START/END OF ROAD TRIP	⛊
STOP	●
LANDMARK OR POINT OF INTEREST	★
ROAD	13
ROAD TRIP	═══

600 MI

THE WONDERS OF LYSEFJORD

Your journey through Western Norway begins in **Stavanger (1),** a city that is easily explored on foot. Stavanger is notable for its mix of styles, the variety of its museums, and its casual atmosphere. It is also the access point to the superb **Lysefjord,** where hikers will love climbing to the **Preikestolen;** the more daring might even attempt the **Kjeragbolten.**

The Preikestolen is an astonishing cliff cut in the rock that overlooks the green waters of the Lysefjord. At 1,982 ft (604 m), it's almost twice the height of the Eiffel Tower. What a view! It is certainly one of Norway's most impressive natural phenomena, all the more spectacular as you have to climb a bit to see it. Frightened, amazed, dizzy, perched on shaky legs between sky and sea, you will be overwhelmed by this magnificent natural creation. Be careful, as there is no guardrail or barrier up there. To see what's going on below, do like everyone else does: Get on all fours and carefully crawl to the edge. Take a look, and then crawl the same way, but backward. Phew!

To get there, you have to take the ferry to Tau from the port of Stavanger (crossing every 30 minutes; approximately a 40-minute trip). From Tau, take Road 13 toward Jørpeland, and then take the small, well-signed road on the left for about 4 mi (6 km). There is paid parking at the starting point of the walk.

Kjeragbolten
Kjeragbolten is best described as a large rock that is stuck, as if by magic, between two cliffs on the south shore of the Lysefjord. Be prepared for an adrenaline rush if you decide to pose for photos there—and the amazement of friends who see them.

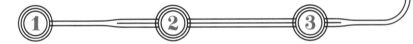

BETWEEN FJORDS AND MOUNTAINS

After following Road 13 for about 110 mi (175 km) from Stavanger, you will reach **Odda (2),** which is, at first glance, an industrial city in decline; it can feel especially dreary in the evening. But on closer inspection, you will discover the superb natural surroundings. Odda is the starting point for an exploration of two national parks: the **Hardangervidda** plateau (whose imposing snowcapped peaks reach over 3,930 ft/1,200 m and form a somewhat menacing backdrop) and the Folgefonna glacier. You'll also see the spectacular **Trolltunga,** ("the tongue of the troll"), a well-known rocky outcrop makes for an amazing photo. The region rises 3,609 ft (1,100 m) above sea level and looks out on to the beautiful Lake Ringedal. Skip it if you are afraid of heights!

The road that leads from Odda to **Eidfjord (3)** runs alongside the **Sørfjord** and winds along the ragged coast. Delightful Eidfjord village, nestled on the edge of the fjord, isn't extraordinary, but as it is located on the crossroads between the east and west of the country, it's worth an obligatory stop. There is an interesting little 11th-century church, which resembles that of Kinsarvik, but it is unfortunately closed to the public to protect its fragile floor.

*Nine miles (15 km) between **Skåre** and Odda, on Road 13, don't miss the Låtefossen, two impressive waterfalls on the right side of the roadside, which flow in raging torrents. Almost 2 mi (3 km) farther on, you'll find another beautiful fall on the left. Windshield wipers required!*

Preikestolen

FROM AURLAND TO LOM: ON THE SOGNEFJORD ROAD

The Sognefjord is the deepest fjord in the country at 4,291 ft (1,308 m), the longest in Europe at 127 mi (204 km) long, and the second longest in the world (after Scoresby in Greenland). It cuts Norway from west to east along more than half the width of the country, to the foothills of the Jotunheimen and Breheimen massifs. The latter is covered by Jostedalsbreen, the largest glacier in Europe. The fjord runs alongside high peaks, the highest of which reaches 7,890 ft (2,405 m). You'll see steep and sparsely populated banks, impressive waterfalls, and small fjord branches like the **Nærøyfjord.** The mood of the scenery changes with every variation in the light: mysterious when the cloudy ceiling is low, colorful and festive when the orchards bloom under the sparkling spring sun.

The scenic Aurlandsfjellet road, which connects **Aurland (4)** to **Lærdal (5),** is particularly beautiful. This road is usually only open from around June to mid-October (depending on the weather), but the first almost 4 mi (6 km) to the Stegastein viewpoint are generally accessible all year

round. Then, over some 25 mi (40 km), at the start of the season you will discover a moving landscape of snowdrifts and frozen lakes. In the heart of summer, the snow gives way to a landscape of stones and peaks, with spots of snow here and there.

But the most striking stretch of road is undoubtedly the one that connects **Sogndalsfjøra (6)** to Lom. Road 55, the Sognefjellet National Tourist Route, is simply sublime! You may think that the superlatives are an exaggeration, but just wait and see. . . . It becomes particularly beautiful from Gaupne, as it runs along the west bank of the **Lustrafjord.** As you travel through this corner, stop for a meal break at **Luster (7),** and once you're refreshed, set off to storm the Sognefjellet Pass, located at an altitude of 891 ft (1,434 m). The road then runs between two national parks: **Breheimen** (literally "the land of glaciers") and grandiose **Jotunheim,** highland plains with glaciers in the background. The route is punctuated by interesting architectural rest areas: Nedre Oscarshaug is a viewpoint like no other, the area of Liasanden is truly

original, and Mefjellet offers a unique setting for this magnificent landscape. Road 55 is only open from May to mid-September (depending on the weather).

When you finally arrive in **Lom (8),** you've reached the ideal base for exploring the Jotunheimen. Jotun means "giant". . . and it is! The name originated in the 19th century with the poet Aasmund Vinje Olavsson, who was overwhelmed by the grandeur of the landscape and its wild beauty. In addition to marking the transition between the east and the west of the country, the Jotunheimen holds many records: It is the largest national park in the country (442 sq mi/1,145 sq km) and is home to 255 of its 300 peaks. Among those are the 20 highest in Norway, led by the Galdhøpiggen, which rises to 8,100 ft (2,469 m), closely followed by the Glittertind and its ice cap at 8,090 ft (2,466 m). Add to that a few glaciers, lakes, varied flora, and you will have an idea of the majesty of this region. From here, allow 2 to 3 hours to reach Geiranger by following Road 15, and then 63.

Sognefjord

GEIRANGER: A NORWEGIAN POSTCARD

As you arrive from the south, the spectacle is dazzling. A dizzying descent through a series of incredible twists and turns takes you from 3,280 ft (1,000 m) of altitude to sea level. (Be aware that this road is sometimes closed until mid-May due to avalanches. Make sure to research before you go.) Look out over one of Norway's most iconic panoramas, the Geirangermotiv. Below, the small, touristy village of **Geiranger (9)** is surrounded by grandiose mountains and borders the narrow fjord, which is classified as a UNESCO World Heritage Site.

Do not hesitate to climb to the mountain next to Geiranger, **Dalsnibba,** which is at an altitude of 4,842 ft (1,476 m). The panorama is magnificent, especially in the early evening.

LOVE AT FIRST SIGHT

CRUISE ON THE GEIRANGERFJORD
This fjord, one of the narrowest and most impressive in Norway (68 mi/110 km to the ocean), is dominated by an enormous rock face from which magnificent waterfalls rush down, such as the Seven Sisters and the Bridal Veil. A boat tour on the Geirangerfjord is an unforgettable experience—it's a setting worthy of the gods. The seagulls following your boat are not shy: If you stretch out your arm with bread at your fingertips, they sometimes come and grab it. In summer, if you have a car, arrive well in advance and be patient.

Geirangerfjord

THE ROUTE OF THE TROLLS

Head toward **Åndalsnes (10),** via the famous Trollstigen, also called the Trolls' Ladder, a road that combines its 11 loops with a 10-12 percent slope that winds fearlessly along the mountainside. (The road is closed approximately from November to the end of May.) Note that if you're driving an RV, it's better to take drive the road going up (north-south) rather than going down. On the way, you'll pass Stigfossen, a superb 590-ft (180-m) waterfall that tumbles down toward the valley. Be sure to stop at viewpoints along the way. At the top, at 2,795 ft (852 m), the Stigrøra plateau allows you to park and admire the entire valley from the viewing platforms. From the platform at the end, the view is simply breathtaking. You will also find a visitor center with exhibits, a gift shop, and a cafeteria. This is a popular meeting place for hikers and lovers of extreme sports like BASE jumping and climbing the Trollveggen, the highest vertical wall in Europe at 3,609 ft (1,100 m).

From there, walk 5 minutes along the path to admire the distant series of peaks that rise toward the sky, and the falls that can be seen from the top. From the trail, the view over the valley and the famous switchbacks is wonderful.

A few hundred miles later, you'll arrive in the cheerful city of **Ålesund (11),** a perfect end to your trip.

PLAYLIST

John Olav Nilsen & Nordsjøen	Sigrid	Ane Monsrud	Pom Poko
–	–	–	–
PARIS, BERGEN	**STRANGERS**	**CONFESS**	**IT'S A TRAP**

PREPARE FOR YOUR TRIP

• **visitnorway.com** •
The official Norwegian tourism website. Lots of essential information for all areas, and the free app for iPhone and Android is especially useful.
• **rutebok.no** • All timetables of transportation in Norway. Very useful for planning your itinerary. Available in English and German versions.

GETTING THERE

Almost all international visitors to Norway will arrive at the modern Oslo Airport Gardermoen (OSL), which is also the main domestic hub for connections to all parts of the country. Stavanger Airport (SVG) is right at the start of the route.

DRIVING TIPS

A word of advice: When planning your route according to your schedule, make two itineraries: one for an optimist, and one for a pessimist. Though distances might not seem huge on the map, speeds are limited at the level of the fjords and the roads are narrow and winding, so driving will take longer than you think. Trucks, camper vans, and RVs can cause slowdowns. And don't forget about wait times for ferries—and the extra time you'll want to take for exploring.

WHEN TO GO

The tourist season runs from mid-June to mid-August. During the off season, expect reduced transport and closed sites and accommodations, including some youth hostels and most campsites. That said, in the blazing fall and winter, when the northern lights illuminate the polar sky, the journey takes on another dimension.

A BOOK FOR THE ROAD

The Redbreast by Jo Nesbø

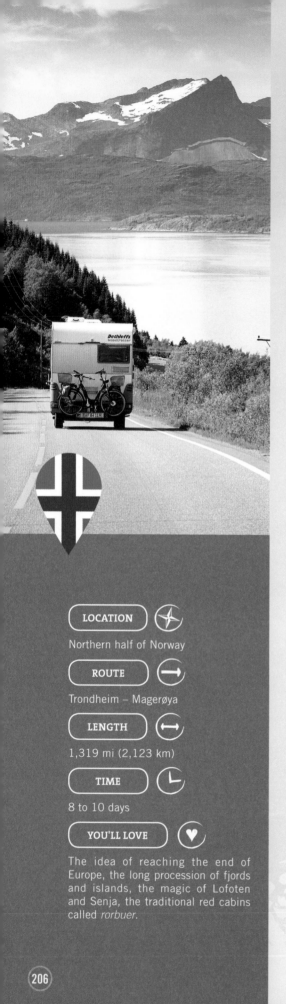

LOCATION

Northern half of Norway

ROUTE

Trondheim – Magerøya

LENGTH

1,319 mi (2,123 km)

TIME

8 to 10 days

YOU'LL LOVE

The idea of reaching the end of Europe, the long procession of fjords and islands, the magic of Lofoten and Senja, the traditional red cabins called *rorbuer*.

6 TROMSØ

SENJA ★

E8

E6

E10

5 LOFOTEN ARCHIPELAGO

STAMSUND

MOSKENES ★   ★ VESTFJORD

BODØ

SALTSTRAUMEN

4

JEKTVIK ★   SVARTISVATNET

SVARTISEN 3

VEGA ARCHIPELAGO ★

TORGHATTEN 2

E6

★ STEINKJÆR

1 ●
TRONDHEIM   **START**
MI 0

8 NORTH CAPE
GJESVÆR ★
SKARSVÅG
MAGERØYA

END
MI 1,319

7

HAMMERFEST

HEADING NORTH

FROM TRONDHEIM ➤⟶ TO MAGERØYA

Tapered like a majorette's baton, the northernmost point of Norway has a cape where Europe ends in a fury of cliffs, strong winds, and stubborn mists spreading over the midnight sun. Along the way, a plethora of mountains, fjords, islands, and islets invite you to wander along the most jagged coastline in the world. The country has over 13,264 mi (21,347 km) of coastline. The south-to-north distance is 1,087 mi (1,750 km), while east to west at the narrowest point is just over 3 mi (6 km).

Alta

Tromsø

NORWAY

Bergen

Oslo

START/END OF ROAD TRIP	
STOP	●
LANDMARK OR POINT OF INTEREST	★
ROAD	E6
ROAD TRIP	——
FERRY	= = = = =

TRONDHEIM, THE FIRST CAPITAL

It was not in Oslo, but in the north that the first capital of Norway was founded: **Trondheim (1),** a merchant and maritime city, anchored at the convergence of the fjords and plains. In the year 1000, King Olaf Tryggvason, a convert to Christianity, founded the city and imposed his new faith on the country. Pagan idols were destroyed, and pagan priests were executed. His successor, Olaf II, made Trondheim the political and ecclesiastical capital of the country. One of the highlights of the city is its stone cathedral, in the Romanesque and Gothic styles, rising toward the heavens, with statues of saints on the facade. Today, Trondheim is no more than a large provincial town, but it remains the spiritual heart of the nation for all Norwegians and the place where its kings are still crowned. Near the mouth of the Nidelva River, tall wooden warehouses on stilts recall the past importance of trade, which remained for four centuries under the control of the merchants of the Hanseatic League.

THE KYSTRIKSVEIEN

Different from other Scandinavian countries leveled by glacial erosion, Norway is two-thirds occupied by mountains, which appear on the horizon as you leave Trondheim via the E6 road. After 77 mi (124 km), in **Steinkjær,** turn off onto Road 17, the Kystriksveien or "national coastal road": a wild, 391-mi (630-km) route along the folds of the Norwegian coast, interspersed with six ferry crossings. It is a grandiose setting of fjords with secret folds, mountains planted in the water, peat bogs frequented by elks at dawn and sunset, and fields dotted with small haystacks. Isolated farms throughout the area recall the tenacity of the Vikings and their descendants, who lived economically independent for centuries. Making nature their gospel, they imagined a country populated by elves and trolls. Thus at the granite coastal massif **Torghatten (2),** the natural tunnel at its center is said to have been pierced by the arrow of a troll.

As you head north, the number of islands increases. There are thousands of them along the Kystriksveien, a few inhabited, most of them deserted or occupied by a few lonely huts. In the **Vega Archipelago,** there are 6,500 islands and islets! On the port side, a different world emerges in the face of the cold Atlantic waves. The forest gives way to the winds and ocean spray, where ports are moored, lining up a few trawlers and *rorbuer* (huts) of iconic red. On the cliffs, kittiwakes, murres, and puffins pile up in groups. On the ground nest eider ducks, whose soft down was once harvested by the Vikings. These lands have been largely unchanged for 1,500 years, which has earned the archipelago recognition as a World Heritage Site by UNESCO.

(3) (4)

THE ARCTIC CIRCLE

From Kilboghamn, the fifth ferry of the Kystriksveien sets sail toward **Jektvik:** to the starboard side stretches a mythical line, beyond which, after the summer solstice, the sun stops setting. The sun just looks like an orange disc bouncing on the horizon, before spreading a strange golden light in normally dark hours. For a few weeks, the rhythm of the days change: Grass is cut for cattle at midnight, people bathe at 3am, and go fishing at 4am. Summer is too short not to take advantage of these long days.

Your journey resumes in dimly lit single-lane tunnels that plunge in and out of the mountains. **Svartisen (3)** (translated as "black ice"),

initially hidden from view by the rocky fences, can be seen past Halsa. Its two twin glaciers, nestled around Snøtinden, form Norway's second largest ice cap (143 sq mi/370 sq km). Just across the inlet, guarded by a tribe of white peaks, **Lake Svartisvatnet** collects the meltwater from the Engabreen glacial tongue—which recedes every year, uncovering fragments of black rock. About 90 minutes later, as you approach the town of **Bodø,** Road 17 grazes a strange phenomenon: the **Saltstraumen (4).** In this strait, just at the foot of the road bridge, one of the most powerful tidal currents in the world forms. Its whirlpool effect may well have given rise to the maelstrom of Norse legends.

TO THE LOFOTEN ISLANDS

Port of Bodø, 9pm. The screeching of the seagulls and the last farewells of the passengers on the platforms signal your departure. After a 2-hour break, the *MF Landegode* resumes its back-and-forth trips to the famous **Lofoten archipelago (5),** under a stormy sky filtering rays of sun. The light is soft, golden, almost warm. Plunged in darkness, the enormous **Vestfjord,** separating the mainland from the archipelago, is ominous, swept by strong westerly winds. The hull echoes at times with the dull sound of breaking waves. Three and a half hours later, the ferry finally docks at **Stamsund,** at 68° 08' north latitude. In the inertia of the white night, an entire fleet of fishing boats emerges. At the dock, the gusts diffuse and then dissipate into a powerful smell of fish.

Jagged peaks seem to float on the sea, encircling the harbor of Stamsund and its islets. One hour to the south, the island of **Moskenes,** accessible by an underwater tunnel, looks like a picture from a postcard. Here stand the highest mountains, as if emerging from the ocean, and the most beautiful villages (Reine and Å) with their *rorbuer* (fishermen's huts) of red wood clinging to the bare rocks. In the spring, you'll see cod laid out to dry on racks. From the coastal road, a steep path interspersed with stones and ropes climbs up the rear flank of Mount Reinebringen, leading to an unmissable overlook: 1,476 ft (450 m) below, a puzzle of the islets and peninsulas and the village nestled in its mini fjord, seemingly at the mercy of the cascades of cliffs that surround it. Farther on, toward Utakleiv Unnstad, the winding roads lead through tunnels to green pastures and inlets carpeted with white-sand beaches and turquoise waters. In the evening, the sun is still shining, orange, stubbornly refusing to set.

DETOUR TO THE ISLAND OF SENJA

The largest island in Norway (612 sq mi/985 sq km), Senja is sparsely populated (with just 7,800 inhabitants) and often unfairly overlooked. You get there via road, leaving the E6 at Anselv, and crossing a large bridge over the Strait of Gisundet. Bypassing immense peninsulas and grandiose fjords dotted with wooden houses, a small road ventures to the village of Mefjordvær, soaked by the spray of the North Atlantic. A tunnel farther on stands out on a green valley grazed by sheep, and a dreamy beach, Ersfjorden. The water temperature in summer is 46°F (8°C). At the edge of the fjord, a palisade of sharp peaks reaching more than 1,640 ft (500 m) covers a mirrored sea, flooded with golden reflections at midnight.

HVALBIFF, ANYONE?

Whale-watching is offered in the Vesterålen Islands (north of Lofoten), departing from Andenes and Stø. In this country, whale hunting has been practiced again since 1993, despite international outcry against it. In all of northern Norway, *hvalbiff* steak is on restaurants' summer menus. It seems archaic, placing the country in conflict with ecology. In 2017, Norway again adopted the largest fishing quota in the world: 999 fin whales, more than Iceland and Japan combined (the only other two whaling nations). Most of the meat is not sold locally; it is exported to Japan.

Lofoten archipelago

FROM TROMSØ TO FINNMARK

Tromsø (6) is the largest city in northern Norway (70,500 inhabitants), located on its own island, 45 mi (73 km) from the winding course of the E6. Tromsø owes its growth to the arctic expeditions in the late 19th century. Remains from this heyday include the old wooden houses of Storgata, a large university, a museum devoted to Roald Amundsen (the first person to reach the South Pole) and other polar explorers, the Polaria museum/aquarium, and two cathedrals (Catholic and Protestant).

As soon as the warm weather returns, the E6 is filled with vehicles from all over Europe, making their slow climb to the North Cape. In the fjords, watched over by snow-capped peaks, increasingly scattered farms affirm the human determination to make this hostile land fruitful. The forest gives way to an onslaught of cold and wind. Low clouds and squadrons of mosquitoes fly over the bogs, which are covered with the fluffy white pompoms of cottongrass. The tundra is not far away—and with it, the first reindeer. There can be no doubt about it: You have reached Lapland. In spring, the reindeer herds, herded by the Sámi people who are indigenous to this part of the county, begin long migrations from the central plateaus to the coast. Some herders even take their reindeer on the open sea to graze on the soft grass of the islands, before returning in the fall.

DETOUR THROUGH HAMMERFEST

Reached by bridge, Hammerfest, located on the island of Kvaløya at 70° 39', 48", has proclaimed itself "the northernmost city on the globe." The claim is debatable, but the town is still home to the Royal Polar Bear Society. Not that you'll see a lot of them in these areas: the closest polar bears live in Spitsbergen, an hour away by plane. Polar bear hunters used to leave from here on expeditions in the Arctic. The polar bear even adorns the city's coat of arms.

MAGERØYA, THE NORTH CAPE ISLAND

Rocks, snowfields, cloudy slopes, reindeer wandering on the barren earth: You are approaching **Magerøya (7)**. Detached from the European continent, the island of the North Cape is now reached by an underwater tunnel. Past the utilitarian village of Honningsvåg, its capital, **Skarsvåg,** "the most northerly fishing village in the world," brings together over 50 houses, a school, and a Santa Claus shop. You're getting closer to the pole. An often-overlooked detour leads to the adorable **Gjesvær,** whose red houses on stilts nestle in a bay along the Arctic Ocean beneath a messy sky, streaked with gulls and puffins. To the far north, the **North Cape (8)** (71° 10', 21") on the mainland emerges. The "real" North Cape at Knivskjellodden, extending even farther at 71° 11', 48", can only be reached on foot, after a beautiful almost 6-mi (9-km) hike.

THE NORTH CAPE BY THE COASTAL EXPRESS

Hurtigruten ships have tirelessly sailed along the country's coasts for more than 125 years. The weekly service initially only included nine stops between Trondheim and Hammerfest. But the ports have now entered a new era—now that the cold winter is no longer synonymous with paralysis. Today, the Hurtigruten ships serve no less than 34 ports, large and small, with a daily passage on board one of their 12 vessels in all seasons.

PLAYLIST

A-Ha –	Kings Of Convenience –
TAKE ON ME	**MISREAD**
Madcon	Mari Boine
BEGGIN	**REINDEER OF DIAMOND**

PREPARE FOR YOUR TRIP

- visitnorway.com •
- nordnorge.com •
- lofoten.info •

GETTING THERE

Your trip will likely start in Oslo Airport Gardermoen (OSL) with a connecting flight to Trondheim Airport (TRD). You can also reach some of the major airports farther north (Bodø, Tromsø, and Alta) via Oslo. The small airports of Hammerfest and Honningsvåg (on the North Cape Island) are served by the local company Wideroe.

RENTING A CAR

It is possible to rent a car in Norway, but the prices are high, especially the drop-off costs if you plan to take your vehicle from the south of the country and leave it in one of the northern cities. Some rental companies (like Hertz) are found at Hammerfest, others are not.

WHEN TO GO

From June to mid-August (50-68°F/ 10-20°C during the day).

WHERE TO STAY

To minimize costs, go for a campsite (often open from June to mid-August only), which also frequently offer wooden cabins called *hitter*. Some are very basic, while others look like small cabins, just like the *rorbuer* of the fishermen of Lofoten. Otherwise, there are quite a few hostels in Norway. In the North, there are eight: in Bodø, Lofoten, Finnsnes, and Finnmark. If you opt for a hotel, the price climbs very quickly. There are also many option—often in interesting homes—with Airbnb.

- camping.no •
- hostels.no •

WHAT TO EAT

Norwegians are not known for the excellent gastronomy. A good option is *lunsj* (lunch) cafés, for their small dishes and *smørbrød* (sandwiches), as well as bakeries, supermarkets, and ports for fresh shrimp and smoked salmon. Pizzas, burgers, kebabs, and hot dogs can be found everywhere. Make sure to taste *gravlaks*, marinated salmon.

A BOOK FOR THE ROAD

The Bridal Wreath by Sigrid Undset

AFRICA

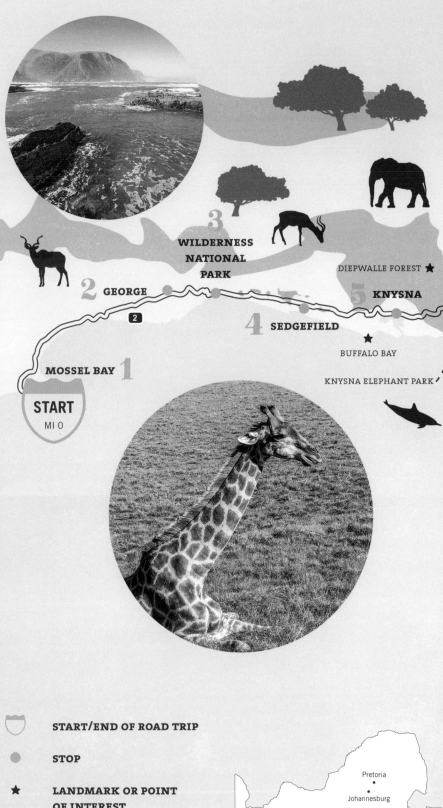

3

WILDERNESS NATIONAL PARK

DIEPWALLE FOREST ★

2 **GEORGE**

2

KNYSNA

5

4 **SEDGEFIELD**

BUFFALO BAY ★

MOSSEL BAY 1

START
MI 0

KNYSNA ELEPHANT PARK

LOCATION

South Africa's Western Cape region

ROUTE

Mossel Bay – Jeffreys Bay

LENGTH

190 mi (300 km)
470 mi (750 km) for the longer route from Cape Town to Port Elizabeth/ Gqeberha

TIME

2 to 3 days without stopping; allow more time to stop for frequent swims.

YOU'LL LOVE

Wild forests populated with rare species, monkeys and gazelles frolicking in fynbos scrubland, the chance to see whales and dolphins, immense deserted beaches, oyster-tasting in Knysna.

⬡ **START/END OF ROAD TRIP**

● **STOP**

★ **LANDMARK OR POINT OF INTEREST**

2 **ROAD**

═══ **ROAD TRIP**

Pretoria
•
Johannesburg
•

Bloemfontein
•

SOUTH AFRICA

Port
Elizabeth/
Gqeberha
Cape Town

NATURE'S VALLEY

7

STORMS RIVER

9

★ TSITSIKAMMA NATIONAL PARK

2

BLOUKRANS BRIDGE

8

PLETTENBERG BAY

6

END
MI 190

JEFFREYS BAY

10

THE
GARDEN ROUTE
FROM MOSSEL BAY ➤➤➤ TO JEFFREYS BAY

Nature lovers will not be disappointed on the Garden Route, which runs along the coast of the Western Cape region, where the Indian Ocean and the Atlantic Ocean meet. Considered one of the most beautiful scenic routes in the world, it crosses through part of Tsitsikamma National Park and many other reserves, as well as endless native forests, vast beaches, creeks, lagoons, and peaceful lakes. These varied landscapes are populated by elephants, gazelles, and monkeys, while in the ocean, you can observe sea lions, dolphins, and whales in season. The temperate climate makes this coastline a permanent deep blue.

MOSSEL BAY AND GEORGE

The Garden Route is a bit of a misnomer; this untamed landscape is better suited to lovers of wild nature. Don't expect to see the magnificent private and public botanical gardens that are common on the nearby Cape Peninsula.

Start your trip east of the Cape of Good Hope by getting on the N2 at **Mossel Bay** (1). The city and its beaches owe their name to the mussels that once thrived here, long before the construction of offshore drilling stations and the real estate boom. The historic center is worth a visit. The Bartolomeu Dias Museum Complex documents the history of the European explorers who cast their anchors here: Portuguese navigator Bartolomeu Dias helmed the first European ship to round the Cape in 1488, followed by Vasco da Gama nine years later. Note the Post Office Tree, a milkwood tree that sailors used to exchange messages starting in the 16th century, leaving their mail in a shoe hung from the branches. Nowadays, a post box shaped like a shoe can be found under the tree. In the same complex, see a wide variety of shells at the Shell Museum and its aquarium before getting a table at one of the many restaurants around town, or having a picnic on Santos Beach. You may be able to spot whales and dolphins from the Cape St. Blaize Lighthouse. Between June and November, the extraordinary right whale comes here to give birth to its offspring.

If you're not in a hurry, stop in **George** (2), a town renowned for its golf and rugby competitions. The Garden Route Botanical Garden offers a small botanical summary of the surrounding environment, where cape reeds and wild daisies rub shoulders with forested areas, giving a taste of the nature you are going to observe on your drive.

THE WILD ROAD

The region around **Wilderness National Park (3),** between the Outeniqua Mountains and the Indian Ocean, is a nature lover's playground. Canoe or kayak up the Serpentine River, admiring the quick, colorful flight of the tiny kingfisher by your side, or take a walk along the 11 undeveloped miles (18 km) of Wilderness Beach.

The Saturday markets west of **Sedgefield (4)** are tempting with their fresh produce and local handicrafts, including Zulu beadwork.

Dunes and lakes populate this landscape alongside the Indian Ocean. Wooded scenery, beaches, and estuaries are home to remarkable birds, including the famous green, red-beaked Knysna turaco, or lourie, whose cry resembles a bark. One of the best places to hear it is the lagoon around **Knysna (5)** (pronounced "nai-zna"), framed by limestone cliffs. Learn about the history of this city at the Millwood House Museum; George Rex, reputed to be the illegitimate son of George III, made this city the base of his extensive network of farms at the begin-ning of the 19th century. Afterward, taste some oysters, a specialty of the city, and wash them down with an irresistible beer on the waterfront terrace of Mitchell's Brewery, a Knysna institution since the 1980s. Take a ride to chic Leisure Isle nearby, or drive 4 miles (7 km) up the Heads Cliffs, where you can get a view of the most dangerous maritime pass in the world, between the Knysna Lagoon and the ocean. Insurance no longer reimburses damage done to ships who try to ply this route.

Though most of the beaches in this area are similarly dangerous to swimmers because of strong currents, you can instead take a safe dip in **Buffalo Bay** (aka Buffelsbaai) or in freshwater Lake Groenvlei, where fishing is also allowed.

There are more beaches around the gigantic bay of seaside resort **Plettenberg Bay (6),** very popular with South Africans. Robberg Beach, the largest in the area, invites you with more than 2.5 mi (4 km) of surf and relaxation; you'll see a ballet of dolphins in summer and whales in winter. For children and adults alike, searching for the pansy shell, a member of the sea urchin family, is a fun activity. They're known as sand dollars in the United States, and you'll recognize them by the five-petaled, flower-like engraving on the flat shell.

HIKING

In Wilderness National Park (65,000 ac/26,000 ha):

- The *Half-Collared Kingfisher Trail* (3 hours round-trip), with a waterfall and chance of spotting rare bird species, including the Knysna turaco.

- The *Pied Kingfisher Trail* (3 hours round-trip) around the Serpentine River.

- The *Woodville Tree Circular Walk* (1 hour round-trip), an easy forest circuit to see the 800-year-old Yellow Wood Tree.

North of Knysna lies the **Diepwalle Forest,** one of South Africa's largest native forests, where you can learn how to spot the stinkwood, the Cape pear tree, the ironwood, and the white alder in the middle of proteas and calodendrums.

To the west, on the N2, the private **Knysna Elephant Park** is home to some baby elephants from Kruger National Park. You can approach them with a guide and even sleep at the park's lodge.

Tsitsikamma National Park

NATURAL WONDER

For even more natural wonder, travel along the Robberg Peninsula Coastal Trail to look for fur seals basking in the many coves.

The Garden Route becomes wild and the cliffs steep as you skirt the Groot River estuary and the remote village of **Nature's Valley (7),** worth a slight detour via the R102. On the N2, around Nature's Valley, the Jukani Wildlife Sanctuary cares for big cats including a blind white tiger. In Kurland village, walk through the gigantic Birds of Eden aviary, which houses 250 species of birds. Finally, Monkeyland provides sanctuary to monkeys formerly kept in cages or laboratories.

This far-flung sector, with a beach hidden by trees that invites you to relax, opens onto **Tsitsikamma National Park,** South Africa's third most visited reserve. On 45 mi (70 km) of coastline, the park is home to protected fynbos, a kind of primitive African shrubland where monkeys and antelopes frolic, as well as native forests where you can find stinkwood, yellowwood and white milkwood. Unfortunately, 19th-century forestry has also left its traces, and the current replanting of pines and eucalyptus is intended for paper pulp manufacturing.

Thrill seekers should stop at **Bloukrans Bridge (8),** reputed to be the highest bungee jump in Africa at 709 ft (216 m). Pass through the peaceful village of **Storms River (9)** and continue to the mouth of its eponymous river, the eastern edge of Tsitsikamma National Park and the Garden Route. Here, you can surf the Supertubes in **Jeffreys Bay (10),** some of the most powerful waves in the world.

The entrance to **Tsitsikamma National Park** is located halfway between its western and eastern limits. It's a narrow coastal strip 3 mi (5 km) wide and 45 mi (70 km) long, ending at the mouth of the Storms River, west of Port Elizabeth/Gqeberha. You can sleep in an oceanette or a self-equipped seaside chalet, as well as eat, camp, and—of course—hike. Most of the park is only accessible on foot. A top pick is the Waterfall Trail (4 mi/6 km round-trip), which travels along the sea to a waterfall.

PREPARE FOR YOUR TRIP

- southafrica.net •
- visitmosselbay.co.za •
- visitknysna.co.za •
- plettenbergbay.co.za •

GETTING THERE

Fly into Cape Town International Airport (CPT). From here, Mossel Bay is a 4.5-hour drive away.

WHEN TO GO

Avoid December and January, when South Africans are on Christmas and summer vacation—prices go up by 20 percent, and accommodations are often full. To avoid rains at the beginning and end of winter, the best time to go is September-October or April-May.

MAIN EVENTS

- Knysna Oyster Festival in July.
- LGBTQ Festival in early May.
- Rasta Festival at the end of July.

WHERE TO STAY

In Mossel Bay

- **3 Colors Blue Guest Houses:** • 3coloursblue.co.za • A stay to remember, with beautiful rooms with terraces and panoramic views of the bay.
- **Wilderness Beach House Backpackers Lodge:** • wildernessbeachhouse.com • A beautiful lodge with impeccable hospitality.

In Knysna

- **The Graywood Hotel:** A beautiful hotel with beautiful woodwork throughout the rooms and public spaces.
- **Stannards Guest Lodge:** • stannards.co.za • Very comfortable, stylish lodge set in a lush garden.

In Plettenberg Bay

- **Bitou River Lodge:** • bitou.co.za • This lodge is known for its large garden.
- **Nature's Valley Guest House:** • naturesvalleyguesthouse.co.za • A guest house surrounded by nature.

A BOOK FOR THE ROAD

Coconut by Kopano Matlwa

CAPE ROUTES IN SOUTH AFRICA

1 ★ ★ 2
★
3

①

CHAPMAN'S PEAK DRIVE

One hundred and fourteen turns over nearly 6 mi (10 km)—don't let that scare you! Even the sign at the start of this drive clearly states that drivers should undertake this road trip, located 12 mi (20 km) south of Cape Town, at their own risk. But for experienced drivers, driving what many call "the most beautiful in the world" is worth the risk. Fortunately, there are also rest areas where you can slow down.

Classified as a national monument, Chapman's Peak Drive was constructed between 1915-1922 in the hopes of developing tourism in the southern tip of the Cape Peninsula. It was a real feat of engineering at the time. A bronze leopard on the beach at **Hout Bay** serves as a reminder that these felines were present here not so long ago.

After visiting the Hout Bay fish market, you can try snoek from the seafood shacks that line the quayside. Served salted, smoked, or accompanied by a curry sauce, this firm-fleshed migratory fish is only caught in the vicinity of Cape Town. It is also possible to take a boat trip from the port to **Duiker Island** to observe its large colony of sea lions and migratory fur seals from Antarctica.

Located south of Hout Bay Beach, the entrance to Chapman's Peak Drive has a toll (47 R). The granite and sandstone cliffs of Chapman Peak (1,942 ft/592 m) overlook the road and the ocean.

The road descends toward **Noordhoek,** a coastal suburb on a huge, deserted beach. This is the setting for the two biggest marathons in South Africa. Note: Chapman's Peak Drive is often closed due to scree; inquire before undertaking the drive.

CAPE OF GOOD HOPE ROAD

Why not extend your route south to Cape Point or Cape of Good Hope? Though this is not Africa's southernmost point (that honor belongs to Cape Agulhas, located 120 mi/200 km east of Cape Point), you'll feel like you're at the end of the world. Pass by **Scarborough,** a small village nestled between two hills that's a paradise for surfers, fishermen, and canoers. The mythical Cape of Good Hope, a popular tourist attraction, is located below a nature reserve. From the lighthouse, the view is incomparable; you can either drive there, or go on foot on paths through the fynbos (a sort of Mediterranean bushy scrub, typical of South Africa). Baboons and ostriches parade in the bushes and the dunes, to the delight of photographers.

THE CAPE WINE ROUTE

A few kilometers from Cape Town, the Cape Wine Route is one of the country's major tourist attractions. The tastings are frequently crowded, but the welcome is always warm, and the botanical gardens of these magnificent estates can often be visited in complete privacy against a backdrop of romantic, mountainous landscapes.

Elegant **Stellenbosch,** the historic capital of the Cape wine region, is full of colonial Dutch architecture. Cape Dutch is known for its thatched roofs and impeccable white-limed facades. Its rectilinear streets are lined by oaks, full of activity from the students at the town's university. The luxurious craft shops of Dorp Street are tempting, not far from the old church, landscaped with white rosebushes, and the streets near the botanical garden and its charming tea room are characterized by historic villas. A good night out is guaranteed at any of the cool bars in the city center, around the Village Museum.

To the east, discover the French Huguenot village of **Franschhoek,** a flowery settlement leaning against the bluish Drakenstein Mountains. The vast majority of estates here today once belonged these French families, who fled their native country in the 17th century to escape religious persecution. Start with a visit to the Huguenot Memorial Museum at the end of town before strolling along the river and up Main Street for some shopping. Head back north toward **Paarl,** where Nelson Mandela spent three years imprisoned in a private house before eventually walking free, ending 27 total years of imprisonment. After visiting the city's small museums, the cellars await.

LOCATION

From the Madagascar Highlands region to the far south of the island

ROUTE

Antananarivo – Toliara

LENGTH

584 mi (941 km)

TIME

Allow at least 8 days; 15 days gives enough time to truly delve into the region.

YOU'LL LOVE

A unique glimpse into Malagasy culture, the beauty of the national parks, rich and unique flora and fauna, the paradisiacal beaches of the south.

START
MI 0

ANTANANARIVO

1

7

2 ANTSIRABE

7

3 AMBOSITRA

ANTOETRA ★

4 FIANARANTSOA

5 AMBALAVAO

7

ANDRINGITRA NATIONAL PARK

ISALO NATIONAL PARK

7

6

ILAKAKA

8

END
MI 584

7

9 TOLIARA

★
ANAKAO

ROUTE N7
IN MADAGASCAR
FROM ANTANANARIVO ➤━━━➤ TO TOLIARA

The 584-mi (941-km) RN7, from Antananarivo to Toliara, is not only one of the most practical routes on the big island of Madagascar, but it also offers a great diversity of landscapes. Traveling along the road also gives a privileged view into the cultures of the ethnic groups that have lived in Madagascar for centuries, including the Merina, the Zafimaniry, and the Bara. For a true dive into Malagasy life, take a ride on a bush taxi, minibuses that, no matter how crowded, are never considered full. These rides are an opportunity to meet the locals and learn the basics of Malagasy.

━━━━★ MANAKARA

START/END OF ROAD TRIP	⬭
STOP	⬤
LANDMARK OR POINT OF INTEREST	★
ROAD	7
ROAD TRIP	═══
FCE TRAIN ROUTE	▪▪▪▪▪

ANTANANARIVO – ANTSIRABE

The Malagasy capital, **Antananarivo (1),** often called Tana, developed on a set of 12 sacred hills, each once held by a different kingdom. The upper town's narrow streets, cobbled and winding, deserve to be wandered, to enjoy views over the capital. Poverty and overcrowding are an unfortunate fact of life in Tana, even in the shadow of the magnificent Queen's palace, and that of the King in Ambohimanga, a park outside the city limits. Stop by the Andravoahangy market to buy wonderful handicrafts.

If you're up for the adventure of taking a bush taxi, you'll have to wave off a throng of touts to find a vehicle bound for Antsirabe, where you'll negotiate the price of the trip and soon be on the road, characterized by omnipresent green rice fields and undulating hills. The journey is not long (about 3 hours) to reach **Antsirabe (2)** (105 mi/169 km), domain of the Merina.

Rizières près d'Antsirabe.

AMBOSITRA AND THE ZAFIMANIRY VILLAGES

Sixty miles (100 km) farther south, you'll stop at **Ambositra (3),** where the Zafimaniry, a community of master wood carvers about 25,000 people strong, reside in the surrounding forest, in villages that are only accessible on foot. Reaching **Antoetra,** the starting point of the hike, is itself a journey, with the bush taxi stopping every 2-3 mi (3-5 km) to load goods, and it takes several days of walking to reach the most isolated settlement. Each Zafimaniry village has its own speciality. In Vohitrandriana, the sawyer trade is passed from father to son. In Sakaivo, accessible in just a few hours, it's clear that the artisan tradition is building houses. Tucked into the depths of a deep green valley, the architecture of this small village, built into the

hillside, is amazing. In 2003, Zafimaniry woodworking was added to UNESCO's list of the world's Intangible Cultural Heritage. The houses, nestled closely together, are oriented toward the southwest, to keep out the heat of the afternoon. Built by hand without any nails or metal parts, the homes are a works of art, with windows and doors carved with geometric patterns. The Zafimaniry are known for the famous rosewood chairs that can be found for sale all over Madagascar.

But little by little, as the resources of the forest have become scarcer, the Zafimaniry have had to diversify. Women cultivate rice and weave small straw hats. Still, the only mark of modernity is a small grocery store that sells beers and soft drinks.

FIANARANTSOA – AMBALAVAO: THE FCE TRAIN AND ZEBUS

At mile 254 (km 410), **Fianarantsoa (4),** Madagascar's second city, is located in the heart of the country's most productive agricultural region. It is famous for its tea plantations and its vineyards, as well as the only passenger rail link still in service in the country, the Fianarantsoa-Manakara line, or FCE train (Fianarantsoa-East Coast).

In **Ambalavao (5),** barely an hour from Fianarantsoa, you'll leave the highlands to descend into countryside characterized by the island's famous red dirt. This road is pure wonder. Ambalavao is known as the kingdom of the zebu, and exiting the city to the south it's clear why: Dozens of herds of these humped cattle often take over the roadway, forcing the bush taxi to a halt.

On Wednesday mornings, the great zebu herds converge in Ambalavao for the Zebu Market in an impressive ballet, with a grandiose mountainous landscape as the background. On a hill a few hundred meters from the village, the cattle are surveyed by potential buyers, a serious business: Zebu can sell for up to 500,000 ariary, or $130. The Bara people who live in this region are truly devoted to their livestock, roaming the great outdoors with huge herds of zebus, symbols of wealth and power.

DETOUR ABOARD THE FCE TRAIN

This colonial-era train is not only a tourist attraction, but also a means of survival for the local population, enabling local products, like bananas and coffee, to be transported from the most remote regions to the markets. Its relatively slow cruising speed (12 mph or 20 km/h) and many stops (17, or one every 6 mi/10 km) give passengers the opportunity to taste the specialties offered by the multitude of street vendors, who rush to the windows as soon as the train has stopped to sell crayfish, samosas, banana fritters, and seasonal fruits.

The trip through lush nature, rice fields, and forests is an adventure in itself, though the poverty here can be sobering: When a "Vazaha" (white man) takes a packet of cookies out of his bag, crowds gather, and children look to tourists in the hopes of getting something to eat or even an empty water bottle.

Ten hours later, you'll arrive in **Manakara,** where a canoe trip on the Pangalanes Canal is highly recommended. You'll visit fishing villages, have a lunch of grilled fish, swim in the Indian Ocean, and visit fields of medicinal plants.

the FCE train

TSARANORO – ISALO: MALAGASY WESTERN

A few miles from Ambalavao is the magnificent and tranquil **Andringitra National Park** (6), reached by bush taxi followed by an easy 6-mi (10-km) hike that leads you to the impressive granite cliffs of Tsaranoro (6,240 ft/1,910 m).

You'll pass a myriad of small, self-sufficient villages, and seemingly endless hiking possibilities. The panoramas are extraordinary and the people are welcoming. You can also observe lemurs, rare birds, and chameleons.

Next stop: **Isalo National Park** (7), a gigantic massif of eroded sandstone (110 mi/180 km long and 15mi/25 km wide) that looks like the setting for a Western movie. Depending on the light, the stone is tinted with gold, green, or ocher. There are several hikes to choose from through rock chiseled by erosion, ranging from 1 to 7 days: You can walk along the bottom of green canyons, swim in natural pools, hike on the massif, or meet with lemurs and the typical, arid vegetation of the south.

After Isalo, the landscapes only become drier, with vast plains as far as the eye can see, no village in sight and nothing but a few baobabs, a lot of cacti, and yellowed grass on the horizon. Astonishing, gigantic, high-speed clouds of locusts, a calamity for the local population, may smash against the windows of your vehicle.

Isalo National Park

Anakao

⑧ ⑨

ILAKAKA – TOLIARA: THE BLUE GOLD OF THE RED ISLAND

The south, the most arid region of Madagascar, is also the poorest, despite the sapphire mines in the ground beneath in **Ilakaka (8),** attracting tens of thousands of fortune-seekers only a few years ago. Many Malagasy people here still hope to get their hands on a precious stone that will change their lives.

Mile 584 (km 941), **Toliara (9),** is the end of the road. The city, languid in the sun, is the gateway to the beach and the small, picturesque Vezo village of **Anakao,** which can only be reached by the sea. The site is wild and the beach is magnificent. The Vezo people depend on the sea, and most of them are comfortable on the water from childhood. The canoe is the Vezo's tool for work and for transportation; carved from a tree trunk with a square sail, it's also the sign of a Vezo person's wealth.

In front of Anakao is a small island refuge for a colony of white-tailed tropicbirds, which makes a great day trip, with a white-sand beach and turquoise water wonderful for swimming. From July to September, whales come here to give birth in the warm waters of the Mozambique Channel, easily seen from the shore or by boat. At sunset, the canoes lined up on the beach shine in a cluster of shimmering colors.

PLAYLIST

Régis Gizavo – MALASO	Quiet Island – EDGE OF THE WORLD
Jaojoby – TIA ANAO ZAHO	Motorama – TO THE SOUTH

PREPARE FOR YOUR TRIP

• **madonline.com/?lang=en** •
An online magazine on Madagascar with articles on all subjects, from political news to society, environment, culture, and the economy.

GETTING THERE

Madagascar's main airport, Ivato International Airport (TNR) is located in the capital city of Antananarivo.
Note: A visa is compulsory for all travelers entering Madagascar.

RENTING A CAR

In major cities and tourist resorts throughout Madagascar, you'll find tour operators and agencies offering car rentals. They're usually expensive and often come with a driver, who can sometimes also act as a guide. If you are on a tight budget, try hiring a bush taxi, which will leave you with incredible memories.

WHEN TO GO

The dry season, from April to November, is the best time to travel the RN7. Temperatures remain cool, even cold. July and August are the busiest months.

WHERE TO STAY

Depending on your budget, you can find everything from simple, inexpensive palm huts to chic hotels in Madagascar.

In Tananarive

- **Moonlight Hotel:**
Lalana Rainandriamampandry, Antananarivo. Very clean rooms in a good location at an excellent value.

In Antsirabe

- **Chez Billy:** *Near the market.* One of the best budget accommodations in town, with simple, cozy, well-kept rooms. The owner is able give advice on almost any aspect of your travel, and it's not uncommon for musicians to perform in the dining room.

In Anakao

- **Safari Vezo:** • **safarivezo.com** •
Fifteen nicely decorated brick, wood, and bamboo bungalows right on the water, with plenty of day trip and diving possibilities.

A BOOK FOR THE ROAD

The Aye-Aye and I by Gerald Durrell

Isalo National Park

START
MI 0

1 MARRAKECH

N9

2 TIZI N'AIT
IMGUER PASS

3 AIT BARKA

JBEL TISTOUIT
★

5 TELOUET

4 TIZI N'TICHKA
PASS

KASBAH
OF TELOU

P 1506

N9

P 1506

6 AMERZGANE

7 EL MDINT

8 TADOULA

CLA STUDIOS

LOCATION ⊕

Central Morocco

ROUTE ↔

Marrakech – Ouarzazate

LENGTH ↔

150 mi (250 km)

TIME ⏱

3 days if you're in a hurry, otherwise
4 days.

YOU'LL LOVE ♥

The variety of landscapes and climates,
interacting with local people, the contrast between the energetic atmosphere of the souks and the calm of
the mountains.

START/END OF ROAD TRIP

● STOP

★ LANDMARK OR POINT OF INTEREST

46 ROAD

ROAD TRIP

HIGH ATLAS MOUNTAINS

TIZI N'TICHKA ROAD

FROM MARRAKECH → TO OUARZAZATE

Approximately 150 mi (250 km), this route through the High Atlas connecting Marrakech and Ouarzazate is one of the most beautiful in Morocco. Everything is rocky, the mountains are bare, and languid valleys are crossed with improbable greenery. Traversing rugged landscapes that alternate between lunar and bucolic, this road is for travelers looking for nature, adventure, and wide-open spaces. Drivers of this route will need to be attentive, as the mountainous road is a series of twists and turns that culminate at Tizi n'Tichka pass at an elevation of nearly 7,550 ft (2,300 m).

تيزي نتيشكة
COL DU TICHKA
ALT. 2260

TAMEDAKHTE **10**

 AIT BEN HADDOU **9**

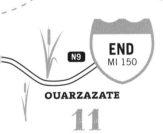

N9 END
MI 150

OUARZAZATE
11

Rabat
Casablanca

MOROCCO

Agadir

(1)————————————————————

MARRAKECH: THE RED CITY

Marrakech (1) is one of those places that inspires reverie. This city will stir something in you, as long as you take the time to bask in its essence. You'll need to stay for at least three nights. You'll see this imperial city as the jewel that it is, set against the gorgeous backdrop of the High Atlas Mountains.

The immense, bustling Jemaa el-Fnaa square alone is worth the trip. And then there are the colorful, noisy souks where you can immerse yourself in the maze of stalls, where seemingly thousands of crafts and wares entice the senses. Marrakech is also full of architectural delights, from superb mosques to remarkable palaces, and, perhaps best of all for travelers, riads that have been turned into guesthouses.

Add in the neighborhood hammams and gregarious merchants, and the city will cast an unforgettable spell.

There's something for everyone here, for Marrakech is not a place frozen in time. Culturally, it's always on the move, with fascinating new museums, flourishing art galleries, and a contemporary art scene that's gaining international attention. While the Red City preserves its memories and values its past, it also bursts with creativity, making it deeply modern and connecting it with the world around it. And of course, let's not forget the food, which highlights both tradition and modern Moroccan cuisine. All this and more make Marrakech an essential stop on any trip to Morocco.

THE ATLAS MOUNTAINS: A GRAND ROUTE

After spending a few days in Marrakech, it's time to leave the hustle and bustle of the city for the sweeping landscapes of the Atlas Mountains, where the adventure really begins. The view from **Tizi n'Ait Imguer pass** (2) (4,820 ft/1,470 m) is stunning, with **Jbel Tistouit** as a backdrop, dominating a group of snow-capped mountains, and kasbahs and small villages below.

After **Ait Barka** (3), the road winds between pine trees, oleander, and terraced fields. Nature mingles with the rust-colored earth on this stretch of undeveloped hills. The view of the valley nestled at the bottom of a deep canyon is superb. Here and there, as you pass through small towns, you may want to stop at a snack stand or a small restaurant for a quick refreshment in the sun. A patchwork of colors runs along the road, ranging from pink to mineral gray to ocher—colors you also see in the villages you pass. From turn to turn, you will also encounter souvenir stands selling a variety of geology-inspired wares, such as geodes.

Marking the border between the provinces of Marrakech and Ouarzazate, the **Tizi n'Tichka pass** (4), the "Pass of Pastures," is the highest road crossing in Morocco at 7,410 ft (2,260 m).

Kasbah of Telouet

TELOUET – TADOULA: TRADITIONAL VILLAGES AND A KASBAH

HIKING

Telouet (5), perched 6,130 ft (1,870 m) above sea level, was once a commercial hub for caravans; in the 14th century, it was a place of exchange and tolerance, where Jews, Muslims, and Christians all coexisted together. The village is dominated by a superb kasbah that once served as a residence for Thami El Glaoui of Marrakech, a powerful leader of the Glaoua tribe of Berbers. You can skip the village, where the offers of merchandise and services are constant; instead, go up to the **Kasbah of Telouet,** set in the hills that dominate a small green valley (4 mi/7 km from Tizi n'Tichka pass; heading toward Ouarzazate, take a narrow, paved road on the left. It's about 13 mi/20 km to the Telouet sign, marking the road up to the kasbah. Access to the road is not very visible, and there are some damaged areas). This large earthen kasbah, where a few storks have taken up residence between migrations, is the first of a number that you will encounter. This is the traditional type of home used by the Berbers of the High Atlas and beyond, in the Draa and Dades valleys.

The road then passes the commune of **Amerzgane (6);** farther on, the village of **El Mdint (7),** easily spotted by its beautiful pink adobe granary; and finally, you are in **Tadoula (8),** where there is a pretty kasbah ruin.

From **Telouet,** you can reach **Ait Ben Haddou** by following the old caravan route that passes through the beautiful Kasbah of Anmiter at 7 mi (11 km). The course is magnificent. To do this long-distance hike, you should hire a guide or have an excellent guidebook. Allow 2-3 days of walking to cover the 25 mi (40 km) to **Tamedakhte** before reaching Ait Ben Haddou, with a stopover in **Assaka.** There are nice little gardens between Assaka and **Tizgui.** You can also just do a portion of the route if you want a shorter hike. For example, you can reach the red village of **Tasga** via a 3-hour round-trip loop.

AIT BEN HADDOU – TAMEDAKHTE: A MOVIE SET!

At about 20 mi (30 km) away from Ouarzazate, **Ait Ben Haddou (9),** a UNESCO World Heritage Site, stands as one of the best preserved *ksars* (fortified village) in all of southern Morocco. In this fortress of earth and reeds, a maze of alleys and open passages weave between the fragile mud houses. Beautiful views can be had from the top of the hill where the *agadir* (fortified granary) of the kasbah is located. The images from this visit will stay with you. In addition, many directors came to shoot their movies here, adding elements of décor that can sometimes be seen today. At the bottom of the village, movie buffs will want to ask about the Plaza of Gladiators, where several scenes from the film *Gladiator* were shot with Russell Crowe, though unfortunately, there is not much left.

Tamedakhte (10) lies 4 mi (6 km) north of Ait Ben Haddou, along a paved road. Located amid a splendid landscape, it is a wonderful walk to do on foot. Coming upon Tamedakhte and its kasbah from the bottom of the village is a real pleasure. It, too, was also often used as a movie set, including for *Gladiator.* You can visit the citadel for 20 Dh, but the kasbah is mostly in ruins. Other nearby kasbahs have been transformed into hotels.

> TO MAKE THE MOST OF YOUR VISIT TO THE KSAR, WHICH IS BEST SEEN IN THE EARLY MORNING OR AT THE END OF THE DAY, SPEND THE NIGHT IN AIT BEN HADDOU.

Ait Ben Haddou

⑨ ⑩ ⑪

OUARZAZATE: GATEWAY TO THE DESERT

Your journey ends in **Ouarzazate (11),** a portal to a world of jagged rocks, stony plateaus, and secret valleys swept by the desert wind. Located at the confluence of the Draa and Dades Valleys, Ouarzazate, like Errachidia farther east, is one of the gateways to the desert and also serves as an important road junction.

In town, you can wander, with or without a guide, through the adobe lanes of the *ksar*—the old town is still inhabited—surrounding the kasbah. It may not be easy to avoid all the salespeople pitching their goods and services, but try to dismiss them nicely. Within the *ksar,* you will come across Arab, Jewish, and Berber quarters and the mosque. You can cross the square where weddings are celebrated,

browse in the Berber pharmacy, and perhaps even meet the local star, "the man with the beard," who has appeared in a dozen films.

At nightfall, Ouarzazate really wakes up. Hundreds swarm into El Mouhadine Square. Under the eyes of their elders sitting on the stairs, kids come to play kickball, skid on their bikes, slide their yo-yos, or gather in an improvised chorus around a pair of musicians. Around the square, there are plenty of cafés where you can sit and enjoy the entertainment while sipping tea. Those who have not yet quenched their thirst for adventure can continue on from Ouarzazate to Merzouga (see Other Road Trips in Morocco).

• **maroc.ma** • The official site of the Moroccan government.
• **www.visitmorocco.com** • Website of the Moroccan National Tourism Office.

GETTING THERE

Marrakech-Menara International Airport is about 3 mi (5 km) west of Marrakech. There are direct flights from European hubs, but flying from North America involves at least one stop.

WHEN TO GO

Spring and fall are the ideal seasons. Summer in Marrakech can be excessively hot, while winters in the Atlas Mountains can be harsh, and nights cool year-round.

GOOD TO KNOW

- In winter, find out about road conditions before setting out by contacting the **gendarmeries** of Ait Ourir (☎ 05/24-48-00-18), of Touama (☎ 05/24-48-49-98), or of Ighrem (☎ 05-24-89-06-15). The pass can be closed between December and March.

- **Fuel up** before departing: There are no service stations between Aït Ourir and Agouim. You will also notice a lot of "hitchhikers" along the way, including false guides, touts, as well as souvenir sellers.

WHERE TO STAY

Marrakech offers a wide range of accommodations for all budgets: tents, hotels and riads for rent by the room or in full. Not to mention apartment rentals for even more independence.

- **Le Lion d'Or:** *Telouet*
• **kasr-telouet@hotmail.com** • This excellent little property, a stone's throw from the splendid kasbah, offers simple, pleasant rooms, some with a view of the ruins. Impeccable. There's also a nice restaurant with a terrace and excellent tajines.

- **Kasbah Hajja:** *Ait Ben Haddou*
• **elhaja-aitbenhaddou.com** • The original structure of this kasbah makes it a unique place. The rooms, which have Berber decor, are small and neat and have patios. The lounge area is set up in a cave, and a very pleasant shaded terrace provides a place where you can have breakfast while admiring the ksar. Solar energy is used for hot water and lighting. Moroccan cuisine. Excellent reception.

A BOOK FOR THE ROAD

Lords of the Atlas: The Rise and Fall of the House of Glaoua 1893-1956 by Gavin Maxwell

Menara Gardens, Marrakech

OTHER ROAD TRIPS IN MOROCCO

① OUARZAZATE AND THE SOUTHERN OASES

South of Ouarzazate, the Draa River leads to a string of villages and ksars. It runs through the compact green mass of the Agdz palm grove as far as **Mhamid** and **Zagora,** the final outposts before the great desert. Farther east, the "valley of a thousand kasbahs," with the Dades River winding its way through, is a constantly changing spectacle. Palm groves and verdant gardens stand out against the ocher and red of the mountains, as do the earthen villages and the kasbahs pointing toward the sky. A little farther to the east, the Todra Gorge is equally impressive, with two 980-ft-high (300-m-high) cliffs forming a sort of open-air cathedral. Finally, the Ziz Valley leads to the gates of **Tafilalt,** once the stronghold of the Alaouite dynasty. Nearby, the magnificent dunes of Erg Chebbi tower over the town of **Merzouga.**

② MOROCCO'S ATLANTIC COAST

An endless road runs along the Atlantic Ocean from Tangier all the way to La Güera, in the extreme south of the country on the Mauritanian border. One of the most beautiful stretches is the 440-mi (700-km) route between Tangier and Essaouira.

Tangier has an atmosphere all its own. Beautiful and peaceful between two continents and between two seas, Tangier is a magical place. A former haunt of bad boys and a refuge for femme fatales, Tangier has inspired many novelists and served as the backdrop for countless adventure and spy films. A city with a scent of scandal, where intrigue and extravagance are the order of the day.

The route to Essaouira is lined with rich remnants left by the great Berber dynasties (especially in **Rabat**) as well as by Spanish and Portuguese conquerors (in **Asilah, Larache, El Jadida,** and **Essaouira**). You'll find unexpected treasures (the Belghazi House Museum, the town of Salé, the Boulaouane Kasbah) and little-known natural sites (such as the lagoon at Moulay Bousselham), not to mention beautiful excursions in the hinterland. Farther south, Essaouira, an endearing city enclosed in ramparts, is the starting point of a sublime coast that stretches all the way to **Agadir.**

ROAD TRIP THROUGH THE NORTH

This part of Morocco is not the most visited, yet it is one of the most interesting—a real crossroads of civilizations at the hinge of two worlds: here, Europe ends and Africa begins.

Let's start in **Tangier** and drive along the Mediterranean coast to reach the **Rif.** This beautiful road overlooks often-deserted sandy coves and crosses through rolling landscapes. It is not uncommon to meet shepherds accompanying their flocks, or to cross paths with local women in traditional dress. After **Ksar es Seghir,** a small port surrounded by modern buildings, you'll pass the new **Tanger-Med** cargo port. The expressway continues to an even more mountainous landscape. On the first foothills of the Rif, **Tetouan** is a piece of Andalusia that feels like it's on the wrong continent. This former capital of Spanish Morocco hides its wonders behind the facades of its white houses, decorated with ceramics and adorned with wrought iron balconies. Its medina is one of the most beautiful in the North.

Chefchaouen, embedded in the mountains that gave it its Berber name meaning "horns," surprises with its astonishing colors. Much of the town is painted in varying shades of blue, and its narrow blue alleys open onto large squares where you'll find Andalusian influences in ornate doorways and arches. This is often regarded as one of the prettiest towns in Morocco.

The capital of the Rif province is **Al-Hoceima,** a newer city on the shores of the Mediterranean. In the background, you'll see large forests of cork oaks and a scrubland covered with lavender, which gave the town its name ("The Lavender"). The drive from Al-Hoceima to Melilla takes about 2 hours, running along the sea and its wild coves.

Northern Morocco is also home to two small pieces of Spain, exiled on the other side of the strait: the enclaves of Ceuta and **Melilla.** The last vestiges of colonialism, these two ports savor their dreamy climate. They proudly display their Spanishness in architecture, gastronomy, and more—and you will have to wait at the border to get there.

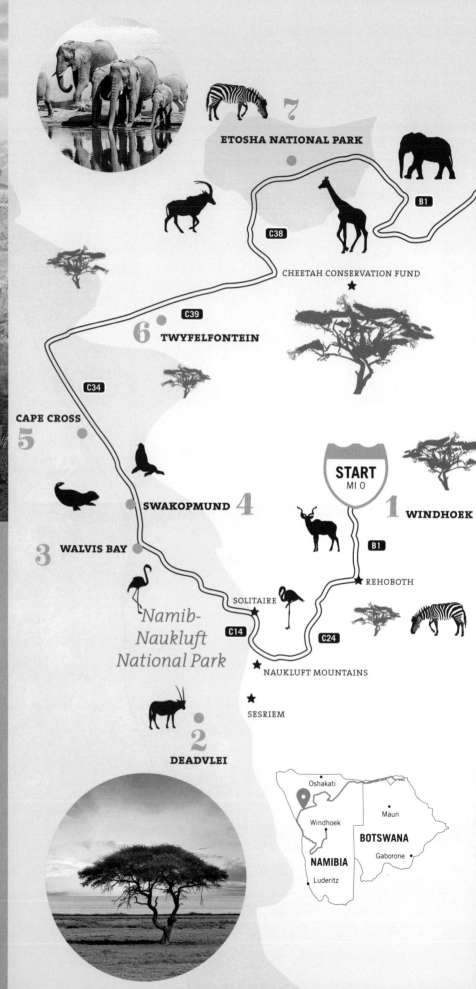

ETOSHA NATIONAL PARK

7

B1

C38

CHEETAH CONSERVATION FUND

★

C39

6 TWYFELFONTEIN

C34

CAPE CROSS

5

SWAKOPMUND 4

START
MI 0

1 WINDHOEK

B1

3 WALVIS BAY

REHOBOTH ★

SOLITAIRE
★
C14

*Namib-
Naukluft
National Park*

C24

★ NAUKLUFT MOUNTAINS

★
SESRIEM

2

DEADVLEI

Oshakati

Maun

Windhoek

BOTSWANA

NAMIBIA

Gaborone

Luderitz

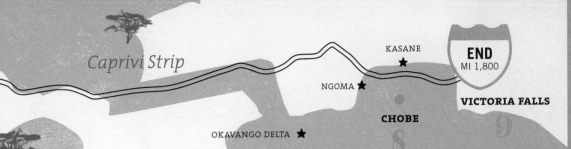

Caprivi Strip

KASANE

END
MI 1,800

NGOMA ★

VICTORIA FALLS

CHOBE

OKAVANGO DELTA ★

UP TO VICTORIA FALLS

FROM WINDHOEK ➤ TO VICTORIA FALLS

Southern Africa has been growing in popularity as a tourist destination, especially Namibia and its neighbor Botswana, both beloved for their wilderness. There's no longer any reason to hesitate: Rent a big 4WD with a roof tent to crisscross through the Namib Desert, following the trail of the rhinoceros in Etosha National Park, and slaloming between the elephants in Chobe. At the end of the road, you'll find the spray and rainbows of the famous Victoria Falls in Zimbabwe. What an adventure!

①

WINDHOEK: WHERE PAST MEETS PRESENT

In Afrikaans, **Windhoek (1)** means "the corner of the wind." The welcoming Namibian capital combines the present, with its modest skyscrapers, and the past, with its many buildings dating back to the time of German colonization. Among the most emblematic structures: the Christuskirche (1910), the Kaiserliche Realschule (1908), the old fortress of the Alte Feste (1890), and the Tintenpalast (1913), the "ink palace" (read: bureaucracy), the seat of Parliament. Some museums offer an interesting perspective, notably the transport museum, installed in the old German railway station. Once your visit to the city is over, it's time to hit the road and head south.

The ribbon of pavement unrolls straight ahead in semi-desert steppe landscapes. The stage is set. After **Rehoboth,** a wide track takes over. Scattered villages, crushed by the sun, emerge from nothingness. As a backdrop, the **Naukluft Mountains** assert themselves little by little. The track twists and turns, climbing toward a campsite situated along a stream in a grove of trees, at the foot of high walls. On the slopes, you might hear the echo of hooves of Hartmann's mountain zebras (very rare) or see the twisting horns of greater kudus.

START/END OF ROAD TRIP

STOP

★ **LANDMARK OR POINT OF INTEREST**

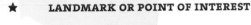
B1 **ROAD**

═══ **ROAD TRIP**

THROUGH THE NAMIB DESERT TO THE SOSSUSVLEI

The mountains are still rolling on the horizon, and huge orange dunes are emerging, too. The highest ones, not yet visible, peak at over 1,000 ft (300 m) in height. Covering an area roughly the size of South Carolina, the Namib Desert stretches for 900 mi (1,500 km), parallel to the shore of the South Atlantic, in a strip 50-100 mi (80-160 km) wide. It is a world apart, seemingly inhospitable, but still home to relatively abundant fauna. In the morning, the landscape is watered by dew droplets from oceanic mists, nourished by the cold Benguela Current, that meet the hot sand heated by the sun of the day before.

A stopover in the hamlet of **Sesriem** is essential, at the gates of the most famous valley of the Namib: **Namib-Naukluft National Park.** From here, a track plunges like a thorn into the side of the great erg through the dry valley of the Tsauchab River. The first oryx, with long straight horns, appear quickly, wandering among the thin brush. They're funny animals: Seen in profile, you might mistake them for unicorns! With your engine off, the slight clop of their steps barely disturbs an intimidating silence. As you continue on, the first sand behemoths gradually emerge. Climbing Dune 45, 500 ft (150 m) high, is a classic adventure. It takes half an hour to reach the top, and when you crest the summit, the sand runs away under your steps like time in an hourglass. A hundred oryx—and a few kilometers—later, get out of the car to see **Deadvlei (2):** Between high orange dunes, ghostly silhouettes of dead acacia trees seem to float in this basin of white clay. This is the Namib in all its splendor.

NOT TO BE MISSED

Have you heard of sandboarding?
Take a snowboard, a thin board of plywood, or even a large square of vinyl, and climb to the top of a high dune and slide down its steepest side. This is sandboarding. Some even try it in a kayak!

WALVIS BAY: ALONG THE ATLANTIC COAST

Former British enclave on German soil, and then part of South Africa, **Walvis Bay** (3) has a cooler climate thanks the Benguela Current. From the lost hamlet of **Solitaire,** via the succession of hairpin turns of the Kuiseb pass, the track to Walvis Bay is long (a good 180 mi/300 km). A new flock of dunes, less bulky and more golden, announces the small town, which is surrounded by lakes that are home to thousands of pink flamingos. The birds are innumerable on the seafront, too: a real forest of legs moving to the rhythm of the tide in synchronized dances. Some 40 percent of all southern African flamingos live in the area.

Farther on, **Swakopmund** (4), the only seaside resort in Namibia, features old Germanic buildings with 1900s charm, rising up in between date palms. Sights in town include the emblematic Woermannhaus museum, the former court of the Kaiserliches Bezirksgericht (now the State House), the Evangelical Lutheran Church, the former Prinzessin Rupprecht Heim military hospital, and the neo-Renaissance railway station converted into a luxury hotel, not to mention the Altes Gefängnis, a prison that looks like a Bavarian inn. At the Hansa Backerei, order *brötchen, apfelstrudel,* and black forest cake. Or take a seat at Café Anton to enjoy some creamy chocolate. The beach and its icy waters are just a stone's throw away, too.

CAPE CROSS – TWYFELFONTEIN: TOWARD THE HINTERLAND

Head north. Unrolling in solitude, the C34 sails between an ocean half hidden in fog and dry coastal plain. This is the Skeleton Coast—named for the skeletons of the whales that have been stranded here, and for the multiple ships that drifted along this lonely coast, condemning their crews to die of thirst. The Portuguese called the area the "Gates of Hell," and even the people who lived here called it "the land God made in anger." After an hour and a half of this atmosphere, you'll reach **Cape Cross (5),** where, during breeding season (at the beginning of the austral summer), nearly 100,000 fur seals make up one of the largest pinniped colonies in southern Africa. Wooden footbridges allow you to approach the odorous and roaring ocean, where the bleating of seal pups mingles with the grunts of the older males.

Dust, sand, and stones accompany your progression in the hinterland toward the Brandberg Massif and Damaraland. This remote area of rugged mountains and arid plains is famous for its petroglyphs and rock paintings made by hunter-gatherers 2,500-6,000 years ago. In the valley of **Twyfelfontein (6),** some 2,000 drawings (classified as a UNESCO World Heritage Site) have been listed, testifying to a time when the climate was milder: giraffes, lions, elephants, antelopes, and other animals were carved on the stone, next to slender human silhouettes drawn in red ocher.

DETOUR TO THE CHEETAH CONSERVATION FUND

A long road leads to the small town of Otjiwarongo, and, to the east of it, to the foot of the small red sandstone massif of Waterberg, emerging above the confines of the Kalahari Desert. At its feet, the Cheetah Conservation Fund camp has taken on the mission of saving cheetahs, which are often hunted by Namibian livestock farmers. A 4WD ride through a large enclosure and a "nose to nose" encounter allow you to observe the fastest animal on the planet in action . . . or in the middle of a nap.

• cheetah.org •

ETOSHA NATIONAL PARK
– THE CAPRIVI STRIP

OKAVANGO DELTA DETOUR

Namibia's flagship attraction, **Etosha National Park (7),** is one of the most beautiful national parks in Africa, and it's also one of the largest (8,600 sq mi/22,270 sq km). Only a third of its territory is open to individuals, but this third is more than enough. You won't find vast savannahs here, but instead a colossal salt pond, dry for most of the year, and scorched lands that push the abundant wildlife to congregate around water during the dry season. A little patience is all it takes, and after a few hours, you'll get to witness the parade: herds of elephants, cohorts of thirsty giraffes, rhinos, zebras, antelopes, and more. A real Noah's ark.

Past Etosha, many people turn back to return to Windhoek. But the temptation to continue the adventure is strong, too. Toward the east, the Namibian **Caprivi Strip** unwinds over an endless finger of land between Botswana to the south and Angola and Zambia to the north. It's 600 mi (1,000 km) to the Botswanan border at **Ngoma,** in the heart of increasingly green landscapes. The pavement runs along the course of the Cubango (Okavango) River for a long time before crossing it and moving away from it.

When you get to Bagani, you're faced with a choice. On the left, the Caprivi Strip and Victoria Falls. On the right, Botswana and the famous animal oasis of the Okavango Delta. The latter has a major drawback: It is only partially accessible by road, at the Moremi Game Reserve. And you need an adapted 4WD and an experienced driver who can navigate the sandy tracks, which can be drowned under half a meter of water during the austral summer. Most visitors rely on local guides who know better than anyone else how to find lions, leopards, and rare wild dogs in the vast savannah. Several camps, scattered throughout the reserve, are only accessible by small plane. Between January and April, only a few scattered ponds remain, from which animal trails radiate like so many veins. If the rains, concentrated during this period, are too weak to water the delta, real downpours then fall on the nearby Angolan mountains before flowing gently in the sand, reaching the Okavango between May and July. This is how the desert turns into a small inland sea in the middle of the dry season.

Etosha National Park

CHOBE NATIONAL PARK AND VICTORIA FALLS

The triangular signs strewn on the road connecting Ngoma to **Kasane** are unmissable: here an "Antelope X-ing," there an "Elephant X-ing"—with the sign showing a pachyderm, ears erect, as a warning. The elephants of **Chobe (8)** are at home everywhere here, often hogging the road or trail. In the dry season, nearly 50,000 elephants live in the park, bounded to the north by the Chobe River and its marshy plains, where they love to splash around. You'll find entire families, the youngest playing and learning to use their trunks as snorkels. Many are political refugees, coming from Namibia and especially from Angola, where wars made poaching more popular. As a result, Chobe, and Botswana more generally, have the highest density of pachyderms in the world.

The icing on the cake is **Victoria Falls (9).** On the agenda: a good hour of red tape at the Zimbabwean border (where you must buy a visa), followed by the shower of spray from the falls, which fall into their long trench (1.1 mi/1.7 km) with a deafening crash. The name for the falls in the local language is Mosi-oa-Tunya, "The Smoke that Thunders." The Zambezi River pours an average of nearly 290,000 gallons (1,100 cubic meters) of water every second, tumbling down 300 ft (100 m) in height in an endless curtain of interwoven waterfalls. Its power is such that, in autumn, the period of the strongest waters, the spray rises up to 1,600 ft (500 m) high!

PLAYLIST

Habib Koité	Oscar Sulley	Lafayette Afro Rock Band	The Funkees
—	—	—	—
BATOUMAMBÉ	BUKOM MASHIE	SOUL MAKOSSA	AKULA OWU ONYEARA

MIDDLE EAST, ASIA, AND THE PACIFIC

END
MI 250

PORT FAIRY

15

14
WARRNAMBOOL

B100

12
PORT CAMPBELL

LAVERS HILL

PETERBOROUGH

13

PRINCETOWN

11

YUULONG

GLENAIRE

LOCATION

Southern Australia, Victoria

ROUTE

Melbourne – Port Fairy

LENGTH

250 mi (400 km)

TIME

Between 4-7 days, depending on your pace and travel interests, including 2 days in Melbourne.

YOU'LL LOVE

Dynamic Melbourne, local cuisine, paradisiacal landscapes, surf spots, diverse fauna.

🛡 **START/END OF ROAD TRIP**

🔴 **STOP**

★ **LANDMARK OR POINT OF INTEREST**

M1 **ROAD**

—— **ROAD TRIP**

===== **OFF-ROADING**

AUSTRALIA

Perth

Brisbane

Sidney

Adelaide

Melbourne

START
MI 0

1 MELBOURNE

M1

GEELONG 2

TORQUAY 3

BELLS BEACH

B100

ANGLESEA 4

AIREYS INLET 5

LORNE 6

7

WONGARRA

SKENES CREEK 8

APOLLO BAY

9

GREAT OTWAY
NATIONAL PARK

C157

CAPE OTWAY

10

GREAT OCEAN
ROAD
FROM MELBOURNE ➤➤➤ TO PORT FAIRY

The Great Ocean Road: A legendary route in the state of Victoria's southwest region, where nature and breathtaking landscapes reign supreme. With white-sand beaches, deserted coves, cliffs, rock formations, tropical forests, and waterfalls, this is an enchanting journey starting in Melbourne through a wild and unspoiled region. Spot kangaroos, koalas, and whales, and indulge in the joy of surfing. The Great Ocean Road is quintessential Australia.

MELBOURNE – TORQUAY: A FEAST FOR THE SENSES

Melbourne (1) is a great strategic base for exploring the state of Victoria and for embarking on the Great Ocean Road, located about 60 mi (100 km) away. Bohemian and arty, Australia's second city delights lovers of culture and gastronomy. Typically Australian, yet so different from the country's other metropolises, Melbourne is not a place to visit, but to experience. Walking its streets awakens the senses, past walls that are an open-air gallery of street art.

For a taste of this unique city, attend an outdoor party or event at Federation Square before losing yourself in the bustling alleyways of the Chinatown district, where it will be hard to choose just one of the many restaurants.

Don't miss the penguin parade on St Kilda Beach or strolling through the Queen Victoria Market among 600 food stalls. You could also attend a footy (Australian football) match at the Melbourne Cricket Ground, a grandiose stage housing up to 100,000 spectators.

Melbourne is also famous for its coffee, claiming to serve the best espresso in the country. Once you've gotten your caffeine fix, head for the Great Ocean Road on the Princess Freeway. Along the way, stop off at **Geelong** (2), a town renowned for its waterfront, beaches (especially Eastern Beach), and botanical garden. From here, the sublime Great Ocean Road is not far away, and the wild coast of Victoria awaits.

NOT
TO BE
MISSED

Fitzroy *is Melbourne's quintessential bohemian district, with an effervescent nightlife scene. Locals like to gather around a beer or a glass of wine on* **Brunswick Street.**

Melbourne

Bells Beach

TORQUAY – LORNE: SUN, SAND, AND SURF

The Great Ocean Road officially begins in **Torquay (3),** an ideal stopover to get to know Australian surf culture, experience the locals' zest for life, and soak up the idyllic vibes of this region.

Torquay, renowned worldwide as one of the cradles of modern surfing, remains a benchmark for those of love riding the waves. This is where the cult brands Rip Curl and Quicksilver were born; you can even get a custom board made. There's also museum totally dedicated to Australian surfing, the Surf World Museum. Among the most famous surf spots a few minutes' drive from Torquay is **Bells Beach,** where the Rip Curl Pro, the oldest surfing competition in the world, takes place every April. Be careful; this spot is not recommended for beginners. If you prefer staying safe and dry, head to the top of the cliffs, an ideal vantage point for observing the waves and surfers.

Ten minutes farther by car brings you to **Anglesea (4),** also renowned for its surf beaches, but with a more relaxed atmosphere than neighboring Torquay, ideal for a family stopover. Don't miss a trip to the town's golf club, famous for the resident kangaroos, which squat on the green all day long. Continue your journey toward Lorne with a stop at the village of **Aireys Inlet (5),** known for its famed Split Point Lighthouse and magnificent sunsets over the jagged coastlines. Afterward, a long stretch follows Fairhaven Beach before ascending into the Otways Forest, where the Great Ocean Road Memorial Arch pays homage to those who built this legendary route.

LOVE AT FIRST SIGHT

For nature lovers, the **Surf Coast Walk** covers 27 mi (44 km) of trails, from Lorne to Fairhaven, to explore on foot or by bike. This walk allows you to experience the enchanting colors of this region, from the deep blue of Bass Strait to the ocher cliffs of Bells Beach to the green eucalyptus forests, at your own pace.

LORNE – APOLLO BAY: FROM TROPICAL FORESTS TO PARADISIACAL COVES

This is without doubt the most majestic portion of the Great Ocean Road. Tropical forests, rivers, waterfalls, cliffs, and small idyllic coves intermingle on this 27-mi (44-km) stretch from Lorne to Apollo Bay. The charming coastal town of **Lorne (6)** is the ideal starting point to hike the majestic forests of **Great Otway National Park,** where the Aboriginal Wadawurrung people have gone to connect with nature for centuries. You'll see kangaroos, koalas, and dozens of species of eagles (about 40 of which are found nowhere else on the planet). Your best chance of spotting one of these animals is to take one of the many hiking trails (ranging between 2.5-5 mi/4-8 km of easy walking).

Among the must-sees are Lower Kalimna Falls and Cora Lynn Cascades, with their natural pools and spectacular waterfalls. Six miles (10 km) northwest of Lorne Erskine Falls is a 100-ft-high (30-m-high) waterfall that's an ideal hangout spot in good weather. Check at the information center before venturing out to make sure the waterfalls have not dried up during the warmer season.

On the outskirts of Lorne, Teddy's Lookout offers breathtaking views of the Great Ocean Road and the Saint George River meandering through fern-covered valleys. The road to Apollo Bay continues along the cliffs, with the ocean on one side and the forest on the other. You'll feel like you're at the end of the world passing wild and peaceful coves of fine sand. Not far away, the Cape Patton Lookout offers a spectacular panorama of the ocean, the crescent of the bay, and the surrounding green hills. In **Wongarra (7)** and **Skenes Creek (8),** just before Apollo Bay, surfers try to catch the waves directly under the cliffs.

Make a stop at **Kennett River,** *head for the hills, and look up: You'll see dozens of koalas, especially at the end of the day when they are feeding. It's one of the best spots in Australia to observe them.*

APOLLO BAY – PORT CAMPBELL: THE TWELVE APOSTLES

The road gently leaves the edge of the ocean to climb inland and though rain forest. The unforgettable rocky mounds of the Twelve Apostles, as the limestone rock formations off the coast are called, will be in view.

Apollo Bay (9) is a great stopover for a few days if you want to explore Otway National Park, where sublime white-sand beaches are framed by picturesque hills. Kayak out to observe a colony of fur seals. Apollo Bay is also famous for its Saturday morning local fruit and craft market. Back in the car, the road begins to wind up to **Princetown** (11) (visibility can sometimes be reduced around Lavers Hill due to fog; drive with caution). Along the way, stop at **Cape Otway** (10), the southernmost point of the coastline, an area as splendid for backpackers as it is dangerous for ships (nearly 200 shipwrecks in a century have given the area the nickname "the Shipwreck Coast").

This is where Australia's oldest lighthouse, the Cape Otway Lightstation, is located. As a bonus, the Lighthouse Road that leads there is an ideal spot for observing koalas. The nearby towns of **Glenaire, Lavers Hill,** and **Yuulong** are the best stops for a lunch break or some hiking.

Once you pass the Otways, the road stops climbing. You are now in Port Campbell National Park, a flat region atop 230-ft-high (70-m-high) cliffs, limestone rocks, gorges, and cavities, which make for a breathtaking spectacle. Quiet Princetown is a peaceful haven and a fisherman's paradise, another ideal base for getting to know the local flora and fauna. Go for a walk along the river, where kangaroos like to take their rest.

THE TWELVE APOSTLES

A few kilometers from Princetown stand the Twelve Apostles, the most photographed sight on the Great Ocean Road. Created by erosion, these impressive rock formations rise up dramatically from the ocean not far from the shore. Get up close on a boat tour, or, even better, by helicopter.

Port Campbell National Park

PORT CAMPBELL – PORT FAIRY: SERENITY AND PLEASURE

This last, straight drive of your journey may not be the most memorable portion, but there are enough attractions here to keep you busy for a day. Some travelers pass through **Port Campbell** (12) without a passing glance, unfortunately missing all the charm and tranquility of this city of 400 souls perched on the edge of a magnificent bay of sculpted limestone cliffs. The city boasts a fine sand beach (the safest for swimmers on this part of the coast), hiking trails, diving spots, and renowned seafood restaurants.

Resume your journey west, where you'll see new rock formations (notably the famous London Bridge), small isolated beaches and coves, and splendid bays, offering a colorful spectacle at sunset. Highlights include the Bay of Martyrs and Bay of Islands. **Peterborough** (13), a small coastal town, is renowned for its rich and varied fauna, including egrets, pelicans, swans, and penguins.

The Great Ocean Road then leaves the shore to end at the Princess Highway junction in Allansford. Continue your journey to **Warrnambool** (14), a few kilometers away, whose historic buildings are the background for observing southern whales, cetaceans that can measure up to 60 ft (18 m). You'll see them breaching and giving birth from July to September off Logan's Beach, an unforgettable spectacle. Finally, finish at **Port Fairy** (15), an adorable little town with a charming and historic main street.

Diving enthusiasts should not miss the **Arches Marine Sanctuary** *near Port Campbell, a breathtaking and unspoiled spot. At this veritable underwater labyrinth of caves, arches, and walls, you can dive to the wreck of the Loch Ard clipper, near the splendid Loch Ard Gorge, one of the most beautiful sites on the Great Ocean Road.*

PREPARE FOR YOUR TRIP

• **visitvictoria.com** •
Lots of info and an events calendar.
• **visitgreatoceanroad.org.au** •
Good maps of all the stages of the route.

GETTING THERE

Melbourne's two airports, Avalon (AVV) and Tullamarine (MEL), are served by major national and international airlines.

RENTING A CAR

From Melbourne, the best way to travel the Great Ocean Road is to rent a car, motorbike, or van. There are many rental outlets in town and at the airports. It's also possible to see the Great Ocean Road by bicycle, or with the bus company V/Line. Remember, Australians drive on the left!

WHEN TO GO

Between November and April, temperatures are around 77-86°F (25-30°C), warm and ideal for swimming. Between June and September, temperatures are quite cool (50-60°F/10-15°C), but chances of rain are low. Note that night falls early in the region (around 6pm), and always remember to pack warm clothes if you are going for a hike.

PLAYLIST

The Temper Trap	Angus & Julia Stone	Bee Gees	Nick Cave & the Bad Seeds
–	–	–	–
LOVE LOST	**JUST A BOY**	**STAYIN' ALIVE**	**RED RIGHT HAND**

WHERE TO STAY

Melbourne is home to dozens of hotels, B&Bs, and hostels; for any taste or budget, you'll be spoiled for choice. The Great Ocean Road also has an extensive selection of hotels, but they tend to be expensive. These three accommodations offer excellent value for the money.

- Torquay Foreshore Caravan Park:
35 Bell St., Torquay.
• **torquaycaravanpark.com.au** •
Worth the detour to camp or park your van, facing the sea on Torquay Surf Beach.

- Great Ocean Road Cottages & Backpackers YHA:
10 Erskine Ave., Lorne.
• **greatoceanroadcottages.com** •
Wooden cottages and tent sites nestled in the bush, close to the river and the beach. Wake up to the sound of cockatoos, with a chance of seeing koalas from your bed.

- YHA Eco Beach:
5 Pascoe St., Apollo Bay.
This youth hostel is very ecologically oriented, designed with pleasant common areas, outdoor terraces, and a beautiful garden.

A BOOK FOR THE ROAD

True History of the Kelly Gang by Peter Carey

Great Ocean Road in Lorne

9 DARWIN

END
MI 1,870

★ KAKADU NATIONAL PARK

8

KATHERINE

1

7

DALY WATERS

TENNANT CREEK 6

★ DEVILS MARBLES

87

HERMANNSBURG

ALICE SPRINGS 5

WATARRKA NATIONAL PARK ★

KATA TJUTA   ULURU

4

COOBER PEDY

A87

FLINDERS MOUNTAINS ★

3 **PORT AUGUSTA**

A1

2
BAROSSA VALLEY

START
MI 0   **ADELAIDE**

1

KANGAROO ISLAND ★

LOCATION

Central Australia, from south to north

ROUTE

Adelaide – Darwin

LENGTH

1,870 mi (3,010 km) from Adelaide, including 1,760 mi (2,834 km) on the Stuart Highway. It's a 470-mi (760-km) detour to Uluru, Kata Tjuta, and Kings Canyon.

TIME

10 to 14 days

YOU'LL LOVE

The rocky red massifs of the central Australian desert, encounters with Aboriginal culture, animals in Kakadu National Park.

STUART
HIGHWAY
FROM ADELAIDE ⟫⟶ TO DARWIN

Ever thought about driving through an entire country? Here's your chance! Follow the path traced by Scottish explore John McDouall Stuart in 1860 and the first trans-Australian telegraph line through the desert heart of the Australian continent. It's a journey unlike any other, with sections of the highway used as an emergency landing strip for the Royal Flying Doctor Service. Though it's now paved from start to finish, locals still call it "The Track."

AUSTRALIA

Perth

Brisbane

Sidney

Adelaide

Melbourne

START/END OF ROAD TRIP

STOP ⬤

LANDMARK OR POINT OF INTEREST ★

ROAD 1

ROAD TRIP ═══

SOUTH AUSTRALIA: CRICKET, BOWLING, AND VINEYARDS

Though the Stuart Highway technically starts in Port Augusta, drivers usually start in in **Adelaide (1)**, the capital of South Australia, 200 mi (300 km) to the south. This large city of 1.3 million people still retains a small-town feel, the sweet coastal air and relaxed pace reminiscent of the Mediterranean. An emerald necklace of parks encircles the historic center, bounded to the north by the wide, meandering Torrens River. Adelaide residents take full advantage of all the outdoor space, often taking a lunch break to jog, canoe, sail, or tan on meticulously mown lawns.

On weekends, the beach is the place to be. Accessible by car or tram, the suburb of Glenelg has one of the area's best marinas and stretches of sand, decorated with araucaria trees. October to March is cricket season, when fans pack the Oval to take in a Redbacks or Strikers match. And when the season is over, the harvest begins in the **Barossa Valley (2),** 45 minutes away. It was in this gently rolling countryside that grapevines first took hold in Australia in the 1840s, thanks to a few Central European immigrants. Today it is the country's wine-growing center, renowned for its riesling and syrah (here called shiraz). The legacy of German settlers is apparent in the town of Tanunda, where the Lutheran churches vie for space with wooden buildings decorated with historic balconies. You'll even a find a *Kegel* (bowling) club, and the Liedertafel choir, which has been singing (half in German, half in English) for more than a century and a half.

DETOUR TO KANGAROO ISLAND

Even though you haven't gotten to Stuart Highway yet, you won't regret taking a detour to **Kangaroo Island.** An hour south of Adelaide, Cape Jervis is the gloomy and lonely starting point for ferries to the island, across the strong, white-capped currents of the Backstairs Passage, subject to winds blowing from Antarctica. True to its name, this large island of 4,500 inhabitants a true Noah's ark: In addition to kangaroos, you'll find wallabies, friendly koalas, a colony of sea lions sprawled on an idyllic white-sand beach, fur seals basking on the rocks, and even echidnas and platypuses (though those are harder to find). Another highlight is watching the pelicans feed at Kingscote Harbor every evening at 5pm. Though the boat passage is expensive, it's a once in a lifetime chance to see such a huge variety of wildlife all in one place.

THE OPAL ROAD

When you reach **Port Augusta (3),** you'll notice the thermometer start to climb. The sky above the dry coastal plain is perpetually blue and cloudless; only the distant **Flinders Mountains** add dimension to the seemingly unending flat horizon. This is true outback less than 3 hours from Adelaide, a wild territory of red cliffs and dry gorges interspersed with intoxicating groves of large eucalyptus trees, inhabited by troops of emus, kangaroos, and goannas (Australian lizards). In the morning at your campsite, you'll be awakened by the morning concert of the kookaburras, which sounds a bit like loud, sardonic laughter.

This is the true start of the long, straight Stuart Highway. Ten, twenty, thirty miles of sparse bush will flash by as you drive at the posted speed limit of 70 mph (110 km/h). You'll share the road with "road trains" flying over the seemingly endless ribbon of tarmac in a thunder of wind, triple-trailers unique to Australia making their way north.

There's a strict ban on getting out of your car here. For a long stretch, the Stuart Highway crosses through the Woomera military zone, one of the largest missile-testing grounds in the world at almost a quarter the size of France. But the flat, empty, semi-desert steppe is truly best seen from the car, the only vegetation a smattering of yellow spinifex and stunted bushes. From time to time, you'll see the blinding salt crust of evaporated lakes, waiting for an improbable rain shower to bring them to life

After more than 5 hours (340 mi/540 km) of watching the odometer tick up, the horizon lost in the haze of heat as you drive the driest part of the continent (a territory two-thirds the size of Europe), you'll finally reach **Coober Pedy (4).** True, the first impression isn't great: a building site in the desert, with mounds of rock dug up by prospectors diving ever-deeper for opals. The rich veins discovered here in the early 20th century made Coober Pedy the opal capital of the world, the source of 80 percent of the world's supply of these iridescent green, blue, red, and yellow "firestones." Here, life takes place mainly underground: Many old mines have been converted into homes and even churches.

DETOUR THROUGH THE RED HEART

From Coober Pedy, the Stuart Highway continues, winding its way through the Australian desert. In what truly seems like the middle of nowhere, 672 mi (1,082 km) from Adelaide, you'll pass the hamlet of Marla ("kangaroo" in the local Aboriginal language), with a gas station, mini-market, motel, campsite, self-serve bar, swimming pool, post office, and laundromat—and not much else. It's the perfect stop for a sandwich or ice cream, though you won't want to linger long, as the temperature can reach 108°F (42°C) in the shade.

Here you'll find the turnoff for **Uluru,** reached via the Lasseter Highway, a "short" detour of 244 km (151 mi). Starting from Coober Pedy later in the day, the sight of the iconic red sandstone rock enveloped in the setting sun is truly breathtaking. Sacred to the Aboriginal population, it's forbidden to climb Uluru, but you can circumnavigate it by car or on foot (a 5.8-mi/9.4-km hike), the best way to take in every fissure and crack. If you're lucky enough to be here during the austral summer, rains propelled by monsoon winds create incredible waterfalls pouring from the monolith's sides, descending toward equally temporary pools. Only the Mutitjulu Waterhole, populated by frogs, remains year-round.

West of Uluru, the 36 domes of **Kata Tjuta** rise up to 2,000 ft (600 m) above the endless infinity of the outback. Six hundred million years of erosion make themselves evident on every stone and every square meter of land here, giving the land an ancient feel. Park in front of the funnel of Walpa Gorge, one of the few accessible pathways through this sacred site, where plant and animal life takes refuge between two colossal red sandstone walls. In the Valley of the Winds, you'll reach a splendid viewpoint of Karingana, a huge amphitheater of crimson rock.

Many now retrace their steps to the Stuart Highway, but others extend their detour to **Watarrka National Park,** where the scarlet walls of Kings Canyon rise to the sky. After rain, the desert is covered with purple carpets of *Calandrinia balonensis* and funny vermilion bouquets of black-lipped Swainsona flowers emerging from the sand. The Rim Walk (4 mi/6 km) crosses a collection of eroded domes called the "Lost City" before plunging down a long wooden staircase into what's called the "Garden of Eden," an oasis of eucalyptuses and large cycads framing precious waterholes.

The adventurous should try the Larapinta Drive, accessible to all vehicles in the dry season, 79 mi (128 km) of road that's by turns rolling, brittle, sandy, and interspersed with corrugated iron, riverbeds to ford, and donkey- and camel-crossings. At the end is the village of **Hermannsburg,** with an out-of-place wooden Lutheran temple, left by the proselytizing of the German missionaries who came here to convert the Aboriginal Australians. At Simpsons Gap, in the MacDonnell massif, 15 mi (25 km) before Alice Springs, a breach in the reddish rock reveals another precious waterhole, inhabited by small, friendly wallabies.

Uluru

BACK ON THE STUART HIGHWAY

Alice Springs (5) is a town of roughly 25,000 inhabitants, the biggest outpost within a 200-mi (300-km) radius. Called simply "Alice" by locals, this doorway to the outback bakes under the sun 300 days a year, astride the Todd River, dry 345 days out of 365. Average temperatures range from 96°F (36°C) in January to 40°F (4°C) in July.

Far from everything and close to nothing, the city is content to play the part of oasis, with its streets lined by date palms and eucalyptus. It's home to swimming pools, green lawns, and a golf course, and its air-conditioners are constantly running. Visit Aboriginal art galleries, an old telegraph building, and two museums on desert flora and fauna, or stop by the grocery store, where you can buy kangaroo tail. Or visit on the second Saturday in July for the Camel Cup, a wild race on the back of Afghan camels, brought here by pioneers in the 19th century.

Refreshed by this oasis, it's time to hit the road again. **Tennant Creek (6),** 750 mi (1,200 km) away, is the next town of any importance. Renamed Jurnkurakurr by its inhabitants, the majority of which are of Aboriginal descent, this hamlet of 3,000 people is still the fifth largest in the northern territories.

Flying by at the posted speed limit, now 80 mph (130 km/h), the landscape is hypnotic, with occasional clusters of rocks, like the big red stones of **Devils Marbles,** interrupting the flat expanse of burnt-looking bush and dry riverbeds.

Alice Springs

Kakadu National Park

NORTHERN AUSTRALIA IN THE RAIN

Stop by **Daly Waters (7)** for a drink in its historic pub, straight out of *Crocodile Dundee*. Broad-brimmed hats hang above the bar, license plates decorate the wall, and the outhouse is made out of corrugated iron.

The landscape here is still bleak, but trees begin to emerge from and the red earth and the air grows heavier and sticker, evidence of the rain that falls here even in summer. From **Katherine (8),** Nitmiluk National Park is 20 minutes away. Behind a curtain of bush, you'll find Katherine Gorge, best viewed from Baruwei Lookout, where a river traces a silvery furrow between two old, glowing cliffs. Crocodiles bask on the orange riverbanks.

The widening of the highway means your trip is coming to an end. First the lampposts, and then the grass and sidewalks of **Darwin (9)** appear. Munch on a crocodile burger at the Mindil Beach Market on Thursday or Friday evenings, after meeting some saltwater crocodiles (which can grow to up to 20 ft/6m and weigh up to a ton) up close at Crocosaurus Cove. The Stuart Highway finally ends at a large clump of coconut palms and tropical trees in front of the Timor Sea.

DETOUR TO KAKADU NATIONAL PARK

From Pine Creek, Route 21 heads north toward the star of the region: **Kakadu National Park,** a UNESCO World Heritage Site. From November to April, rain colors the landscape, and jabirus and geese splash through carpets of water hyacinths. Beware: Both freshwater Johnston crocodiles and their giant marine cousins, saltwater crocodiles, inhabit these swamps. In dry season, hike to the serene pools below Gunlom Falls, Twin Falls, or Jim Jim Falls, whose diaphanous streams of water flow into an amphitheater of red rock protecting a vast natural swimming pool. No crocs here! Among the 25 trails crisscrossing the park, some lead to beautiful examples of Aboriginal rock art, animals and deities painted in red ocher.

PREPARE FOR YOUR TRIP

- australia.com •
- guide-australia.com •
- southaustralia.com •
- discovercentralaustralia.com •
- traveloutbackaustralia.com •
- northernterritory.com •
- parksaustralia.gov.au •

GETTING THERE

There are few direct international flights to Adelaide or Darwin. Fly into Sydney or Melbourne first, and then transfer to a domestic flight on Qantas, Virgin Australia, or Jetstar. There are also frequent connections to Alice Springs and even Uluru.

RENTING A CAR

Car or camper van? A van is a little more expensive, but it allows camping with a bit more comfort. Whatever you decide, make sure to ask the company if you're allowed to take your vehicle on unpaved trails; otherwise, any damage will not be covered by insurance. 4WD enthusiasts will find a host of routes through the outback, but it's imperative to be experienced and well-equipped. The drive is more dangerous during the rainy season.

WHEN TO GO

March-May and October-November.

WHERE TO STAY

Accommodations are expensive in Australia, even motels, but the outback offers a huge selection of campsites, from wild to more organized. Some are even free! Otherwise, a camper van gives you a lot more freedom.

WHERE TO EAT

Before embarking on the Stuart Highway, make sure to stop by the supermarket to stock up on fuel, water, and food. Outside cities, there are some gas stations for supplies and refueling, but they are few and far between.

A BOOK FOR THE ROAD

Oscar and Lucinda by Peter Carey

PLAYLIST

AC/DC	INXS	Julia Jacklin	Yothu Yindi
–	–	–	–
THUNDERSTRUCK	NEED YOU TONIGHT	POOL PARTY	TREATY

Jim Jim Falls, Kakadu National Park

START
MI 0

PENELOKAN

MUNDUK

PURA ULUN DANU BERATAN

JATILUWIH
RICE TERRACES

SECRET GARDEN VILLAGE

PURA LUHUR
BATUKARU

TEGALLALANG

UBUD

LOCATION
Island of Bali in Indonesia

ROUTE
Munduk – Ubud – Mount Batur

LENGTH
About 80 mi (130 km)

TIME
1 day. The route can be done on a motorbike or by car. But make sure to stop along the way to discover local life, explore nature, and learn about Balinese heritage. Allow at least 3-4 days for a deeper experience.

YOU'LL LOVE
Rice terraces, picturesque villages, lakes, volcanoes, mountains, traditional shows, and local cuisine.

  START/END OF ROAD TRIP

● STOP

★ LANDMARK OR POINT OF INTEREST

── ROAD TRIP

BALI

Negara

Gianyar

Denpasar

Kuta

END
MI 80

MOUNT BATUR

KEDISAN

THROUGH THE
BALINESE
RICE FIELDS

FROM MUNDUK ➤ TO MOUNT BATUR

Explore the roads of Bali on a motorbike and treat yourself to a fabulous trip through rice fields, jungles, and mountains. On this trip, you'll cross lively and picturesque villages and get a taste of the local way of life, with the wind in your hair and your sunglasses on. It's not just a trip—it's a unique and authentic adventure, far from the crowds and buses filled with tour groups.

① —————————————————

MUNDUK: AUTHENTIC BALI

Fifty miles (80 km) north of Denpasar (the capital of the island, where the international airport is located), you'll find the village of **Munduk (1),** a small, authentic gem, located in the middle of wild hills and terraced rice fields. Start your journey here to enjoy the most beautiful landscapes of the island.

Perched on the side of a hill at an altitude of 2,600 ft (800 m), Munduk is an ideal home base for exploring the region with its many natural treasures. Rice terraces west of the city, crops, and orchards form a green patchwork, nestled in a wild jungle. In the late 19th century, when the Dutch settled in northern Bali, they imported with them coffee, vanilla, cloves, and cocoa. These plantations can still be found in the region today. It's an ideal setting for a ride on two wheels and is a real feast for the eyes—and the nose. The scent of cloves perfumes the surroundings.

Tip: Be careful on small, winding roads, which aren't always in good condition.

HIKES AND WALKS BY THE LAKE

Munduk is also an ideal starting point for hikes, which range in length from a few hours to a full day. (Many of the accommodations in the area can organize guided tours for you.) You'll find superb waterfalls here, such as GitGit Waterfall, located at the bottom of a valley about 9 mi (15 km) northeast of Munduk. Then, return to the summits to admire the magnificent sunrises or sunsets that the surroundings offer, undoubtedly among the most beautiful on the island.

Next, heading south toward Ubud, take the road for about 20 mi (30 km), passing even more superb landscapes along the way. It's a spectacular route with incredible views of Lake Tamblingan, Lake Buyan, and the mountains. There are numerous lookouts along the road, which are ideal for photos.

NOT TO BE MISSED

Two miles (3 km) before the town of Bedugul, at Lake Beratan, you'll find the Hindo-Buddhist temple of **Pura Ulun Danu Beratan,** *the second largest temple in Bali. Built in the middle of the lake, it seems to float on the water. It is dedicated to Dewi Danu, the goddess of lakes and rivers. It makes for a superb panorama thanks to the surrounding mountains, and it acts as a symbol throughout Indonesia—the temple is depicted on the 50,000 rupee banknote.*

EN ROUTE TO THE RICE FIELDS

Continuing toward Ubud, take a detour west toward **Pura Luhur Batukaru.** Along this road, you'll also reach the **Jatiluwih Rice Terraces (2),** considered the most beautiful rice terraces on the island (*jatiluwih* means "magnificent" in Balinese). They are classified as a UNSECO World Heritage Site. The crops spread out at the foot of Mount Batukaru (another wonder of the region) and sculpt the landscape in shimmering staircases, displaying their extraordinary palette of different shades of greens. From the top of the hills, the view is breathtaking—sometimes you can even see all the way to the south coast of Bali. A winding road of about 12 mi (20 km) crosses this grandiose landscape, enough to offer you a magical adventure on your motorbike. It's also nice to explore on foot, getting lost in the labyrinthine paths between the rice fields.

FOCUS

Rice Terraces:
Emblems of Bali

Listed as a UNESCO World Heritage Site, the rice terraces of Bali are a true trademark of the island. Rice, water (flowing first through temples and then into fields), and *subak* (a cooperative social system that manages the network of canals and dams allowing irrigation) have shaped the Balinese landscape for a thousand years and are an integral part of religious life. The rice terraces are also an ode to Dewi Sri, the goddess of fertility.

SECRET GARDEN VILLAGE: A SWEET AND SAVORY BREAK

Secret Garden Village (3) is well worth a little detour. Three miles (5 km) as the crow flies east of Jitaluwih, this complex with modern and traditional architecture is lost in the middle of the countryside. Its aim is to promote local products. For example, you can discover how to make a soap using natural products, see how coffee is prepared (tasting included), and learn some great secrets of Balinese cooking (with the possibility of lessons, as a bonus). You can also sleep, eat, and visit the large rice fields in the surrounding area. All in all, it's a fun way to discover the products of Bali.

UBUD: STROLL IN THE MIDDLE OF BUCOLIC LANDSCAPES

Next stop: **Ubud (4)**, 20 mi (30 km) south of Secret Garden Village (about a 50-minute drive). It's an essential stop on your journey, both for the city and for the surrounding region. Ubud was made famous as a setting in the book (and movie) *Eat, Pray, Love*. Countless celebrities and artists have stayed here to recharge their batteries or to be inspired: Julia Roberts, Walter Spies, Charlie Chaplin, Noel Coward, Barbara Hutton, Elizabeth Gilbert. . . . The list goes on!

Located in the geographical center of the island, it is considered the food capital of the archipelago, a wellness city par excellence, and the cultural heart of Bali. Balinese history, tradition, and art are all concentrated here. Highlights include the Ubud Food Festival, which takes place every spring, and the abounding spas and yoga schools in town. You'll also love the folklore of daily dance and music shows, the gamelan (traditional Balinese orchestra) concerts, and the traditional clothing worn by residents. Don't miss a visit to the lush Sacred Monkey Forest and its free-roaming monkeys, or the many museums promoting Balinese art (Puri Lukisan Museum, Neka Art Museum, Agung Rai Museum of Art).

To taste the plenitude, move away from the city center and turn the corner. . . . Here is the countryside, with its rice fields, creeks and rivers, and farm animals.

Here, forgo a set route. Just let yourself be guided by the country roads. Forests, rice fields, villages—the bucolic landscapes unfold and reveal the sweetness of Balinese life. Do not hesitate to leave your two-wheeler behind to better walk along a path or cross a river. It's a setting of peace and wonder.

Pura Ulun Danu Batur

ON THE ROAD TO MOUNT BATUR: BALINESE CRAFTS

Head back to the north of the island, but this time farther east. Your objective: reaching Mount Batur, the third highest peak in Bali, culminating at 5,633 ft (1,717 m). To get there, you have several options (Ubud is the hub of a multitude of small roads). The best option is to take the road toward Tegallalang. The first 12 mi (20 km) are bordered by villages, each specializing in a different craft industry. In Gentong (2 mi/3 km away), it is small wood animals. In Sapat (2.5 mi/4 km away), it's flower painting. In Penusuan, the next village, sculpture of wooden masks and figurines. In Sebatu (10 mi/16 km away), it's . . . phallic statuettes! The last 12 mi (20 km), straight north, cross bucolic countryside and small villages (avoid leaving early in the morning to escape the flood of tourist buses leaving for the day; the roads will be more peaceful and pleasant during late morning). Along the way, do not miss the rice terraces of **Tegallalang** (6 mi/10 km): It's a view worthy of a postcard. To reach Mount Batur, head north toward Batur.

ON TOP OF BALI'S THIRD PEAK

This is one of the most beautiful vistas on the island. The arrival on the site of **Mount Batur** (5) is grandiose and often a bit chilly (wear layers, especially if you are on a motorbike). The last kilometers bring you to the village of **Penelokan** (paid access), at the top of a huge volcanic caldera. In the center is the majestic throne of Mount Batur. On its slopes, traces of ancient lava flows are still visible (the last eruption was in 2000). At the foot of the volcano, you'll find the lake of the same name. In front of it to the east, outside the caldera, is Mount Abang (the second largest peak in Bali). What a show! Take a walk along the ridge to admire the site: You'll find no shortage of lookouts (be careful, the road does not go all the way around the caldera; you will have to retrace your steps). But the best option is to go down into the Penelokan caldera via a winding 5-mi (8-km) road (traffic is often heavy, especially with trucks going up). You will reach the small village of **Kedisan** 1,600 ft (500 m) below, the ideal point to begin a beautiful road trip along the lake.

Walk along the shore on the east side to visit the rural villages of Buahan and Abong. It's possible to extend the walk (about 30 minutes on a path from Abong) to the village of Trunyan, known for its ancestral funeral rites (in which the dead are deposited on the ground under a structure of woven palm leaves). It's best to take a guide and go by boat (departure from Kedisan) for a more interesting visit. The west bank leads to the Air Panas site in Banjar, 2.5 mi (4 km) away via a narrow, winding road. It's a traditional but toursity place, famous for its hot springs, where you can go for a swim. You'll see an unusual volcanic landscape with abandoned houses under construction—the government has banned all construction because of the risk of eruption. These two escapes allow you to admire the lake and its changing colors in a peaceful atmosphere.

HIKING

It's possible to hike all the way up **Mount Batur,** with frequent departures from Air Panas and the Pura Jati temple. Guides are strongly recommended for the ascent (guides can be found on site, or ask at your accommodation). Allow around 2 hours for the ascent and a little less for the descent. The hike is not too strenuous, but remember to be well equipped (layers, raincoat, walking shoes, flashlight, snacks). The hikes often begin early in the morning—around 4am—in order to reach the top to see the sunrise. From above, the view of the surroundings is simply exceptional—a highlight of any trip to Bali.

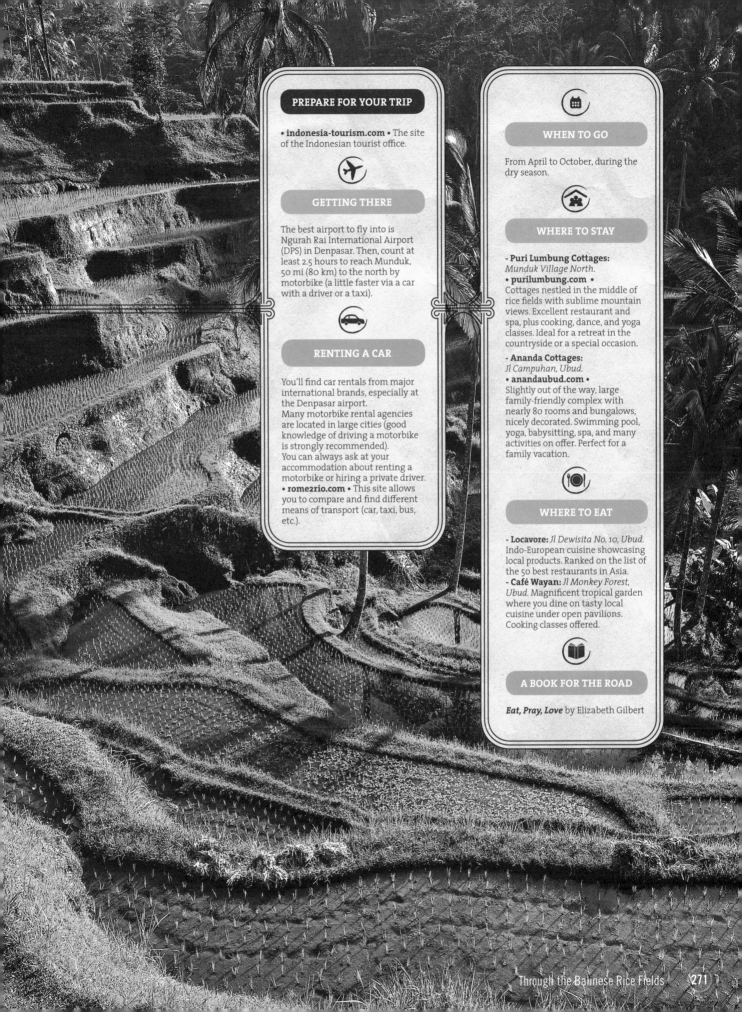

PREPARE FOR YOUR TRIP

- **indonesia-tourism.com** • The site of the Indonesian tourist office.

✈ GETTING THERE

The best airport to fly into is Ngurah Rai International Airport (DPS) in Denpasar. Then, count at least 2.5 hours to reach Munduk, 50 mi (80 km) to the north by motorbike (a little faster via a car with a driver or a taxi).

🚗 RENTING A CAR

You'll find car rentals from major international brands, especially at the Denpasar airport.
Many motorbike rental agencies are located in large cities (good knowledge of driving a motorbike is strongly recommended).
You can always ask at your accommodation about renting a motorbike or hiring a private driver.
- **rome2rio.com** • This site allows you to compare and find different means of transport (car, taxi, bus, etc.).

📅 WHEN TO GO

From April to October, during the dry season.

🏠 WHERE TO STAY

- **Puri Lumbung Cottages:** *Munduk Village North.*
- **purilumbung.com** •
Cottages nestled in the middle of rice fields with sublime mountain views. Excellent restaurant and spa, plus cooking, dance, and yoga classes. Ideal for a retreat in the countryside or a special occasion.

- **Ananda Cottages:** *Jl Campuhan, Ubud.*
- **anandaubud.com** •
Slightly out of the way, large family-friendly complex with nearly 80 rooms and bungalows, nicely decorated. Swimming pool, yoga, babysitting, spa, and many activities on offer. Perfect for a family vacation.

🍽 WHERE TO EAT

- **Locavore:** *Jl Dewisita No. 10, Ubud.* Indo-European cuisine showcasing local products. Ranked on the list of the 50 best restaurants in Asia.
- **Café Wayan:** *Jl Monkey Forest, Ubud.* Magnificent tropical garden where you dine on tasty local cuisine under open pavilions. Cooking classes offered.

📖 A BOOK FOR THE ROAD

Eat, Pray, Love by Elizabeth Gilbert

LOCATION

West Jordan

ROUTE

Amman – Aqaba

LENGTH

250 mi (410 km); 290 mi (465 km)
with round-trip to Wadi Rum

TIME

1 week

YOU'LL LOVE

The Byzantine mosaics, the fortified
castles, the fabulous city of Petra, the
ochres and oranges of the Wadi Rum
desert, the warm waters of the Red Sea.

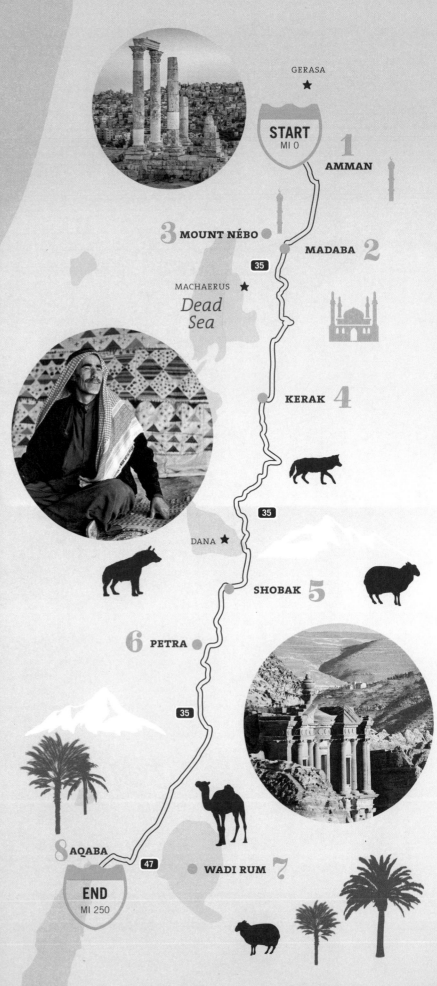

GERASA
★

START
MI 0

1 AMMAN

3 MOUNT NÉBO   **MADABA 2**

35

MACHAERUS ★

*Dead
Sea*

KERAK 4

35

DANA ★

SHOBAK 5

6 PETRA

35

8 AQABA

47

END
MI 250

WADI RUM 7

THE KING'S ROAD

FROM AMMAN ➤➤➤ TO AQABA

This is one of the oldest roads in the world: More than 5,000 years ago, people traveled here between Egypt and Mesopotamia. The Nabataeans, who traded in frankincense and spices, carved the fabulous city of Petra, torn from the red rock of the desert, along this road. The Romans came next, followed by Byzantine pilgrims who went in search of the tomb of Moses, and then Arab armies, then the Crusaders. Their castles remain, anchoring their majestic ruins to the ridges dominating the route.

START/END OF ROAD TRIP

STOP

LANDMARK OR POINT OF INTEREST ★

ROAD 35

ROAD TRIP

NATURE RESERVE

AMMAN: 4,000 YEARS OF HISTORY

Perched at an altitude of 2,600 ft (800 m), at a distance from the Jordan Valley, **Amman (1),** the Jordanian capital, shares its antiquity with Rome, as well as the fact that it was built on seven hills. The city is baked by the sun in summer and regularly dusted with snow in winter. On the peaked summit of Jebel al-Qala'a, cluttered with tangled ruins, the citadel has seen the city grow, collapse, and be reborn several times. Remains of the temple of Hercules, a Roman road, a Byzantine basilica, and an Umayyad palace (among others) are juxtaposed in a disorder that is made all the more difficult to decipher because some buildings are built with stones recycled from older structures.

Below, the heart of the ancient city beats in a concert of horns, clustered around the sparse Roman ruins of the forum (which was one of the largest in the empire), the odeon, and a nymphaeum (large fountain). Right in the middle, a theater, inaugurated around the year 170 under Marcus Aurelius, is much better preserved. Shows are given here in summer, and in 2017, the first opera festival in the Arab world was held here!

Throughout the day, the call to prayer spreads over the city, broadcast from the two slender minarets (in the Ottoman style) of the King Hussein Mosque. Rebuilt in the 1920s after Arab Jordan was liberated from the Turks, it stands on the site of one of the very first sanctuaries of Islam. Behind it, the bazaar is a jumble of shops, jewelry stores, and fruit and vegetable stalls.

DETOUR TO GERASA

It takes 1 hour, thanks to traffic jams, to travel the 30 mi (50 km) that separate Amman from Jerash. The modern town, without much charm, hides the exceptional ancient city of **Gerasa,** founded, it is said, by Alexander the Great. At the top of a short hill, Hadrian's Arch announces the atmosphere. Erected in the year 129 in a style combining Greek and Oriental influences, it commemorates a visit by the emperor that marked the beginning of the golden age of the city and of the 10 Romanized cities of the Decapolis. Enter through the south door to discover a superb oval square delimited by a colonnade of Ionic columns. To the west, the remains of the temple of Zeus are located next to the south theater, excellently restored. Every summer in July, it returns to its original role, attracting troupes and folk groups from all over the Mediterranean basin. Below is the main avenue, the *cardo maximus,* making its way to the north gate. This porticoed street, once lines with market stalls, stretches its Ionic columns with Corinthian capitals over nearly half a mile (800 m) toward the pretty little north theater and the holy of holies of Gerasa: the temple of Artemis, patron goddess of the city, with colossal pink columns.

ancient site of Gerasa

MADABA AND MOUNT NEBO: BIBLICAL HISTORY

From Amman, the King's Road ignores the three-lane highway that runs directly south, preferring to follow a route in the mountains, on the ridges overlooking the Dead Sea from the east. It takes the name of Highway 35 here, and it initially runs flat toward **Madaba (2),** just 20 mi (30 km) southwest of Amman, crossing a succession of villages baking in the sun and stony fields with furrows and skinny olive trees.

Mentioned in the Bible, Madaba is a city that trades minarets for bell towers. Half of its inhabitants are Christian—and have been since the Byzantines made it a major pilgrimage center in the 6th century. At that time, there was a large school of mosaicists here, whose remarkable works still partly decorate the floors of St. George's Church (famous for a map of the Holy Land), Church of the Apostles (goddess of the sea, animals, and fruit trees), and the Burnt Palace. Other mosacis have been gathered at the local museum and the archaeological park.

There are plenty of viewpoints from which to take in panoramas of the area: Views over the city, from the bell tower of the St. John the Baptist Church. Views from the remains of the Fortress of **Machaerus,** anchored to a bald promontory overlooking the blue scar of the Dead Sea. And views from **Mount Nebo (3),** from where Moses contemplated the promised land for the first and last time. In good weather, you can see Bethany, where Christ was baptized, and across the waters to Jericho and the Judean Mountains. The church on the summit, rebuilt in modern times, houses a splendid mosaic dating from 531, on which lions, hunters, and two men stand together with an ostrich, zebra, and dromedary on a leash.

DETOUR TO THE DEAD SEA

From the heights of the King's Road, several roller-coaster-like roads slide from bump to bump, then between bare knolls, finally descending in hairpin turns toward the bowels of the earth. Of all the points of the globe, the **Dead Sea,** spread out at 1,410 ft (428 m) below sea level, in the depths of the great Rift fault, is the lowest. Why this name? For the simple reason that no species, except bacteria, can survive here: Its salinity is 10 times higher than that of the oceans. On the south shore, potash, bromide, and magnesium are mined. Depleted by the massive diversion of water from the Jordan River (80 percent), its only tributary, the Dead Sea is a shadow of its former self; it could disappear completely by 2050. There is now talk of digging a canal to replenish it by pumping water from the Red Sea, at the risk of upsetting several ecosystems. In the meantime, you can always check the theory that you can float here without swimming—it's true! You can also smear yourself with mud, reputed to be excellent for the skin.

Madaba

Shobak

IN THE FOOTSTEPS OF THE CRUSADERS

Clinging to its rock, your next stop is **Kerak** (4), a town known for its fortified castles built by Crusaders to ensure their presence in the Holy Land during the Middle Ages. Following the capture of Jerusalem and the founding of Crusader States in 1099, Baldwin of Boulogne erected fortresses near Petra, at Shobak (then called Montreal), at Aqaba (Aila), and in Kerak. Founded to protect the east wing of the Crusader settlements and trade routes to the Red Sea, these anchor points also served as a base, in the 1170s, for the murderous raids of the cruel Raynald of Châtillon, Lord of Oultrejordain.

Then, the Arab reconquest began. Aqaba fell, Kerak and Shobak were besieged, resisted for a time, and were eventually conquered. Today, the citadel of Kerak is only a shadow of its former glory. Its obvious power nevertheless remains, as do a good part of its underground passages, the dungeons, the residence of the knights, and the ramparts from which Raynald of Châtillon would hurl his (numerous) enemies. **Shobak** (5), about 60 mi (100 km) to the south, has preserved a church and later constructions.

To connect the two castles, the King's Road crosses the depths of Wadi al-Hasa. The gorge, usually dry, is almost entirely devoid of vegetation. A little farther on, **Dana,** a popular tourism spot, stands in contrast. This tiny village with centuries-old yellow stone houses is anchored on the edge of a biosphere reserve, in the immediate vicinity of five springs—a luxury rare in these latitudes. Hyenas, wolves, and wild cats inhabit the area.

PETRA: THE PEARL OF THE DESERT

The King's Road reaches its most beautiful stopover: **Petra (6),** the "city of stone," made famous on screen by *Indiana Jones and the Last Crusade.* The Nabataeans, a semi-nomadic Arab people, carved out this city in the canyons of ocher and orange rock of Wadi Musa.

Hidden in a basin surrounded by mountains—perfectly hidden from view, located nevertheless at the confluence of trade routes—the city grew in size from the year 300 BC. Via the King's Road, the caravans then made their way to Syria and the port of Gaza. From Arabia came myrrh and dates, spices and silks. Petra prospered, first independent, and then as a Roman colony. In the soft sandstone and limestone, the Nabataeans hollowed out and chiseled palaces and masterly tombs.

You'll approach the city through the narrow Siq. Carved out by the once ferocious waters of Wadi Musa, the gorge, more than 0.6 mi (1 km) long, winds between narrow walls. Its sides have been carved with niches, where the damaged statues of protective deities still rest.

Finally, the cliffs open up. Bathed in the morning sun, the facade of the extraordi-nary Al-Khazneh (treasury), carved out of a mountain of pink sandstone, appears. Its two levels combine all the cultural influences of the eastern Mediterranean basin: Corinthian columns, representation of deities including the Egyptian Isis, Greek Castor and Pollux, and Dushara, patron goddess of the Nabataeans. Hollywood has attempted to make it a secret entrance to the shrine of the Holy Grail, but Al-Khazneh is actually the monumental tomb of an unknown king.

On foot, or on the back of a donkey or a camel, dozens of tombs, palaces, temples, and buildings are revealed in an immense and rugged setting. The most beautiful are all carved from red, ocher, or golden rock—such as the theater enlarged by the Romans, and the royal tombs, some of which have been converted into paleochristian churches. A long staircase carved into the rock leads to the impressive Ad Deir (monastery), a temple dedicated to another unknown monarch. Everything is immense: the 150-ft-high (45-m-high) facade, the size of the rooms, the enormous columns and gables crowning the building with pomp.

WADI RUM: IN THE FOOTSTEPS OF LAWRENCE OF ARABIA

The King's Road leaves the heights to join the Desert Highway, crowded with trucks coming and going between the capital and the port of Aqaba. An hour later, the pavement, bordered by the tracks of the old Hejaz railway, crosses a vast expanse of pink sand guarded by towers of ruiniform sandstone and granite.

Of all the deserts, **Wadi Rum (7)** is neither the largest nor the best known. It is sometimes called "Valley of the Moon" for its bare appearance, but it much more colorful than the moon. Wind and heat sculpted the stone, creating arches. And the rocks, covered in places with petroglyphs engraved by nomads, gradually break up into sand, forming dunes that are sometimes pink, sometimes orange, sometimes glowing.

Domain of the Bedouins, Wadi Rum is a living desert. Young shepherds still guard their flocks of sheep here. Lawrence of Arabia, the archaeologist who became a spy in the service of the queen during the World War I, knew these people well, and made them his hero in his fight against the Ottomans. It was here, in Wadi Rum, that he had established his headquarters. In 1918, he achieved his final victory at Damascus. Four years later, the "Emir Dynamite" embroidered his own myth in a book with mystical overtones: *Seven Pillars of Wisdom.* Today, the iconic rock pyramid of Jebel Rum (5,689 ft/1,734 m), watching over the village, has become a playground for climbing enthusiasts.

THE RED SEA ON THE HORIZON

The Desert Highway abandons its straight line and plunges down, carving its way between tall rock formations. In the opposite direction, trucks struggle to make the climb. Through an alley of date palms farther on, the blue of the Red Sea spreads over the horizon.

Aqaba (8) has long been a place where goods and convoys pass through. Built around springs around the 8th century BC, the oasis was for a long time an essential stopover for caravans heading toward the heart of the country on the King's Road. Some even see it as the incarnation of Eziongeber, King Solomon's port on the Red Sea.

Anxious to protect this strategic location, the Crusaders built a bastion on the seafront, later reinforced by the Egyptian Mamluks—and, above all, an authentic castle on Pharaoh's Island, 4 mi (7 km) away, now located in Egyptian territory.

Now surrounded by hotels, crowded every weekend by beachgoers from Amman, Aqaba is both the only port and the only seaside resort in the country. If sunbathing on fenched-in beaches is not to everyone's taste, the translucent waters of the marine reserve, stretching a dozen kilometers to the south, are unmissable. Under the waves, the explosion of life contrasts with the bareness of the surface. Between the brain and table coral, and the soft coral oscillating to the rhythm of the current, a multitude of small colored fish—butterflyfish, parrot fish, clownfish—glide by. Moray eels, Napoleon snake eels, scorpionfish, and others show themselves to divers, at 50-65 ft (15-20 m) deep. And on the wreck of the *Cedar Pride,* a transport vessel sunk in 1986, life is everywhere. If you're lucky, you'll even meet a turtle or two.

Wadi Rum

PREPARE FOR YOUR TRIP

- **visitjordan.com** • Official tourism website of Jordan. Gives a good overview of classic tours to do in the country.
- **visitpetra.jo** • Official website of the Petra Development and Tourism Regional Authority, with good general information.

GETTING THERE

The most common entry point into Jordan is the Amman Airport, officially known as the Queen Alia International Airport (AMM). You'll need a visa to enter the country, which can be obtained on arrival at the airport. It costs 40 JOD (approx. $56) for a single entry and is valid for 30 days. The visa is included with the Jordan Pass, a tourist pass that includes entry to almost all of the country's sights and museums.

RENTING A CAR

Most of the major international rental brands are present in Jordan and the rates (with unlimited mileage) are not too high. It is possible to pick up the vehicle in Amman and leave it in Aqaba (for an additional cost).

WHEN TO GO

From March to May and from September to early November.

WHERE TO STAY

You can find everything in Jordan: inexpensive rest houses managed by the government, affordable small hotels, establishments designed for groups (especially in Petra and Aqaba), and luxury hotels up to international standards. At the cheaper options, check to see if there is a fan (or air-conditioning) in summer and heating in winter. Prices are at their highest from March to May and from September to October/November. You can also camp in the reserves (Mujib, Dana) on your own and in Wadi Rum with a guide.

WHAT TO EAT

A good option in Jordan is dining at a hotel, or head to a popular eatery for falafel and shawarma. In small restaurants, the menu is generally very simple: grilled chicken or stew with rice and/or salad. At more high-end options, you can opt for a traditional assortment of mezze (hummus, tabbouleh, labneh, etc.), or treat yourself to the Jordanian king's dish: Bedouin mansaf (lamb and rice with pine nuts).

A BOOK FOR THE ROAD

Appointment with Death by Agatha Christie

MILFORD SOUND

END
MI 90

THE CHASM

HOMER
TUNNEL

94

HOLLYFORD
VALLEY

LAKE GUNN 4

MIRROR LAKES 3

EGLINTON VALLEY 2

94

START
MI 0

TE ANAU 1

LOCATION

Extreme south of South Island

ROUTE

Te Anau – Milford Sound/Piopiotahi

LENGTH

90 mi (150 km)

TIME

3 to 4 hours minimum

YOU'LL LOVE

The feeling of entering a nearly inaccessible area, the rain forest, crystal clear lakes, waterfalls, and the majesty of Milford Sound/Piopiotahi.

THE MILFORD ROAD

FROM TE ANAU ➤➤➤ TO MILFORD SOUND

At the end of South Island, the peaks of the Southern Alps/Kā Tiritiri o te Moana slide straight toward the Tasman Sea with a backdrop of exuberant vegetation, watered by rainfall that is frequent—to say the least. The ocean infiltrates here in a collection of deep, isolated, and nearly inaccessible fjords. A single small winding road ventures into the region to access the most beautiful of them all: Milford Sound/Piopiotahi. This dive into Fiordland National Park, part of the Te Wahipounamu reserve, a UNESCO World Heritage Site, is a life-changing experience.

Auckland

NEW ZEALAND

Wellington

Christchurch

Queenstown

START/END OF ROAD TRIP	⬯
STOP	⬤
LANDMARK OR POINT OF INTEREST	★
ROAD	`94`
ROAD TRIP	═══

MIDDLE EAST, ASIA, AND THE PACIFIC

NEW ZEALAND

90 MI

TE ANAU AND ITS LAKE

Have you heard of the takahē, a kind of big blue chicken with orange-red legs and beak? It is the largest member of the rail family, redis-covered in 1948 on the slopes of the Murchison Mountains, when the species was thought to be extinct. This says a lot about the isolation and impenetrable nature of the New Zealand fjords region. The bird can be seen in the flesh and feathers at the nearby Te Anau Bird Sanctuary, along with other endemic birds: the kākā (a parrot), kererū (a pigeon), and tūī (a large songbird that can imitate the human voice).

Besides the takahē, another (re)discovery, on the opposite side of the lake, helps to place **Te Anau** (1) on any tourist's itinerary: that of a narrow cave crossed by an underground river, where you can jump onto a boat to observe the glowworms that line the walls like a starry sky. For 20 mi (30 km), State Highway 94 progresses along-side Lake Te Anau, the largest lake on South Island (133 sq mi/344 sq km), of glacial origin. Very deep, it stretches over 40 mi (65 km) long at the foot of the powerful coastal massifs to the west, inter-sected by three fjords. On the other side of the river, pastures and green hills alternate with woods and beautiful views of the distant snowcapped peaks of the Southern Alps/Kā Tiritiri o te Moana. It is not uncommon here to find yourself blocked by packs of sheep shamelessly invading the road, under the guidance of a shepherd and his dogs.

VALLEYS AND TEMPERATE RAIN FORESTS

Winding its way up the Eglinton River, the road follows a natural cor-ridor framed by steep, dark mountains. At the foot of the mountains, pink and purple lupines brighten the landscape. Emerging from the woods, State Highway 94 leads into the broad **Eglinton Valley** (2); a glacier once flowed into this vast natural enclosure, and today it's carpeted in golden tussock—a cold-weather grass growing in dense clumps. After crossing the river, **Mirror Lakes** (3) hold out their reflec-tive surfaces at the foot of giant massif: the Earl Mountains.

Despite the thin humus, southern beeches, podocarps, and ferns thrive here, watered by 10-20 ft (3-6 m) of annual rainfall! It rains an average of 300 days a year in the area, sometimes for weeks on end. It should come as no surprise, then, that the West Coast of New Zealand has earned the nickname the "Wet Coast." Perfectly translucent, miraculously sheltered from the wind, the waters of **Lake Gunn** (4) offer another reflection of the mountains covered with vegetation. If you go for a short stroll along the lake's shores, you'll see the clouds split into two, their reflections dancing on the blue and emerald waters. New Zealand director Peter Jackson shot several scenes of the first *Lord of the Rings* movie in the peaks surrounding this natural sanctuary, reinvented for the film as the Misty Mountains. And, indeed, mist does cling to these mountains.

UNDER THE MOUNTAIN

Past Lake Fergus, the road branches west, gliding through the Darran Mountains, straddling the beautifully forested **Hollyford Valley (5),** and then offering a view of Falls Creek rolling down the cliff barely 65 ft (20 m) from the road. A few kilometers—and a good climb—later, you'll reach the highest point of the route (3,100 ft/945 m in altitude). Here, you'll have to wait at the traffic light, sometimes up to 20 minutes, for it to turn green so you can enter the **Homer Tunnel (6).** This single-lane tunnel, which stretches 0.7 mi (1.2 km) long, took 20 years to dig into the granite, and it was finally inaugurated in 1954. Rainy days make for a lovely wait: A string of waterfalls forms on the dark surrounding walls. When the weather is better, you might come across a kea, a large green and red mountain parrot, quite cheeky, who loves to nibble on tires and rubber seals on car windows. The tunnel leads to the Cleddau Valley. State Highway 94 descends the slope in large curves, wandering from panorama to viewpoint, between streams and foxgloves, before returning to the forest. The bare walls disappear, and the vegetation becomes wild. Less than 10 minutes later, the trail to **The Chasm (7)** plunges under a canopy of branches, which protects the large tree ferns. The short loop (20 minutes), interspersed with wooden walkways, leads to a gorge carved by a powerful stream, framed by rocks pierced with round or oval basins polished by the eddies of the water over the millennia.

MILFORD SOUND/PIOPIOTAHI: THE CLIMAX

Captain Cook was the first English-speaking person to note, in his logbook in 1770, the spectacular beauty of the South Island fjords. But he also underlined, with a furious stroke of his pen, the blood-thirsty voracity of the sandflies that proliferate here. Watch out for these gnats, which sting and scratch. According to Māori legend, Hine-nui-te-po, goddess of the underworld, was so overwhelmed by the fjords' beauty that she feared all who visited would never want to leave, and so she released swarms the bugs to keep visitors at bay.

At the end of State Highway 94, **Milford Sound/Piopiotahi (8)** is unmissable, the most beautiful and the most remote of the region's 14 fjords. This 9-mi-long (15-km-long) trough erects its vertical walls above a majestic line of water, watched over by the unmistakable rock pyramid of Mitre Peak (5,522 ft/1,683 m)—often shrouded in the morning by a veil of mist. New Zealand's fjords have been gradually shaped by the slow work of successive glaciations over the last two million years. As recently as 15,000 years ago, an ice cap covered this entire part of the South Island.

The frequent rain makes the trees and moss sparkle and feeds hundreds of waterfalls, some delicate, others thunderous, such as Bowen Falls, whose spray can be seen from 1,600 ft (500 m) away. Everything here is soaked to the point that, at certain times, the vegetation perilously clinging to the sheer drops collapses into tree avalanches. Helicopter flights, boat rides, and kayak trips distill the beauties of the fjord at different speeds. It's magical to approach the place with a paddle, where you can get up close to a few sea lions lazing on the coastal rocks and see, in the distance, the fins of a

troop of bottlenose dolphins cutting through the waves. Fresh water is so abundant here that it forms a sort of sheet on the surface of the fjord, sometimes nearly 30 ft (10 m) thick. Tannin from the forest tints the waters, largely dampening the diffraction of light, allowing bottom-dwelling species, such as spider crabs and black coral, to live here at only 20 ft (6 m) deep.

DID YOU SAY KIWI?

This strange bird is flightless, like many of its fellow New Zealand avians, the result of evolution without predators. The kiwi spends its life hidden low to the ground, where the female lays her egg (which weighs a full quarter of her weight), and the male incubates and raises the young for only three weeks. After that, the chicks are on their own. Emblematic of New Zealand, the iconic kiwi is at risk: there were 5 million of them around 1925, but there are only 25,000 of them today, victims of predators introduced by settlers. Of the six subspecies listed, three live in Fiordland.

FOCUS
Milford Track

The most famous of New Zealand's 10 Great Walks, called the most beautiful hike in the world by some, sets out to conquer Milford Sound/Piopiotahi in its own way, through glacial valleys streaked with waterfalls, humid forests, and windy passes. Though the trek is not very long in distance (33 mi/53.5 km), it is arduous and muddy, and the whole thing takes four days. From the end of October to the end of April, you must book well in advance to be able to embark on the adventure and spend the night in the huts punctuating the route. In low season, there are fewer people, but the climate is even more difficult: This is when the risk of avalanche and flood is greatest. Among the highlights of the walk is a detour to Sutherland Falls, 1,900 ft (580 m) high.

• doc.govt.nz/milfordtrack •

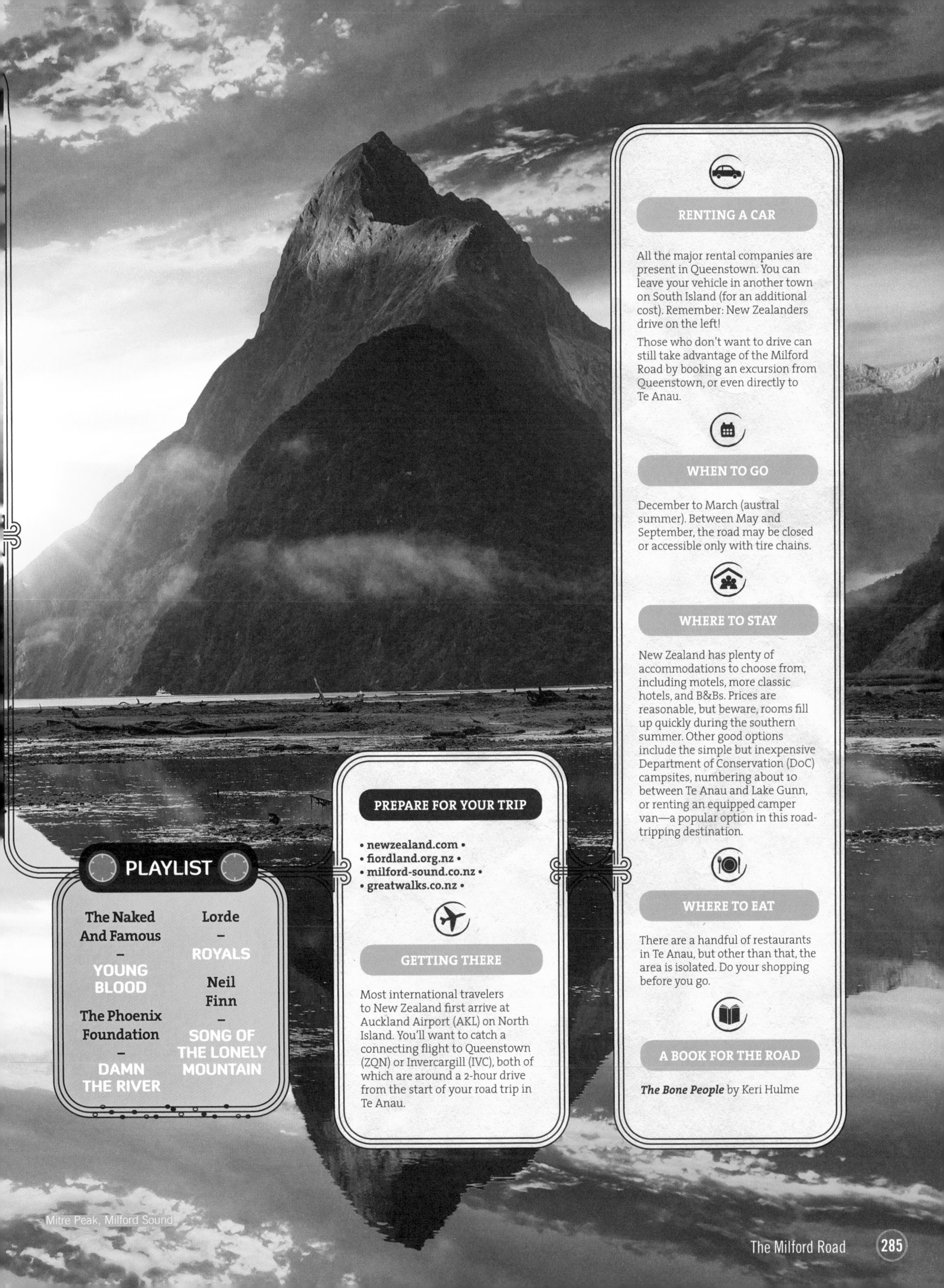

RENTING A CAR

All the major rental companies are present in Queenstown. You can leave your vehicle in another town on South Island (for an additional cost). Remember: New Zealanders drive on the left!

Those who don't want to drive can still take advantage of the Milford Road by booking an excursion from Queenstown, or even directly to Te Anau.

WHEN TO GO

December to March (austral summer). Between May and September, the road may be closed or accessible only with tire chains.

WHERE TO STAY

New Zealand has plenty of accommodations to choose from, including motels, more classic hotels, and B&Bs. Prices are reasonable, but beware, rooms fill up quickly during the southern summer. Other good options include the simple but inexpensive Department of Conservation (DoC) campsites, numbering about 10 between Te Anau and Lake Gunn, or renting an equipped camper van—a popular option in this road-tripping destination.

WHERE TO EAT

There are a handful of restaurants in Te Anau, but other than that, the area is isolated. Do your shopping before you go.

A BOOK FOR THE ROAD

The Bone People by Keri Hulme

PREPARE FOR YOUR TRIP

- newzealand.com •
- fiordland.org.nz •
- milford-sound.co.nz •
- greatwalks.co.nz •

GETTING THERE

Most international travelers to New Zealand first arrive at Auckland Airport (AKL) on North Island. You'll want to catch a connecting flight to Queenstown (ZQN) or Invercargill (IVC), both of which are around a 2-hour drive from the start of your road trip in Te Anau.

♪ PLAYLIST ♪

The Naked And Famous
–
YOUNG BLOOD

The Phoenix Foundation
–
DAMN THE RIVER

Lorde
–
ROYALS

Neil Finn
–
SONG OF THE LONELY MOUNTAIN

Mitre Peak, Milford Sound

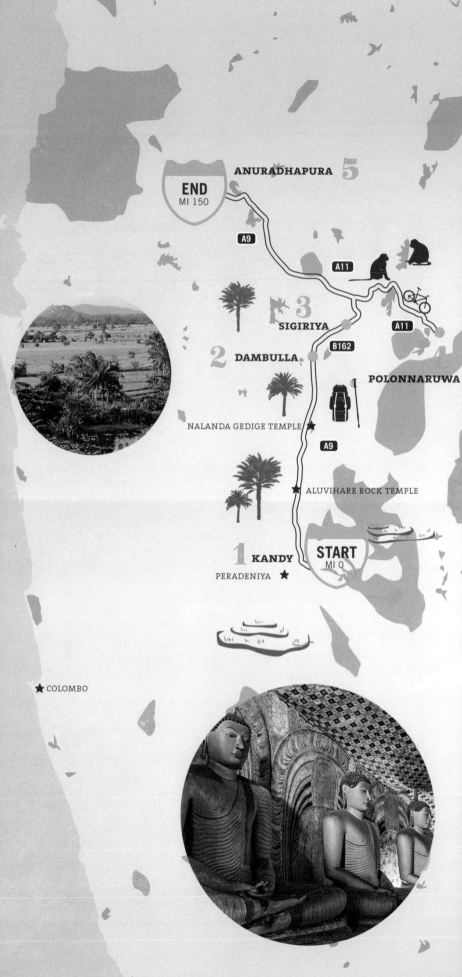

ANURADHAPURA 5

END
MI 150

A9

A11

3

SIGIRIYA

A11

B162

2 DAMBULLA

POLONNARUWA

NALANDA GEDIGE TEMPLE ★

A9

★ ALUVIHARE ROCK TEMPLE

1 KANDY

START
MI 0

PERADENIYA ★

★ COLOMBO

 LOCATION

Central Sri Lanka

ROUTE

Kandy – Anuradhapura

LENGTH

About 150 mi (250 km)

TIME

Allow at least 4 days, 1 day per site.
Dambulla and Sigiriya can be visited
in the same day.

YOU'LL LOVE

Temples, statues of Buddhas, archaeological ruins, mountains, rain forest,
and religious rituals.

THE CULTURAL TRIANGLE OF SRI LANKA

FROM KANDY ➤➤➤ TO ANURADHAPURA

Kandy, Polonnaruwa, Anuradhapura: three exceptional sites, three historical places, three Sri Lankan beauties. Add to that the temple of Dambulla and the site of Sigiriya: Welcome to the cultural triangle of Sri Lanka! It's an epic journey through the heart of the island, where you'll encounter splendid Hindu heritage, royal cities of the past, and sacred religious customs, on roads between rice fields and mountains.

Anuradhapura

Batticaloa

Kandy

Colombo

SRI LANKA

Galle

START/END OF ROAD TRIP	
STOP	●
LANDMARK OR POINT OF INTEREST	★
ROAD	A9
ROAD TRIP	═══

KANDY: THE SACRED CITY OF SRI LANKA

Located 2 hours from the capital **Colombo,** in the geographic center of the island, this is an ideal starting point to begin your journey in the cultural triangle. It's easy to get here from Colombo; a good option is taking the train, for a trip through exuberant nature. With another option, traveling by car, the picturesque scenes of life parade along the kilometers against a backdrop of forests and rice fields.

Once you arrive, **Kandy** (1) reveals itself magnificently, in the midst of green hills and mountains.

Its city center, nestled at the bottom of a valley, is organized around an artificial lake, bordered by the royal palace and the Sri Dalada Maligawa, also called the Temple of the Sacred Tooth Relic. A major place of pilgrimage, it is one of the symbols of the city. Inside, one of the Buddha's teeth is housed (as the name suggests), though you can't actually see the tooth, only the case it is kept in. The holy atmosphere and beauty of the temple and palace are unmissable. The splendid temple grounds are also the backdrop for daily religious ceremonies and processions.

Outside the temple, you'll find yourself in the heart of Sri Lankan life: bustling alleys, stalls full of fruits and vegetables, booths displaying spices, teas, and other local products. Dogs play in the street, and tuk-tuks zoom past buses.

Craving some quiet? Climb the surrounding hills, where some beautiful Ayurvedic centers and local accommodations are located, often hidden behind lush greenery and offering a breathtaking panorama over the entire valley.

NOT TO BE MISSED

*Less than 4 mi (6 km) to the southwest, the Royal Botanic Gardens of **Peradeniya** are worth a visit. Founded in 1371 during the reign of Vikramabahu III, this space of almost 150 acres (60 ha) has an incredible collection of orchids, as well as spectacular specimens such as the singular coconut palm trees (found only here and in the Seychelles), a gigantic Java fig tree, and a majestic avenue of royal palms. You will also be able to observe an impressive population of bats who have made their home here. This is one of the most beautiful gardens in Asia.*

Head in the direction of **Dambulla (2),** 2 hours north of Kandy. On the road, you'll pass several pretty points of interest: the spice gardens and the **Aluvihare Rock Temple** near Matale and, farther north, the **Nalanda Gedige Temple.** Nature lovers will want to visit the botanical garden, which explains the properties of each plant and spice, and for history lovers, the two religious sites are really worth a stop.

Dambulla

DAMBULLA: A TEMPLE IN THE HEART OF A MOUNTAIN

At first glance, Dambulla seems like a junction in the road, a town without any real interest. But no, this treasure is simply hidden in the heart of his mountain: a large granite rock overlooking the city! It's a wonderful place, classified as a UNESCO World Heritage Site. As you arrive at its foot, you'll be greeted by a giant Buddha, 100 ft (30 m) high, completely covered in gold. The tone is set, and this first statue announces nearly 150 others (smaller of course), hidden at the top of the hill in the famous Golden Temple.

The history of this site dates back to the 1st century BC. The king at the time, Valagamba, came to take refuge in these caves, chased by Tamil invaders. Back on his throne, he turned it into a fabulous Buddhist monastery, today a major place of pilgrimage, with 80 caves, 5 shrines, 157 statues, 153 images of Buddha, 22,600 sq ft (2,100 sq m) of murals. It's enough to make your head turn in every direction. There is so much to see, from floor to ceiling.

A 15-minute climb is necessary to reach the top of the temple. At the top, you'll be rewarded with a grandiose view of the surrounding countryside and the entrance to the site. Inside, a large courtyard reveals cave sanctuaries, each containing a specific treasure. Despite all the visitors, the monks continue to go about their days, calmly and solemnly.

SIGIRIYA: A CITADEL IN THE MIDDLE OF THE CLOUDS

To the northeast, 20 km from Dambulla, **Sigiriya** (3) is a breathtaking geological and historical site, classified as a UNESCO World Heritage Site. Culminating at 590 ft (180 m), this red stone rock, nicknamed Lion Rock, emerges from the plains and the jungle. A lookout point and natural bunker, it was occupied in the 5th century, during which a magnificent palace and its gardens were built on its top.

Reaching the top of the site is equivalent to climbing the Eiffel Tower (requiring around 1,200 steps). But your efforts are rewarded along the way: terraced gardens, ponds, mysterious caves at the foot of the rock, and paintings, not to mention the famous frescoes of *The Damsels of Sigiriya* engraved on the cliff. And then at the top of the rock, after passing two emblematic lion's paws that frame the last flight of steps, you'll reach the highlight: the remains of the citadel, its private swimming pool, its royal terraces, and more, all overlooking a sea of forest and clouds. It's a sensational panorama.

THE CITADEL OF SIGIRIYA: A FAMILY TRAGEDY

At the end of the 5th century, Kashyapa, illegitimate son of the king, wants to seize the throne. He kills his father by burying him alive, and then drives out his half-brother Moggallana. The latter swears revenge, and Kashyapa, cautious and paranoid, builds the citadel of Sigiriya, a veritable inaccessible bunker. For 18 years, Kashyapa lives the life of a pasha, surrounded by numerous courtesans, while his brother prepares an army. The time for revenge has come: Moggallana brings his troops around the site. It is impossible to win a battle by trying to seize this majestic citadel. But Moggallana lays siege to the rock and waits patiently. It takes only one week for his brother to surrender.

Polonnaruwa

POLONNARUWA:
THE KINGDOM OF TOQUE MONKEYS

About 1.5 hours east of Sigiriya by road, **Polonnaruwa (4)** is the fourth stop in the cultural triangle. This ancient Sinhalese capital (11th and 12th centuries) is a real archaeological gem (the city's new town is a good place to spend the night). The remains of this city, some of them magnificently preserved, stretch for several miles in the middle of the jungle: an archaeological treasure, a journey through history, an adventure in the kingdom of . . . toque macaques! The site is indeed populated by thousands of monkeys living peacefully between stones, in shrines, or in the middle of statues of Buddha, adding a little more magic to this breathtaking place. Polonnaruwa also served as the setting for the filming of the Disneynature film *Monkey Kingdom,* released in 2015.

The best thing to do here is rent a bike and browse the many trails here, exploring the countless buildings classified by UNESCO. Among the highlights: the statue of King Parakramabahu I, Gal Vihara temple and its giant statues, the ancient structure of Polonnaruwa Vatadage, Thivanka Image House and its superb interior frescoes . . . the list goes on and on.

ANURADHAPURA:
THE HOLY CITY OF SRI LANKA

The last stop on your trip to the cultural heart of Sri Lanka: **Anuradhapura (5),** located to the west, just over 2 hours' drive from Polonnaruwa.

Former capital of Sri Lanka for 13 centuries, this sacred city, classified as a UNESCO World Heritage Site, was abandoned in the year 993 following invasions. Today, the holy city is once again accessible and offers an incredible circuit in the footsteps of past centuries. On the agenda: palaces, monasteries, Buddhist temples, and splendid stupas to be explored in a spiritual atmosphere that invites contemplation.

The ancient royal city stretches for nearly 6 mi (10 km), to the west of the railroad. Some must-see attractions include: Jaya Sri Maha Bodhi, the most sacred temple in the city, in which a branch of the tree of awakening (the sacred tree under which Buddha is said to have meditated and attained enlightenment) has been planted. From the top of its 300 ft (90 m), the Ruvanvelisaya Dagoba impresses with its immaculate white dome and its 360 elephant heads, guardians of the temple housing relics of Buddha. In another genre, the Jetavanaramaya and Abhayagiri stupas were built entirely in red brick and stand out majestically against the landscape. Do not miss the Isurumuniya temple, a rock sanctuary, an ideal spot for admiring the sunset.

PLAYLIST

Pony Pony Run Run	Had To Hear
–	–
HEY YOU	REAL ESTATE
Seals & Croft	Keane
–	–
SUMMER BREEZE	SOMEWHERE ONLY WE KNOW

PREPARE FOR YOUR TRIP

• srilanka.travel • The website of the Sri Lanka tourism office.

GETTING THERE

Fly into Colombo Airport, aka Bandaranaike International Airport (CMB). Then, allow at least 2 hours by road (car or taxi) or 2.5 hours by train to reach Kandy, 70 mi (115 km) to the east by car.

TRANSPORTATION

• rome2rio.com • This site allows you to compare and find different means of transport (rental car, taxi, bus, train, etc.) wherever you are. Renting and driving your own car or motorbike is not recommended because of the challenges and high accident risks of driving in Sri Lanka.

WHEN TO GO

The best season to travel to Sri Lanka is February-March.

WHERE TO STAY

- **Notting Hill Country House:** *37/83, Ampitiya Road, Kandy.* Magnificent white colonial-style building, clinging to the hillside. Nice décor, with a lot of character. Beautiful view over Kandy from the central terrace, where you can enjoy a quality breakfast.
- **Lakmini Lodge:** *126, Sigiriya.* Good value for money at this guesthouse offering rooms for different budgets, the most economical of which are perfectly comfortable. Sleek black-and-white design. Friendly welcome. 10-minute walk from Lion Rock.

WHERE TO EAT

- **Helga's Folly Hotel:** *70, Rajapihilla Mawatha, Kandy.* This is undoubtedly one of the most interesting establishments in Sri Lanka. The décor is a cross between *Alice in Wonderland* and *The Addams Family*, with every square inch of the walls, facade, and even the garden rewarding curiosity. One meal is not enough to discover this unique place.
- **Honey Pot:** *33, Deveni Rajasinghe Mawatha, Kandy.* Pretty spot a little outside Kandy, ideal for leaving the bustle of the city and enjoying the river view that awaits you on the terrace or in the dining room with its large bay window. Tasty local cuisine served.

A BOOK FOR THE ROAD

Running in the Family by Michael Ondaatje

Anuradhapura

INDEX

Dades Valley, Morocco

Ring Road, Iceland

COPYRIGHTS

Legend: v = thumbnail, b = bottom, t = top, l = left, c = center, r = right

PHOTOGRAPHS

HEMIS.FR

Alamy : p113 ; Alba Jeronimo / Alamy Stock Photo : p232 l ; All Canada photo : p76 vtr, p77 b ; Animals Animals : p9 ; Aurora : p109 ; Azam Jean-Paul : p90 vb, p112, p114 ; Berthier Emmanuel : p116, p290 ; Bibikow Walter : p250 vr ; Blend Images : p94 ; Boisvieux Christophe : p135, p137, p170 ; Cavalier Michel : p69, p161 vt, p166 vb, p169 ; Chaput Franck : p160 l, p266 l, p286 ; Cultura : p130 l ; Dagnall Ian / Alamy Stock Photo : p154 ; David Noton Photography / Alamy Stock Photo : p84 ; Degas Jean-Pierre : p104 vt ; Dirscherl Reinhard : p53 l, p150 ; Ducept Pascal : p14 vt, p19 ; Escudero Patrick : p146, p232 vt ; Frilet Patrick : p30 vt, p172 l, p221 ; Frumm John : p272 vb ; Garcia Julien : p204, p278 ; Geogphotos / Alamy : p212 ; Gerault Gregory : p174 ; Giuglio Gil : p226 ; Glyn Thomas Photography / Alamy Stock Photo : p232 vb ; Griger Tomas / Alamy Stock Photo : p210 ; Guy Christian : p73, p85, p87, p89 ; Hagenmuller Jean-François : p95 ; Heeb Christian : p62 l, p64, p22 l, p30 l, p34, p37, p58, p82 l, p93, p128, p238 t, p242, p262 ; Hugues Hervé : p192 vt, p252, p255, p256 ; Image Source : p40, p219, p219 ; imageBROKER : p123, p124, p136, p245, p270 ; Jeremy Woodhouse/Luka Esenko/Blend Images LLC : p295 ; John Warburton Lee : p276 ; Jon Arnold Images : p66, p16, p17, p18, p21, p22 vb, p25, p33, p56, p63, p88, p96, p97, p101, p102, p106, p110 l, p120 vb, p120 l, p130 vc, p130 vt, p134, p161 vb, p163, p172 vc, p180, p194, p195, p208, p239, p250 l, p253, p260, p265, p268, p277, p279, p286 l ; Kauffmann Alain : p66 t ; Krinitz Hartmut : p133 ; Lemaire Stéphane : p168, p250 v, p254, p263, p269 ; Leperi K.D. / Alamy Stock Photo : p46 vb ; Lescourret Jean Pierre : p156 ; lucky-photographer / Alamy Stock Photo : p12 ; Maisant Ludovic : p144 l p192 l, p275 ; Martin Thomas Photography / Alamy Stock Photo : p158 ; Mattes René : p120 vt, p157, p159, p166 vc, p188, p243, p274 ; Mauritius : p122 ; McCormack Gareth / Alamy Stock Photo : p176 ; Minden : p11, p47, p224 vb, p229 ; Mint : p264 ; Moirenc Camille : p164, p165, p166 l, p166 vt, p266 vb, p271 ; Montico Lionel : p238 b ; Morandi Tuul et Bruno : p184, p191, p227, p231, p289 ; Novarc Images : p190 ; Padro Efrain / Alamy Stock Photo : p27, p46 vc, p51 ; Palanque Denis : p72, p75 ; Rabouan-Fiori : p286 vt ; Renault Philippe : p67, p70, p71, p77 t, p23, p28, p29 ; Rieger Bertrand : p155, p160 v, p171, p246, p272 vc ; Ritterbach Juergen / Alamy Stock Photo : p235 ; Robert Harding : p182, p218, p224 l ; Schmid Chris / Eyemage Media / Alamy Stock Photo : p104 l ; Serano Anna : p234 ; Seux paule : p3288 vb, p291 ; Sierpinski Jacques : p237 ; Stroujko Boris / Alamy Stock Photo : p236 ; Szefczyk Borys / Alamy Stock Photo : p233 ; Travel Pix / Alamy Stock Photo : p108 ; vallecillos Lucas / Alamy Stock Photo : p201 ; van Gorkum Harry / Alamy Stock Photo : p280 l ; Westend 61 : p62 vt, p55, p125, p129, p151.

SHUTTERSTOCK.COM

P63 vb, p63 vc, p010, p65 b, p76 vbr, p76 vbl, p76 vtl, p77, p78, p79 b, p79 t, p6 vb, p6 vt, p7, p14 l, p14 vb, p15, p22 vt, p26 b, p30 vb, p30 vc, p38 vb, p38 vc, p52 vb, p52 vt, p54, p59 b, p59 t, p82 vb, p82 vt, p86, p90 l, p90 vc, p90 vt, p98 vb, p104 vb, p110 v, p111 vb, p111 vt, p115, p117, p126 v, p127, p130 vb, p138 v, p142, p144 vb, p144 vt, p145, p152 l, p152 vb, p152 vt, p172 vb, p172 vt, p177, p178 v, p179 vb, p179 vt, p192 vb, p200 v, p206 vb, p207, p209, p216 vt, p217, p223 b, p223 t, p228, p240 l, p240 vb, p240 vt, p241, p252, p252, p258 l, p258 vb, p258 vt, p266 vt, p267, p272 l, p272 vt, p280 vb, p280 vt, p281, p282.

GETTYIMAGES

Akegooseberry : p181 ; Biris Paul : p107 ; Clark Jonathan : p74 ; Copson Alan : p50, p46 l ; David Wall Photo : p257 ; DEA / C. Dani I. Jeske : p283 ; Delimont Danita : p49 ; Fox Laurent : p284 ; Goujon Olivier : p98 l ; Kalaouzis George : p100 ; Kern Rick : p32 ; Leprêtre Pierre : p183 ; Ley A. V. : p48 ; Lomchid Pete : p185 ; Marcoux Yves : p68 vt ; Palanque Denis / hemis.fr : 68 l ; Piyasirisorost Ratnakorn : p178 l ; Primeimages : p285 ; Van Hasselt John / Corbis : p35 ; Wojcik Adrian / EyeEm : p98 vt.

PHOTONONSTOP

AGE : p148 ; AGF Foto : p42 ; Aurora : p92 ; GO Premium : p220, p220 ; Harding Robert : p216 l ; Johnér : p24 ; Look : p10 ; Schneider Danièle : p8, p141, p140, p216 vb ; Sime : p36, p38 vt, p43, p44, p45, p186 v, p187, p189, p192 vc, p196, p197, p198, p199 t, p200 l, p224 vt, p251 l ; Simeone : p199 b ; SimePhoto RF : p186 l ; Warburton-Lee John : p132.

AGE FOTOSTOCK

Angela to Roxel/imageBROKER : p206 vt ; Azumendi Gonzalo : p202 ; Cavalli Angelo : p38 l ; Clickalps SRLs : p175 ; CSP-Harlekino : p211 ; DueÒas Eva : p26 t ; Garcia Julien : p213 ; Glusic Robert : p13, p6 l ; Gottschalk Manfred : p259 ; Guichaoua Yann : p230 ; Harrington Blaine : p41 ; Hernandez Jacobo : p139 ; Janik Maggie : p68 vb ; Kunkel Patrick : p143 ; Remsberg Edwin : p244 ; Staszczuk Slawek : p138 l ; Stuart Mel : p126 l ; Top Photo Group RF : p98 vc ; Vallecillos Lucas : p203 ; Wlodarczyk Jan : p147, p206 l.

DREAMSTIME

Lunamarina / Dreamstime.com: p149; Xbrchx / Dreamstime.com: p162; Fritz Hiersche / Dreamstime.com: p261; Julius Kielaitis / Dreamstime.com: p296.

ILLUSTRATIONS

SHUTTERSTOCK

p64, p67, p73, p74, p20, p49, p54, 93, p96, p102, p133, p140, p175, p185, p189, p191, p191, p205, p205, p235, p247, p252, p255, p284.

MAPS

Clémence Boulay and Camille Neumuller.

WANDERLUST ROAD TRIPS
Avalon Travel
Hachette Book Group
1700 Fourth Street
Berkeley, CA 94710, USA
www.moon.com

Director of Collection and Author: Philippe Gloaguen
Managing Editor: Hannah Brezack
Production: Lucie Ericksen and Rue Flaherty
Cover Design: Erin Seaward-Hiatt
Moon Logo: Tim McGrath
Proofreader: Megan Anderluh

ISBN-13: 978-1-64049-599-9

Printing History
1st Edition — October 2021
5 4 3 2 1